EZRA POUND AND HISTORY

EZRA POUND SCHOLARSHIP SERIES

General Editor, Carroll F. Terrell

James J. Wilhelm, *Dante and Pound: The Epic of Judgement*

Frederick K. Sanders, *John Adams Speaking: Pound's Sources for the Adams Cantos*

Vittoria I. Mondolfo and Margaret Hurley, eds., *Ezra Pound: Letters to Ibbotson, 1935-1952*

Barbara Eastman, *Ezra Pound's Cantos: The Story of the Text*

James J. Wilhelm, *Il Miglior Fabbro*

John J. Nolde, *Blossoms From the East: The China Cantos of Ezra Pound*

Kay Davis, *Fugue and Fresco: Structures in Pound's* Cantos

Marianne Korn, ed., *Ezra Pound and History*

EZRA POUND AND HISTORY

Edited by
MARIANNE KORN

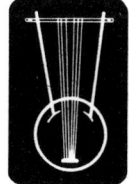

The National Poetry Foundation
University of Maine, 1985

Published by The National Poetry Foundation
University of Maine at Orono, Orono, Maine 04469

Printed by The University of Maine at Orono Printing Office

Copyright © 1985 by The National Poetry Foundation

Library of Congress Catalog Card Number: 85-61155
ISBN: 0-915032-11-2 cloth
ISBN: 0-915034-12-0 paper

PREFACE

EZRA POUND AND HISTORY

The description of Pound's *Cantos* as a poem "including history" echoes through this present book. It is a recognition, however partial, of what is one of the most insistent, persistent and problematic aspects of Pound's work.

There is, of course, a simple sense in which most, or perhaps all, of his writing "includes history"; the peculiarly bookish nature of Pound's earliest poetry was quickly recognized by readers and reviewers. The device of the *persona*, specifically, functions to "include" a historical mode which both preserves and translates the living material of the past which is embodied in literary tradition. The epigraph which Pound devised for the 1909 *persona*-poem, "Sestina: Altaforte" reads in part: "Eccovi! Judge ye! Have I dug him up again?"[1] For this *persona* is the product of Pound's faith in the possibility of reviving the true nature of the historical fact in the voice of the present.

Both these poems and much of the early prose are the expression of a young man revelling in the glamour of history, in the immanence of the very "pastness" of the past. The literary sketches which Pound published in the Philadelphia *Book News Monthly* in 1906 and 1908, for example, are records of a romantic nostalgia. In describing his visit to the city of Burgos, Pound wrote[2] of walking streets haunted by the deeds and words of the poem of *The Cid*, transcending time and even fiction itself: centuries melt away as reality becomes a fiction, and fiction a felt reality. This same conjunction of past and present, literary hero and poet, subject and object, fictional and historical discourse, echoes through Pound's various accounts of his travels in Italy and Provence a few years later; for

---
1. *Personae: The Collected Poems of Ezra Pound* (New York, 1926), p. 28.
2. "Burgos, a Dream City of Old Castile," *Book News Monthly*, xxvi, 5 (October 1906), 91-94.

> I have walked there
>   thinking of old days.[3]

It was not in fact until the transitional poems of 1914 through 1922, or thereabouts—the poems beginning with "Near Perigord" and ending in the historical usages of the Malatesta cantos—that the old certainties of the *persona* vanish in Pound's awareness that historical truth is not necessarily fact to be received, simple and unchanged, unmediated into the twentieth century: but rather a "rag-bag" of details whose status is uncertain, whose truths are unclear, and whose causal links have vanished.[4] It was in fact because of his need to discover and reveal the truthfulness of historical objectivity that Pound developed a discourse for *The Cantos* which presents details in turn, until their contextual significance appears and is perceived in the present, "make it new" replacing the mere "digging up" of men and deeds.

The papers in this book are a selection of the work which was presented at the 1982 Ezra Pound Conference held at Middlesex Polytechnic, London. They do not represent a single approach to the problems of Pound's history, or history in Pound's poetry. Rather, the selection suggests something of the range of approaches which is currently to be found in Pound scholarship, applied here to that essential question of poetry and history: the extent to which the poem *represents* reality, demanding a knowledge of the world to which its words refer, in order that the meaning may be interpreted.

Michael André Bernstein's paper introduces the problem by proposing an "ironical" reading of *The Cantos* as a rag-bag of authorities which reveals Pound's struggles to devise a new relationship between world and word. Pound's search for the *mot juste*, like Flaubert's, is seen as his means of developing that post-Romantic discourse, the productive text whose referentiality is mediated by history. Such innovation is seen also by Alan Durant as the center of our interest in the language of *The Cantos*, although his paper also acknowledges the problems of context and allusion arising from Pound's interrelationships of cultural and linguistic emphases. Durant's paper therefore moves toward a recognition of the ways in which Pound sought to use historical, economic and other cultural perspectives in his work, culminating in his attempts to intervene in history, by poetry, to "make a paradiso terrestre" [117/802]. The disrupting linguistic devices of *The Cantos* must be seen, therefore, in relation to the history in the

---

3. "Provincia Deserta," *Personae, ed. cit.*, p. 121.
4. See my *Ezra Pound: Purpose/Form/Meaning* (London, 1983), Part IV.

poem, in terms of the problematics of authority and subjectivity on the one hand, and of social history on the other.

Martin Kayman's paper questions the validity of the "eccentric" approaches to Pound's writing which accept and perpetuate its separation from the mainstream of contemporary thought; this eccentricity, which is Pound's also, he relates to the poet's radical innovativeness. His survey of critical practice moves through a phenomenological reading, developing an empirio-critical approach to problems of form and referentiality.

Papers by Dennis Brown, Stephen Wilson and Ian Bell deal with similar problems of unity and referentiality in the early *Cantos*. Brown focuses upon the "luminous detail" of Pound's method, concluding that the subject-matter of *The Cantos* is its discourse, and neither the fact nor the fiction of its references. Stephen Wilson's study of the Malatesta cantos records the debate between truth, in the sense of the world of fact, and the truth of epic poetry. The critical turning-point of Canto 8 is seen as preparing the narrative strategy for the rest of the work, that of the "inductive method" which produces the illusion of objectivity in the work, and limits interpretation, or seeks to do so. Similarly, Ian Bell takes Canto 31 as a discursive turning-point which moves the reader from the Renaissance to the world of Jefferson and Adams; he analyses the composition of the canto in terms of a metonymic procedure which provides both method and meaning in the work.

Pound of course *used* history, especially cultural history, in his work. From *The Spirit of Romance* to *Drafts and Fragments*, his texts were written in the consciousness of a literary context: "All ages are contemporaneous. . . . This is especially true of literature, where the real time is independent of the apparent. . . ."[5] Max Nänny's paper is an attempt to displace the Pound canon within the literary tradition; he proposes a Menippean tradition as an alternative to the accepted epic categorization of *The Cantos*, and in so doing offers a new understanding of the structural nature of the work. Alan Peacock, similarly, studies the *Homage to Sextus Propertius* in the context of the neo-classical tradition, taking a view of the mode of "imitation" as a key to understanding the status of the *persona*. This leads at once into problems of language and questions of a political identification between present and past. The paper identifies the elegiac mode, and that linguistic practice which Pound called "logopoeia," as central to this approach.

---

5. Praefatio to *The Spirit of Romance* (London, rev. edn. 1952), p. 8.

The uses which Pound made of a variety of literary texts of all ages has always, necessarily, formed an area of major critical interest for students of his work. In the case of *The Cantos*, of course, the question of his use of preceding texts has always seemed of major importance to the most basic understanding of the work. John Nolde's paper takes up the problem of Pound's use of Chinese history in its various documentary forms; he studies the origins and sources of Pound's knowledge in the work of Giles, Fenollosa, Confucius and his commentators, Morrison, Legge, Pauthier, de Mailla, and others: the references reflect the historical, ethical and linguistic dimensions of the Chinese cantos, 53-61. Mohammad Shaheen's paper adopts a similar strategy in illuminating the nature of Pound's use of Del Mar's *History of Monetary Systems*,[6] and offering an exploration of referential aspects of sections of Cantos 96 and 97.

The two final papers in this collection place Pound and his work in the context of society, and see the work as a social construct. Burton Hatlen's detailed study of Pound's fascism offers an essential understanding of the nature of fascist ideology as a preliminary to an examination of the influence of *New Age* syndicalism, early fascism, and a later fascist nihilism on the assumptions of his politics. *Jefferson and/or Mussolini* is considered within the context of this development. Hatlen argues that *The Cantos* "deconstructs" fascism by its ideogrammic method, in this respect echoing the judgment of other contributors examining the relationships between Pound's world and the word of the poem; the study is especially directed, in this paper, toward understanding the "history" of the cantos of the 1930s, specifically the political patterns of Cantos 31 through 70. David Murray's study of the economic dimensions completes this aspect of the book. He examines the way in which Pound used money to signify a cultural and moral complex which is central to the materials and meaning of *The Cantos*. He explores the parameters and limitations of this usage in a way that reveals a good deal about aspects of *The Cantos* which many readers have found obscure, puzzling, and ultimately contradictory. Murray's study, like Hatlen's, squarely faces the problems of the "usury" image, and the anti-semitic references among Pound's social and cultural concepts; in addition, it places Pound historically in the Populist tradition, an aspect of his thinking which has perhaps been somewhat neglected. These two papers conclude the book, in fact, by offering some evidence to the reader that in both his prose and

---

6. Alexander Del Mar, *History of Monetary Systems* (New York, 1903).

his poetry, Pound fictionalized history: or perhaps, to put it differently, that all historical discourse is, in the end, a complex fiction.

Many acknowledgements could be made, both to the writers of these papers, and to others not represented here, who contributed to the conference by unrecorded discussions. However, I would like to make a special personal acknowledgement of debt to Carroll F. Terrell, of the National Poetry Foundation, University of Maine at Orono. Without his constant efforts on behalf of Pound studies, neither the annual Pound conferences, nor the kind of work which this book represents, would be so extraordinarily flourishing.

Marianne Korn

TABLE OF CONTENTS

PREFACE 7

MICHAEL ANDRÉ BERNSTEIN
    History and Textuality in Ezra Pound's *Cantos* 15

ALAN DURANT
    The Language of History in *The Cantos* 23

MARTIN KAYMAN
    Ezra Pound and Science: Phenomenon and History 37

DENNIS BROWN
    The Translation of History in the Early Cantos 53

STEPHEN WILSON
    A Tentative Intervention in the Argument
    "Sous les Lauriers" 63

IAN F. A. BELL
    The Paralyzed History of Canto XXXI 75

ALAN J. PEACOCK
    Pound and Propertius: The Limitations of an
    Historical *Persona* 83

JOHN J. NOLDE
    Ezra Pound and Chinese History 99

LIONEL KELLY
    Personal History in *The Cantos* 119

MOHAMMAD Y. SHAHEEN
    The Story of Abd-el-Melik's Money in
    Canto 96 and 97 135

BURTON HATLEN
    Ezra Pound and Fascism 145

DAVID MURRAY
    Pound-Signs: Money and Representation in
    Ezra Pound 173

INDEX OF PERSONS, PLACES AND THINGS 199

MICHAEL ANDRÉ BERNSTEIN

HISTORY AND TEXTUALITY IN EZRA POUND'S CANTOS*

I

Ah! oui, c'est beau, l'éducation!
—Flaubert, *Bouvard et Pécuchet*[1]

One way to situate my argument—and no doubt the least promising, considering the occasion and audience—is with a hopelessly naive question: Why do we not read *The Cantos* ironically? Why, that is, does the dizzying torrent of "particulars," the fragments gathered from millenia of diverse cultures and dispersed traditions, often with only rudimentary indications of the context within which these particulars were first articulated and from which they derive their luminous *vertù*, not appear to us as an exuberant parody, subverting by its very insistence the claims of a bibliomania whose references we are still solemnly attempting to catalogue? After all, no one has ever demonstrated with more rigor the effects of an abiding faith in the Library as a store-house of *exempla* than the author Pound himself once called "his true Penelope."[2] Bouvard and Pécuchet are, if nothing else, indefatigable "literalists of the imagination," ever ready to commit their comfort, material substance, and even physical well-being to follow the instigations of their heterogeneous authorities, and the sheer range of their curiosity is as dauntlessly encyclopedic as that of πολυτροπος Odysseus, whether in his Homeric, Joycean, or Poundian incarnation. The paradoxical lesson of Flaubert, a lesson

---
*Preparation of this essay was assisted greatly by a grant from the American Council of Learned Societies and the National Endowment for the Humanities, and I am glad of the opportunity to acknowledge their support. I would also like to thank the Committee on Research of The University of California, Berkeley, for their travel grant which enabled me to present my work at the 1982 Conference.
1. Gustave Flaubert, *Bouvard et Pécuchet*, ed. Edouard Maynial (Paris, 1965), p. 383. "Ah, yes, isn't education a wonderful thing!"
2. Ezra Pound, "Hugh Selwyn Mauberley," in *Personae* (New York, 1971), p. 187.

to which Pound's friend and sometime fellow Vorticist Wyndham Lewis was particularly alert, is that as a literary technique, "Realism," the effort to match word and world without a gap, inevitably ends in a stylized parody, and that as a program for self-improvement the ordering of one's life as an *imitatio librorum* leads either to provincial adulteries and suicide, or more "optimistically," to *Bouvard et Pécuchet*'s relieved decision, "*Copier comme autrefois.*"[3]

Except, of course, so we console ourselves, for the author himself, whose texts, by virtue of their formal mastery of structure and rhythm, participate in an entirely different order, one uncontaminated by—although hardly innocent of a certain mordant connoisseurship in—the ludicrous misinterpretations of the characters themselves. It is Emma Bovary, in other words, as well as Frédéric Moreau, Bouvard and Pécuchet, etc., rather than their creator, who are the only "realists" in Flaubert's novels, readers determined to "put into action" the programs and instigations crystallized in the volumes of their libraries.[4]

But even the author himself, as Flaubert's letters ceaselessly complain, must saturate himself in the very books and reading-habits he scorns, precisely in order to let his own novels' aloofness from their content emerge, not by any direct expression of disgust, but through the creation of an absolute chasm between the writing-as-style and the details of the narrative-as-plot-and-character-revelation. Thus, although our own desire for some humanly attainable shelter from Flaubert's irony prompts the creation of a sentimentally heroicizing myth ("the hermit of Croisset," etc.), strictly speaking, the novels themselves permit no such avenues of escape; indeed, the degree to which they succeed in realizing the status of autonomous texts is directly dependent upon their capacity to subsume, without remainder or evasion, *all* of their constituent elements into a single armature.[5]

---

3. Gustave Flaubert, *op cit.*, p. 389. "Let us take up copying again, just like before."
4. One characteristic attempt to evade the thrust of Flaubert's not-all-that-stoic pessimism is to attribute the flailings of his characters to the *quality* of the books upon which their actions are modelled. If only the *exempla* were less shabby, so the argument runs, their effect would be enlightening rather than destructive. But if this claim is at least theoretically plausible in the case of Emma Bovary, the situation of Frédéric Moreau or Bouvard and Pécuchet cannot be bracketed quite so reassuringly. Flaubert's clerks, for example, as the scholarship upon *Bouvard et Pécuchet* has demonstrated so abundantly, draw upon representative—and by no means always discredited—volumes from virtually the entire canon of nineteenth-century speculative and practical thought. Their problem is not with the kinds of texts consulted, but with a certain way of reading, with what we might call the theme of the Book as a *paideuma*. Just as it is not the *content* of specific utterances that determines their place in the *Dictionnaire des idées reçues*, so much as their iterability *per se.*
5. I suspect that one of the reasons Flaubert's letters have come to be cited as often as his novels is that it is in the correspondence that the myth of the writer as proto-martyr and heroic victim is so seductively developed. It is also just this motif that Flaubert sought, with increasing success, to keep entirely out of the fiction itself.

Ideally, then, the Flaubertian project should leave open only two paths for "the artist who does the next job":[6] either to continue the tradition of the *"livre sur rien,"* probing still further the stylistic possibilities inaugurated by *Bouvard et Pécuchet* (and here by Samuel Beckett, especially the Beckett of *Comment c'est* and *Nouvelles et textes pour rien*), or to fall back into the kind of naive realism I have attributed to Flaubert's fictional characters.[7] But clearly *The Cantos* escape the confinement of either paradigm; they do not aspire to the self-reflexive autonomy of a purely aesthetic artifact, nor, in the main, do they pretend to a transparent and unmediated referentiality. Pound's language presents, represents, and invents all at once, and it does so without privileging any single mode or trivializing essential distinctions between categories. Much of the force of *The Cantos* themselves—and a major portion of their legacy to subsequent writers—stems from the seriousness with which Pound struggled to incorporate the problematic relationship between text and world left by the nineteenth century into a new discourse, a poetics sufficiently flexible to traverse, as if they were only thresholds, the barriers writers like Flaubert had erected with such labored mastery.

Yet I also know that an understanding of *The Cantos'* poetics requires more than merely a descriptive account of its intent, and that the complex logic by which the poem seeks to validate its own procedures is still far from having received a sufficiently precise scrutiny. This task is all the more urgent, because whatever sense we make out of the poem's various thematic concerns is entirely dependent upon the way we come to understand the methodological principles governing their inclusion within *The Cantos*. Perhaps the most fruitful objective I can set myself in the brief span of this discussion, is not so much to presume to any definitive resolution, but rather to let the problem itself appear as starkly as possible in its full singularity. Along the way, I want to indicate *some* of the principal terms which any coherent model will have to engage, but my own effort is directed toward opening a central "domain of description" for more detailed, subsequent research.[8] And in any such effort, to adopt Robert Duncan's

---

6. Ezra Pound, *Literary Essays*, ed. T. S. Eliot (New York, 1968), p. 406. All subsequent citations from this collection are acknowledged in the body of the essay as *LE*: page number.
7. For a more detailed discussion of the degree to which Flaubert's novels did indeed succeed in divorcing themselves from issues of referentiality and contemporary events, see my essay, "Jonathan Culler and the Limits of Uncertainty," in *Poetics and Theory of Literature*, 3 (1977), 589-595.
8. I take this term from Michel Foucault, *The Archaeology of Knowledge*, trans. A. M. Sheridan Smith (London, 1972), p. 114.

fine insight, "definitions are not restrictions, but outlines of energing possible elements of [a] world."⁹

II

> By good art I mean art that bears true witness.
> —Ezra Pound, "The Serious Artist,"
> [*LE*, p. 44].

> A new order is a contention in the heart of existing orders.
> —Robert Duncan, "Man's Fulfillment in Order and Strife¹⁰

Even to consider the possibility of an ironic reading of *The Cantos* such as I hinted at in the opening, must appear, I am certain, little more than a perverse example of critical self-indulgence. Yet I am by no means the first admirer of Pound's work who has experienced that disconcerting possibility. In Book Three of *Paterson*, for example, Williams' "reply to Greek and Latin with the bare hands,"¹¹ we discover a characteristic Poundian letter, which, in its exuberant pedagogy, could easily have fitted into an imaginary American equivalent of *Bouvard et Pécuchet*'s instruction manuals:

   re read *all* the Gk tragedies in
   Loeb.—plus Frobenius, plus
   Gesell   plus Brooks Adams
   ef you ain't read him all.—
   Then Golding "Ovid" is in Everyman lib.¹²

Moreover, I do not believe that in this context we can derive any assistance from the distinction between the discourse of the novel and that of verse. Quite the contrary is true, since if the nineteenth-century novel only gradually, and with at best partial success, began to undermine the notion of its language as primarily representational, the situation of poetry was closer to a total severing of any mimetic ties to an outside reality. What Michel Foucault has called the "radical intransivity"¹³ of post-Romantic literature constitutes not only the syntax and style, but also the major

---
9. Robert Duncan, "Man's Fulfillment in Order and Strife," in *Caterpillar*, 8/9 (October, 1969), 236.
10. *Ibid.*, p. 229.
11. William Carlos Williams, *Paterson* (New York, 1963), p. 2.
12. *Ibid.*, p. 138.
13. Michel Foucault, *The Order of Things* (London, 1970), p. 300.

theme of Mallarméan poetics, and from such a perspective the entire undertaking of a work like *The Cantos* will seem largely a regressive solecism. *Bouvard et Pécuchet* acknowledged, if only by ironizing, the desire to find an accessible link between text and world, but in Mallarmé's verse there is simply no more occasion for even an indirect polemic, and instead of a puppet-theater of mechanical, would-be "factive personalities," there is only *Un coup de des'* lucidly indifferent image of

> UNE CONSTELLATION
> *froide d'oubli et de désuétude*. . . .[14]

For Flaubert, good art can "bear witness" only to its own painfully achieved distance from the realm inhabited by his characters. For Mallarmé, there is, essentially, nothing to which to "bear witness" and only a language of pure absence with which to authenticate the imperatives of art. But for Pound, there is no necessary contradiction between the formal demands of a realized aesthetics and the discourse of historical, ethical, and political ideas. We know that long before Orwell, Pound saw in the *mot juste* a guardian of communal survival, arguing that:

> The *mot juste* is of public utility. I can't help it. I am not offering this fact as a sop to aesthetes who want all authors to be fundamentally useless. We are governed by words, the laws are graven in words, and literature is the sole means of keeping these words living and accurate [*LE*, p. 409].

But what I think is less apparent is just how intricate—and in the actual working-out of his poem even precarious—the effort to harmonize both orders would prove.

III

> *Übrigens ist mir alles verhasst, was mich bloss belehrt, ohne meine e Tätigkeit ze vermehren oder unmittelbar zu beleben.*
> —Goethe, quoted in Friedrich Nietzsche's
> "*Vom Nutzen und Nachteil der Historie für das Leben*"[15] "plus always Τέχνη"
> [85/546]

---

14. Stéphane Mallarmé, *Oeuvres complètes*, ed. H. Mondor et G. Jean-Aubry (Paris, 1945), p. 477. "A Constellation/cold with forgetfulness and disuse." My claim here does not, of course, deny the existence of a considerable and powerfully registered irony in Mallarmé's writings. In the *Poèms en prose*, as well as in numerous individual lyrics, there is an unmistakably ironic tension, but both its sources and its effects are entirely different from Flaubert's scarcely-controlled frustration at human self-deception.
15. Friedrich Nietzsche, "*Vom Nutzen und Nachteil der Historie für das Leben*," the second of the *Unzeitgemässe Betrachtungen* in *Werke*, ed. Karl Schlechte (Munchen,

At its core, the theoretical foundation for any analysis of textuality is an emphasis on language as essentially *productive* rather than reproductive, on a "recourse to polysemy" in which "a single 'word' proves to be conveyed by several 'voices,' to be located at the crossroads of several cultures."[16] And, in the admittedly clangorous jargon of its practicioners,

> To the idealism of a meaning anterior to that which "expresses" it, the text would then oppose the materialism of a play of signifiers that produces meaning effects. To the staticity of a discourse limited by what it has sought to copy, the text would oppose an *infinite play* ("pre-meaning"), divided into readings (or *"lexias"*) according to the endless paths on which the combination and intersection of signifiers take place.[17]

Thus in the first instance, it is precisely Pound's interweaving of so many voices, diverse languages and citations, his refusal to ground the words of the poem in the utterances of a single, unified lyric sensibility, that opens the way for the most wrenching intertextuality ("every text is absorption and transformation of a multiplicity of other texts")[18] in modernist verse. Obviously in a poem throughout which, for all but the most degoted exegetes, many passages function purely as visual (e.g. the Chinese ideograms) or as visual-acoustic stimulants (e.g. the various foreign words depending on whether or not the reader can even "sound" them out loud), the "primacy of the signifier" is already an essential resource. Indeed, the "deferment of recognition," the sometimes never-completed circuit joining signifier to signified, provides *The Cantos* with what is simultaneously a form of heightened textual pleasure (the participatory, sense-*producing* energy demanded of the reader) and of frustration.

But what differentiates *The Cantos* so markedly from other modernist and post-modernist writings in which the "deferment of recognition" has become the work's principal strategy—its guarantee of admission, as it were, into the Debrett's of pure textuality— is that Pound continued to insist not merely upon the potential public utility of his poem in the general sense of its contribution to preserving the communal language, but also upon the existence of an external, independently meaningful set of references to which his text directs its readers. Yet in contrast to Flaubert's "naive realists," *The Cantos*, referentiality is not defined primarily,

---

1954), I, 210. "I hate everything that merely instructs me without increasing or directly quickening my activity."
16. Oswald Ducrot and Tzvetan Todorov, *Encyclopedic Dictionary of the Sciences of Language*, trans. C. Porter (Baltimore, 1979), p. 356.
17. *Ibid.*, p. 357.
18. *Ibid.*, p. 359.

let alone solely, by the immediate world of contemporary phenomena. The link between word and world is neither direct nor totalizing: it is mediated by the categories of history and *praxis*, by a present which is always already seen as fragmented, and a future which the poem can neither predict nor control.[19] Pound's history, moreover, is itself a textual record of momentary and partial narratives of human labor set into an intricate dialogical relationship with one another, a polyphony of voices marked by internal fissures and contradictions as much as by unexpected silences and sudden reversals of priorities.

History provides the category for a genuinely interpersonal and non-reductive mediation between the words of the poem and the various possible worlds with which these words maintain a simultaneously commemorative and projective bond. It is also the one category that can incorporate, without risking annihilation, the ironist's gaze, since irony is itself a historical position, with distinguishable tropes and vicissitudes, and thus properly belongs *within* the confines of historical description. Curiously enough, however, as soon as history is recounted, whether in a poem like *The Cantos* or in a work of conventional historiography, it inevitably participates in all of the ambiguous logic of textuality:

> "History" signifies the totality of past events. It also designates the oral or written records of this totality. Thus there is a "history of history," i.e. a structure . . . of the narrative methods . . . through which the poet has been given memorable form. . . .
>
> Thus "history"—the linguistic presentment of the past—makes "history." It organizes our perception of the past, our cognitive remembrance. . . . What we call "history" is not a cumulative process of evidential elucidation, but a series of interpretive readings or "translations." Each successive era or political culture reads previous readings, and does so in the light of its own linguistic-ideological reflexes. . . . These reciprocities, cross-echoes and reticulations form the semantic field of historical narrative and of historical experience.[20]

Thus Pound's history has a paradoxically double function: itself profoundly textual, it nonetheless serves to direct—without rigidly determining—the productive energy of the verse away from any purely aesthetic transcendence. The worst simplification of

---

19. I am, of course, not asserting that history is the sole mediating category in *The Cantos*. Pound deeply believed that "the gods" did in fact exist, and his language can speak of "Bright gods and Tuscan, back before dew was shed" [3/11], because he was sure a sufficiently acute perception of the world would find something real to which these words exactly correspond. The category of religious and mythic universals profoundly affects the poem's discourse, but the interaction between this level of "reference" and that of historical, contingent *praxis* is too complex and vexed to include in the present discussion.
20. Anon., "The Language-field of Nazism," in *T. L. S.* (April 5, 1974), 353.

the manuals consulted with such avidity by Bouvard and Pécuchet, or of the romances so eagerly consumed by young Emma Roucult, was that each one offered a total explanation of the world, a global set of instructions by which the reader's life could henceforth be guided. I believe that Pound, at times, did indeed hope that *The Cantos* might contain such a "totalitarian" synthesis,[21] and were it not for the terrible price he himself paid for his "errors and wrecks" [116/796] these moments might indeed prompt some of the irony we feel towards Flaubert's helpless "idealists." But the very effect of the historical polyphony I have only begun to describe, the felt pressures of textual fragmentation and thematic contradictions, undermine from within the totalizing impulse, and in the process free the poem from hardening into a univocal—and hence inevitably ironizable—cultural *summa*.

If the dialectic interplay between history and textuality generates the poem's fructifying energy, it also determines the extent to which *The Cantos* succeeded in uniting the modernist preoccupation with art's essentially self-reflexive nature to the oldest tribal impulse towards telling the tale of the tribe in memorable verse. Obviously I am not claiming that Pound negotiated that dialectic with unwavering sureness, but the "record of [his] struggle" still seems to me the most engrossing venture of its kind in post-Enlightenment literature. And even though the commitments of time have made me restrict my comments to the most general methodological issues, perhaps even this beginning can open the field for further analysis among the artists and critics already engaged in taking "the next step." The project of *The Cantos* as a whole continues to gather to itself a tradition of its own, rich in detailed illuminations and new beginnings. For modern poetry *The Cantos* in their paradoxical union of history and textuality, remain—"crags cranks climb" and all[22]—a constant challenge to the safe orthodoxies of critical fashion. To move from the theoretical dilemma I have outlined to the specifics of Pound's actual practice on a canto-by-canto basis requires its own careful series of mediations between structure and realization, but with sufficient patience, perhaps we too

> ... will come to the Commissioner of the Salt Works
> in due course [98/685].

---

21. Pound used the expression "totalitarian treatise" in *Guide to Kulchur* (London, 1966), p. 27.
22. The phrase is from Basil Bunting's "On the Fly-leaf of Pound's *Cantos*" in *Collected Poems* (Oxford, 1978), p. 110.

ALAN DURANT

THE LANGUAGE OF HISTORY IN THE CANTOS

I

The context for discussion of Pound's work has remained, despite the explosion of Pound studies in Britain and in the United States in the 1960s, difficult, either by way of general assessment, or even when focused on specific topics such as China, Pisa, politics or history. It is problematic within literary history because of debates surrounding the poet's life, with local and immediate questions (such as allegiance to Fascism, implications of the trial, the Bollingen prize, madness) obscuring other more general issues; problematic for exegesis, because of the range of allusion and breadth of reference of *The Cantos*, as well as in view of the changing practices within the poem's incompleted, fragmentary composition; problematic for existing forms of criticism, evaluation or commentary, because of the difficulty of understanding ways in which the poetry's tissue of interrelations and repetitions is sustained in articulations of language increasingly subsumed — until closing hesitancies and recantations of the 1960s — under contentious philosophies of language, of meaning, and of culture. These famous complexities of the Pound argument are, if well known, still practical obstacles, troubling the useful development of research and perplexing wider understandings of the continuing and expanding interest in Pound.

But these difficulties for discussion face, always, an urgency and an importance: for if it is widely recognized that a significant transformation of poetic practice occurs in the twentieth century, it is also evident that Pound's writing, as well as his editing and influence, attest crucial innovations and directions within those developments. And if it is usual to trace the developments themselves across two distinguishable domains, the new cultural emphases in poetry and the linguistic innovations of modernism, it is still more importantly the interrelations between these concerns which produce the difficulty of context and, practically, of comprehension.

Yet despite the complexities, it is evidently the ways in which these domains are reciprocally defining—the cultural interest requiring a newness of language, but the language of the poem establishing the terms of the political or the cultural—that is both the mark of Pound's importance (his work energetically, continually, poses the questions), and the difficult terrain of contemporary placings of his achievement or significance.

The two areas of concern are individually familiar:

(1) New cultural perspectives for poetry. The annexation of history as an available resource for poetry, a material whose literary elucidation can produce a capability to understand, and to intervene in, the modern world. The emphasis appears related to the negotiation of a new and more central position for poet and poetry in twentieth-century European and American society, a move to revise the terms of address of the nineteenth-century poet and audience, an impulse echoed across the almost simultaneously emerging, and later extended, varieties of New Criticism. In these terms, the cultural emphasis across the range of forms it assumed has its importance, both in respect of the individual writers— Pound, Eliot, Joyce, etc.—but also as significant focus of twentieth-century literary attentions, with reverberations through Richards, Leavis and others into continuing practices of literary education. Poetry becomes less a diversion or entertainment, more a culturally prophetic source of social meaning; for Eliot there is a tradition and dissociation of sensibility, terms of a history within which a moment of interruption has deformed contemporary living. Restitution of contemporary society would rely upon fullness of restoration, preservation, and reunification. For Pound there is, around the time of *Mauberley*, the apprehension of usury, of evident "repeats" in history—and of possible transformation of the present in political intervention (the developing accent of the polemics, the politics, later the broadcasts). And the operation of history in *The Cantos* has its evident and repeated configuration; recall, for example, the famous pronouncements. First, from "Date Line" in 1934: "An epic is a poem including history. I don't see that anyone save a sap-head can now think he knows any history until he understands economics. . . ."[1] Next, from "History and Ignorance" in 1935: "History that omits economics will not eternally be accepted as anything but a farce or a fake. The gross cloacal ignorance of professors, of reporters who offer

---

1. *Literary Essays of Ezra Pound*, ed. T. S. Eliot (repr., London, 1968), p. 86.

chronicles with no economic analysis, can not forever pass as enlightenment!"[2] Third, from "An Introduction to the Economic Nature of the United States," in 1944: "For forty years I have schooled myself, not to write an economic history of the U.S. or any other country, but to write an epic poem which begins 'In the Dark Forest' crosses the Purgatory of human error, and ends in the light. . . ."[3] Lastly, from Canto 117, in the mid-1960s: "The dreams clash/and are shattered—/and that I tried to make a paradiso/terrestre" [117/802].[4]

(2) The modernist practices of language. Adoption of new processes of composition for poetry, involving increasingly a dissolution of logical or grammatical relations (from Imagism and the famous cutting of *The Waste Land* onwards there is the affirmation of metaphor—"Wisdom lies next thee,/simply, past metaphor" [82/526]—ideogram and ideogrammic method, forces and tensions exposed in juxtaposition and counterpoint); and use of a wide range of historical and cultural allusions. In these allusions, the references function as illustration to the cultural history to be reviewed and restored, in excess of a conventional panoply of figurative literary mythology—as such, an altered and extended condition of literary and cultural reference; use of complex interplays of registers, dialects, colloquialisms, quotations.

These are the two familiar areas of innovation. Such projections of a cultural history within poetry appear relatively unproblematic, when conceived as isolated instances or levels of composition. But what makes the varying modernist configurations of subjectivity, literary language, cultural history, and political position of continuing concern is the way in which these practices disrupt and displace a set of long-standing distinctions or oppositions in terms of which literature has been conceptualized: at least since the Renaissance there have existed, across changing theoretical and practical consituencies, distinctions in effect between consciousness and imagination as source of expression; styles and genres as forms of implementation of expression; substantive or thematic occupations as subject matter.

Beyond all other innovations, it is this set of divisions, effectively between an author, a form, and a content, which some twentieth-century writing—and eminently aspects of the poetry of Pound—most energetically investigate, tracing in language the production of positions of meaning and constitutions of poetic

---
2. *Selected Prose, 1909-1965*, ed. William Cookson (London, 1973), p. 237.
3. *Ibid.*, p. 137.
4. *The Cantos* (London, 1975). Subsequent references in the text will give Canto and page number in this edition.

voice—the very terms of definition of selfhood and of society. If literature always had its forms for treatment of public and historical events (the epic of heroic and national celebration and destiny; the epigram, the epitaph, the ode), what writings of Pound and others have made clear is the constitutive role of language in the productions of literary representations.

To assume a position of social and individual meanings—to take up a position in a set of historically constituted personal, social and linguistic options—is shown by such radical practices of writing to be not simply the adoption of an available range of rhetorical, literary forms for expressing social comment, but a process within which meanings are produced by the specific character of articulations of language. This is exactly the problem of Pound's early writing, until the intermediary stances of *Mauberley* and *Propertius*: *Mauberley* seemingly Pound's last attempt to define poetic voice by casting off *personae*; and *Propertius* with its interfusion of discursive registers and social positions within which poetic voice has to be assumed or rejected. The importance of these two works might now seem to be preeminently that they mark a decisive stage of transformation from the translations and early poems in which Pound experimented with factitious voices of a *persona*, towards the shifting and unfinalized complexity of address of *The Cantos*.

II

Such significances of history within the study of Pound—relations of the past being exactly what is called up to moments of self-definition and of social identification—appear to engage questions which both reflect back upon enunciation and conceptions of an author (the poet's experiences and development, within which the *personae* and work on the troubadours focus a concern for historical representations, ways of deploying contemporary resources of language to conjure meanings for a past), and which address a larger social history—the domains of investigation (economics, Chinese history, Sigismundo, etc.). Such terms of a history for study of Pound also place these concerns of biography and of social reference within considerations of forms of language, and place the question of voice within a material history and changing currency of literature and a reading public.

These elements are a history of poet and poem in which the specific illustrations, quotations and illuminations of *The Cantos* are embedded. But conceived in these terms of a past enfolded within contemporary resources of language, the historical material of *The Cantos* engages important problems when considered alongside other emphases made by Pound—in particular, the continual stress on experience and sight as the source of facts, and a closeness of thought to reality, which can be reflected in a precision of definition and language.

Consider, for example, these affirmations: in the essay "The Serious Artist" in 1913:

> Purely and simply . . . good art can NOT be immoral. By good art I mean the art that bears true witness, I mean the art that is most precise. You can be wholly precise in representing a vagueness. You can be wholly a liar in pretending that the particular vagueness was precise in its outline.[5]

Or, again:

> I am not now speaking of shams. I mean beauty, not slither, not sentimentalizing about beauty, not telling people that beauty is the proper and respectable thing. I mean beauty. You don't argue about an April wind, you feel bucked up when you meet it. You feel bucked up when you come on a swift moving thought in Plato or on a fine line in a statue.[6]

Or, in *Polite Essays*: "Men are good or bad in the year 1935 in proportion as they will LOOK at the facts, new facts, any facts."[7]

But in apparent opposition to these priorities, many of the poem's major aspirations—and, in view of the eminent popularity of the paradisal, lyrical sections, much of its interest—lie precisely outside these spheres of empirical evidence. At least two significant areas contingent to this focus on fact and experience need to be distinguished and explored.

(1) The first such area is the poem's "religious" emphases, which overspill or extend beyond the immediate truth of experience: from the early models of transcendence such as the vortex (the *BLAST* manifesto's "Beyond Action and Reaction, we would establish ourselves"), to the images of crystals and gemmology of the late Cantos, or the Platonic signature inscribing the form of the divine in the forms of the material; metamorphosis and epiphany of Gods; sight, light, vision, illumination—so many ways of conceiving experiences of speculation and faith. Effectively, these extend the register of sight, facts, and truthfulness to reality into an implication of an unseen reality, with metamorphosis and epiphany stressing that this preternatural reality will remain unseen to all except the chosen—prophets, seers, heroes, and poets.

---

5. *Literary Essays, ed cit.*, p. 44.
6. *Ibid.*, p. 45.
7. *Polite Essays* (London, 1937), p. 51.

The claimed continuity between empirical fact and mystical belief, which *The Cantos* across all their variation demand, establishes a form of unarguable justification for the practical emphases of knowledge and polemic. Indeed it guarantees (and this is the very germ of Pound's support for Fascism) the deliberated patterns of world history and contemporary expedient. Relatedly, the major truth of the unseen endorses, as what Fenollosa will call "natural suggestion,"[8] certain effects of metaphor and of the whole fabric of interconnections of *The Cantos* in allusion, juxtaposition, and structures of repetition. It is this "unseen" endorsement which closes off an otherwise far wider range of possible interrelationships between images, sequences and sections. The power of the eye and of simple fact, the assured certitude of the project of the long poem and of the essays until a closing silence, stretches beyond these immediate boundaries of the sensed into "the high air, to the stratosphere, to the imperial/calm, to the empyrean, to the baily of the four towers/the NOUS, the ineffable crystal" [40/201].

(2) A second non-empirical range of concern is the processes of history themselves, which are not offered up for test by experience; these being invisible, what remains of past ages, regimes, civilizations is a set of relics and documents. As signs or evidences, these stress the way in which acts of vision and assumptions of fact rely upon mediating processes of conceptualization and interpretation—stress that there can be, when considering events and relations of a past, no simple immediacy or primacy of facts of sight, no evident and unanswerable certitudes or patterns. Indeed, Pound employs senses of decay of the past on occasion exactly by addressing the deformation of relics, and their overlayering in the modern world—"That, Fritz, is the era, to-day against the past,/'Contemporary.' And the passion endures" [7/25]—in order to evoke the sense of a grandeur of the past being debased—and, correlatively, of a proper or real condition inaccessible to sight, beyond our immediate perception unless in acts of love, faith, or enlightened and charged perception. Specifically, notions of causation are invisible, can only be rationally constructed in argument, and this is a major problem for a poetry which insists upon self-evidence and demonstration by way of presentation, juxtaposition, and association. In context of empirical terms of experience and of immediate, self-evident knowledge, with definition in simple correspondence with reality, the emphasis upon economics is especially significant, since the processes and relations

---
8. Ernest Fenollosa, *The Chinese Written Character as a Medium for Poetry* (San Francisco, 1936), p. 8.

which constitute economics and derivative social relationships are never simply graspable as objects or the epiphenomena which those relations produce. Nevertheless, Pound affirms in "The Liberal: Request for an Effective Burial of Him": "I have pledged for a clear definition of terms, for an adequate international news service, and for a knowledge of economic causes and effects, clearly learnable from history."[9] One consequence of this is a deflection of Pound's writing away from argument into polemic and assertion in the essays, and a displacement of concepts of explanation for usury and/or exploitation (necessitated by the early, radical realization of social relations as concerns of poetry) by anti-semitism and its terminology of "blood, bones, and endocrines."[10] This substitution of bodies and objects for relations and processes indicates a capturing of the invisible with the visible—less what Fenollosa calls "a bridge whereby to cross from the minor truths of the seen to the major truths of the unseen,"[11] than an appropriation and reduction of complexities of constitutive relations (for persons, as for financial institutions and social practices), turning these into simple truths of nature and self-evidence.

III

These two problematic extensions of the Poundian epistemology are interesting in themselves, making possible many of the certitudes of the poem and of the essays, and extending scope from entrenched certitudes of individual experience into imagined, inherent forms of the universe and lessons from a totality of world history. But, for the poem, there is, beyond all the logical difficulties with which these formulations are faced, the difficulty that not only are the relations of history not simply available as empirical evidence, as facts for the eye, but that the poem's ability to refer, to construct and articulate a set of historical relations and associations, is possible only within forms of language—in specific forms of representation available in literary discourse.

In order to speak of world history, it is necessary to take up a specific position of enunciation (in poetry, frequently the articulation of lyrical voice, but, following the Symbolists, possibly a tissue of reading relations). This is the point of intersection

---

9. *Action*, 132 (27 August, 1938), 13.
10. "Race," *New English Weekly*, X, 1 (15 October, 1936), 12.
11. *The Chinese Written Character . . ., ed cit.*, p. 11.

between Pound's insistence upon social explanation and imperative, and his requirement of a new grasp of language and meaning.

The crucial questions of language and the ways in which *The Cantos* are to address a reader Pound negotiates in a series of models and theories: definition, the ideogram, the luminous detail, metaphor. But considering less how the theories appear to be implanted in *The Cantos*, than how reading might establish or vindicate the effects the theories anticipate, a number of complexities of the poem including history become acute. Four distinct sites of interrogation of the power of this means of historical illustration as a basis for an actual and effective literary politics might be thought to require particular comment.

(1) The first such site is Pound's ways of referring, across a variety of radically different kinds of reference. These become problematic with regard to the precision of definition and realism in writing, what the young Pound called the prose tradition in verse, insofar as the constant suggestion of a world against which language is to be tested is undermined by unexplored questions of the existence or non-existence of the entities being referred to. It is not that it is in general impossible to refer to things which do not exist (unicorns, angels, abominable snowmen), or which no longer exist (dodos), but that Pound's understandings of language at stake in *The Cantos* appear to commit the poem to an existence in the world—by way of the simple, ritual acts of incantation and invocation—of a wide range of mythical, divine, and fabulous entities. In this sense, the poem's project to chart movements of history, of knowledge, and of society in processes of language is an important inversion: those movements appear to be not so much recorded by the language (with the poem's meaning reaching out for the reality), as invoked and indeed constituted by features of the poem's discursive organization.

Moreover, whilst these difficulties of prediction, as well as usages of language which are referentially opaque, are constantly at play in *The Cantos*, the problems such usages pose for Pound's simple insistence upon meaning being tied to correspondence with a real world, words reaching to the object, to the bone, and thus to meaning, are never questioned. Against the complexity for analysis of the usages of *The Cantos*, Pound merely continues to affirm: "To communicate and then stop, that is the/law of discourse/To go far and come to an end" [80/494]; or, "And as Ford said: get a dictionary/and learn the meaning of words" [98/689]; or still, at the beginning of the *ABC of Economics*: "Once again, please do not imply. Please do not think I mean one whit more than what I have written. When I want to mean something further I will say it."[12]

Despite the force of these proclamations, description of a world referred to is further problematized by the evocation of paradisal scenes, where language explicitly negates the existence of virtually all the qualities it attributes: "Nor bird-cry, nor any noise of wave moving,/Nor splash of porpoise, nor any noise of wave moving,/. . ./no gull-cry, no sound of porpoise,/Sand as of malachite, and no cold there,/the light not of the sun" [17/76-77]. Incidentally, too, it might be noticed that these famous lyrical sections run against at least one emphasis of Fenollosa, that concerning the "complete sentence . . . which it would take all time to pronounce,"[13] with all other lesser sentences leaking everywhere "like electricity from an exposed wire" in the continual displacement of energies of nature in interminable relations. For Pound, paradisal lyricism involves, repeatedly, a density of nouns (but again, Fenollosa: "A true noun, an isolated thing, does not exist in nature. Things are only the terminal points, or rather the meeting points, of actions, cross-sections cut through actions, snap-shots"[14] and few verbs and, where these exist, often passives or intransitives: a lyricism of immanent and static energies rather than of continuous and transformable forces. Indeed, where there are present indicative verb forms of action ("The sea's claw gathers them outward/Scilla's dogs snarl at the cliff base" [47/236] etc., these remain ambiguous between the specificity of a particular action being watched, and general or habitual processes of nature which are continually repeated.

(2) Image and parataxis offers a second important site of interrogation: grammatically isolated words may be understood to produce not single meanings, but meanings for a reader, changing in time, place and significance. Consider, for example, Pound's use, for the representation of history, of archaism, especially for terms of enunciation such as "saith." In contemporary English, the distinction of "saith" from "said" is not at all one of reference, but of the institutional place of the speaker, or the speaker's position of enunciation. Or again, the changing senses established in particular acts of reading by variations of time and place—the effect, for example, of exoticism (the nationally and educationally shifting effects of Pound's interweaving of different languages).

Indeed, the very necessity of making it new, upon which Pound insists, is the result, within the history of a national language

---

12. *Selected Prose, ed cit.*, p. 203.
13. *The Chinese Written Character . . ., ed cit.*, p. 11.
14. *Ibid.*, p. 24.

and a society, of language change—exactly what his theories of language will evidently seek, in the present and for the future, to repudiate ("the legal or scientific word ... must, at the outset, be defined with the greatest possible precision, and never change its meaning"[15]): making it new assumes a level of control over meaning (meanings for a whole passage or work can be known in respect of a particular period by inspection, and then translated, updated, for a different historical moment), a power of fixing identity across time and place. Remember the famous letter to W. H. D. Rouse, of February 1935: "I don't see that one TRANSLATES by leaving in unnecessary words, that is, words not necessary to the meaning of the WHOLE passage, any whole passage. ... I believe one shd. check up all that verbiage as say 4% BLANKS, to be used where and when wanted in the translation. ...."[16] It is precisely this kind of control over meaning which *The Cantos* demonstrate to rely upon detailed specifications of context and circulation—and to be radically transformed by transplantation into a compound literary work such as *The Cantos*, where a whole new range of determinations of context and of meaning prevail.

(3) Polysemy, ambiguity, and cohesion constitute a third area of investigation. Despite the contradiction that multiple possibilities of meaning pose to what might be called Pound's natural philosophy of language, many of the transitions of *The Cantos* are achieved by puns and rhymes across languages. In terms of fields of force disposed around a central presence, and of a poetic process imitative of that force-field in overlayerings of metaphor and of the repeat in history, it remains a major question how it is that *The Cantos* progress at all, rather than continually circling this central node or axis.

Clearly the poem does not do this: beginning without specified origin, with a coordinating conjunction "and then" referring to antecedents which will never be specified, the poem never affirms its direction or focus, and ends across a series of biographical and thematic displacements fifty years and eight hundred pages later, still in a fragment, and no closer to finality: "i.e. it coheres all right/even if my notes do not cohere" [116/797].

It is largely displacements by way of ambiguity which precipitate the poem's advance. Consider, for example, the grammatical ambiguity of the "so that" with which Canto 1 closes—a rare, explicit logical connective, but ambiguous between its implication of purpose, or of result. For the representation of historical

---
15. "A Visiting Card," in *Selected Prose...*, ed cit., p. 291.
16. *The Letters of Ezra Pound, 1907-1941*, ed. D. D. Paige (London, 1951), pp. 357-358.

connection in the poem there remains always this urgency for analysis of the peculiarities of co-reference in *The Cantos*, which create its effects of continuity and cohesion; of shifters, of enunciation, and the specification of that position in place and time; and of explicit use of connectives, precisely forms of transition which neither specify nor yet annul the processes of language, knowledge, and history which it is the poem's object to elucidate.

(4) Finally, we need to look at the dissolution of Pound's syntax, in favor of juxtaposition and association, achieved in the practice of metaphor. This dissolution disrupts the forms of cohesion which for lyrical poetry before the Symbolists and the Imagists constitute the relations of texture—realizations of a mediating voice of discourse and persuasion. The accent of the ideogrammic method, of signs offering up of themselves, and in their written forms, meanings which they contain by imitation, runs against this emphasis of a subjective lyricism and a voice, producing instead an impact of the documentary, the tabular, and the visual.

But this disruption returns across kinds of discrepancy between visual readings of the poem (the pictogrammic and spatial emphases) and acts of reading aloud, whose intonational contours (Pound's own are exemplary in this) negotiate ambiguities, selecting meanings, stresses, and relations between elements of the ideogrammic fabric, fixing them in the certainty of voice and body. For Pound, the fixing of meanings in vocal stress is simply incorporated into techniques which organize the power of visual readings: this is the sense of his suggestion in a letter to Hubert Creekmore, of February 1939: "ALL typographic disposition, placings of words on the page, is intended to facilitate the reader's intonation, whether he be reading silently to himself or aloud to friends."[17] But whilst generally excised before the "natural" operations of language and the world, it is significant that the effect of a subjectivity intervenes in a number of contexts. Consider, for example, imperatives in Canto 52, such as "Know then" [52/258]: or Canto 77, "To/know what precedes and what follows/will assist yr/comprehension of process/ vide also Epictetus and Syrus" [77/465]; or the confessions of the *Drafts and Fragments*, "I have brought the great ball of crystal;/who can lift it?/can you enter the great acorn of light" [116/795]?

There is continual contradiction between this lyricism and the patterning of nature objectively mirrored and defined in

---
17. *Ibid.*, p. 418.

language. The epistemological question of the poem—its insertion of a knowledge of reality from experience within the major experience of the divine and of nature—is exactly hidden, concealed, here, with the voice and the experience calling up in language patterns which are then taken to represent, if elusively, an objective and material nature.

Indeed, it is this contradiction which is suspended in the structure of the composition of *The Cantos*, in increments and drafts and fragments, with the title itself disavowing continuity and development in favor of the loose cohesion of collected cantos. This form of composition held in abeyance questions about overall relations, or what would be the retroactive importance for the early stages of the poem of its closure of meaning in paradise, knowledge, and plenitude precipitated by an end. Draft, fragment, the poem at first anticipatory, then later retrospective—the references back, the allusions, and the repetitions making closing stages intelligible only by analysis of formative early moments.

These four areas of complexity of language (as well as others) which can disrupt the definition of a history from which knowledge and direction can be simply taken are crucial to contemporary discussion and assessment of *The Cantos*. It is not just that for whatever reason Pound neglects to consider the various kinds of investigation and argument which might have alerted him to the range of contradictions to which such a project of one hundred cantos, or a "cryselephantine," "really LONG, endless, leviathanic" poem would be subject. What is important, now, is that his work enacts, in a particular and problematic realization, a continuing set of concerns about the constitution and circulation of meanings in language.

IV

The HISTORY of *The Cantos* leads in a variety of ways. Substantive questions of a past enfolded within the poem can be seen to be themselves embedded within a set of broader questions—of the language of representation, of ways of referring, and of a subjectivity in development and process. What makes *The Cantos* significant is the way in which the poem exemplifies dimensions of a writing of the self into available positions to be occupied in the configurations of a past, a language, and a present society; more than functioning as a set of illustrations as exempla, the poem's history refracts into a range of considerations: a) Into questions of the notion of author and of subjectivity; the history of writer and poem, of biography—Pound's desired move into a position of meaning embodied in a series of geographical moves, from frontier Idaho into capitals of civilization, with this move traced in the successive models of centers of knowledge, pivots, axes; Pound's various concerns for the position of centralized, unified, and controlled meaning: definition; authority; the phallic seed and fecundity of nature leading to the generation of knowledge; incantation and a voice of prophecy positioned against the displacements of language and social change. b) Into questions of social history; the knowledges deployed; economic speculation; reflections upon history, biology, literature; vilification of other conflicting currencies; the poem within traditions of literature— its development and diffraction of conceptions of the long poem: Pound's radical perception that the destiny of heroes and nations is intertwined with questions of economics and of social relations, but this observation folded back upon the potency of individual men of knowledge and power, Sigismundo, Mussolini, Kung, the history returned to an individual's position of knowledge; the literary tradition for reformation and restoration to be taken within its own history: crisis of European civilization at the time of and after the First World War, circulation of opinion and political radicalizations in depression and slump, social and political upheaval, etc.

These are the historical elements which intersect in the language of the poetry, are what is worked over in the writing and the acts of reading—language in practice as constitution of personal and social identity, in sexuality, in meanings, and in politics. The dilemmas of the Pound argument circle these several interwoven histories: the history included by the poem; the personal history written across the poem; the social history which positions it. The familiar dilemmas of interpretation and assessment revolve around Pound's recognition of this individually and socially constitutive character of language in action. But, for Pound, the recognition is checked always but ineffectually by repression of that radical potentiality in the selection, correction, and proscription necessary to produce a unified meaning for poet as subject, for poet positioned in society as possessor and author of knowledge, and for poet as authority and agent of culture.

MARTIN KAYMAN

*EZRA POUND AND SCIENCE:
PHENOMENON AND HISTORY*

Despite its continued growth, interest in Pound—still less critical acceptance—has always been relatively restricted; and this in face of Pound's undeniable literary-historical centrality to modernism. Pound has been strikingly unsuccessful in finding a suitable place within the dominant intellectual, critical and ideological traditions, be it the school of Leavis, the "New Criticism," or the traditions of Marxist, Freudian and structuralist thought. On the other hand, his acceptance owes itself to a relatively small (but distinguished) body of scholars who, by their dedicated efforts, have generated a considerable apparatus. In other words, in order for Pound to be read, a new space adequate to his work has had to be produced: a space effectively defined by its distance from the "mainstreams."

The industry/profession has engaged with Pound's discourse and constructed a library and a language which enables us, materially and intellectually, to read and discuss the work. Neglected histories, philosophies and buried ideas have been "dug... up out of sepulture," generating virtually a compendium of heresies. Terms have been resurrected and/or invested with new meanings and new terms invented; cultures and historical moments have been juxtaposed into alternative traditions and patterns. This eccentricity of discourse and materials not surprisingly imitates the eccentricity of Pound's own ideas and sources, either by a process of endorsement or by the generation of analogous references.

For some, this relative eccentricity in respect of "mainstream" modern thought is evidence precisely of the radical and positive innovation that is Ezra Pound: a new discourse, technique, a new culture, a chance to escape the contradictions and partialities of the exhausted dualisms and inadequacies of Western intellectual culture in a return to a vital and affectionate cosmos.

This is "the better tradition," kept alive on the margins of the dominant mercantile and capitalist culture.

But, as Ian Bell has recently argued,[1] it can also be seen not as a genuine opening of horizons, but rather, by means of that very eccentricity and its accompanying opacity, as evidence of the closed and circular nature of the Poundian curricular universe. Thus the only way of reading Pound would indeed be to repeat his eccentricity, either literally or analogically, within the pre-ordered totality. In this sense, if the poem is addressed to a member of the tribe, then it equally well constructs the character of the tribe to which one, as reader/scholar, must seek to attain: the curriculum constitutes a sort of shibboleth for initiates and masters.

Whether it be a liberation from decayed thought, or an imprisonment within an eccentric totality, a sort of private language has grown up within a professional circle.[2] This language borrows its terms, references and authorities from central traditions or, more often, from the "heresies," or by invention directs itself, self-referentially, towards a specialized and inter-validating Poundian universe. It hence explicates and justifies what may effectively be called a Poundian "paradigm"—or, to partake in that very process, what we might call a "paideuma."

More recently, however, the now fairly strongly established paradigm has been reaching out and coming closer to recuperating more "mainstream" paradigms and/or analogizing with them—for example, in Herbert Schneidau's and Jacob Korg's attempts to apply Roman Jakobson, or John Steven Child's use of semiotics, also in Jean-Michel Rabaté's encounter with deconstruction, and Christine Brooke-Rose's semiotic analysis.[3] Freud and Marx, needless to say, remain outside the paradigm; and these omissions or incompatibilities are significant. Although Peter Booker, David

---

1. Ian F. A. Bell, *Critic as Scientist: The Modernist Poetics of Ezra Pound* (London, 1981). E.g.: "we find ourselves repeating repeats which in themselves seal the world by their own repetitions" [p. 242]; and "the reader participates in the concealment of origins as in his turn he further decentres the text before him in an effort to reconstruct the hidden harmony that its curriculum promises" [p. 245].

2. The language, that is, for example, of process, palimpsest, paideuma, paraclete, sagetrieb; of logopoeia, melopoeia, phanopoeia, mythopoeia; of image, vortex, *virtù*, ideogram, concetto, forma; of metathemenon, noigandres, phantastikon, polumetis and poliphoibois; of Fenollosa, Frobenius, Agassiz, Antheil, Douglas, Del Mar, of Richard St. Victor, Erigena Scotus, Gemisthus Plethon, Grosseteste, de Gourmont, John Heydon; of the Albigensians, the Manicheans and Eleusis—not to mention the Chinese terminology.

3. Herbert N. Schneidau, "Wisdom Past Metaphor: Another View of Pound, Fenollosa and Objective Verse," *Paideuma*, 5-1, pp. 15-29; John Steven Childs, "Larvatus Prodeo: Semiotic Aspects of the Ideogram in Pound's *Cantos*," *Paideuma*, 9-2, pp. 289-307; Jean-Michel Rabaté, "Pound's Art of Naming: Between Reference and Reverence," paper at the Ezra Pound Conference (Sheffield, 1981); Jacob Korg gave his paper at the Keele Conference in 1977, and one has also heard a Lacanian interpretation (Durham, 1980).

Murray, Stephen Wilson, Ian Bell, Alan Durant and others (including, I might add, myself) work from within either or both of these traditions, in none of these cases do we find the discourses used as supports for the Poundian enterprise, which itself refuses them.

One central area in which a special paradigm has been required, and not lacking, is obviously the question of how to read the technical innovativeness of the poem, particularly at the level of *form*. The problem is focused by Yvor Winters' famous attack, which declared a critique from within a highly classical discourse, opposing a rational category of ideas/concepts to an empiricist category of sensation.[4] Donald Davie's explicit refutation escapes Winters' dichotomy by reference to a Poundian category: "the point to be made is that Pound in *The Cantos* characteristically aims at re-creating not the concept, any or all of them, but rather the *forma*, the thing behind them and common to them all."[5] This *forma* is explicated firstly with references from within the Poundian paradigm—the "immortal *concetto*," and inevitably "the rose in the steel dust" from the "Cavalcanti" article and the *Guide to Kulchur*.[6] When Davie returns to the issue in his later work, he finds a further contemporary analogue in Allen Upward, explicating the *forma* in terms of the *ontwerp*, which he links to another Poundian term, the "vortex," thus giving the double-vortex or water-spout/fountain image.[7]

This sequence is placed not in a traditional historico-philosophical context—from whence came the critique—but rather in relation to an *objective world*, guaranteed specifically by science:

> Upward has too much respect for the honest materialist—in particular, for the physicist of his day—to forget, when he turns to look at the *im*materialist (or as he must call him, following Alfred Nobel, the *idealist*), how the materialist conceives of matter as knotted and equally opposed strengths, as in the wrestlers who tremble as they lock. This *is* the nature of matter....[8]

---

4. Sensory perception replaces idea. Pound, early in his career, adopted the inversion derived from Locke by the associationists: since all ideas arise from sensory impressions, all ideas can be expressed in terms of sensory impressions. But of course they cannot be: when we attempt this method, what we get is sensory impressions alone, and we have no way of knowing whether we have had any ideas or not.

Yvor Winters, *The Function of Criticism* (1957), quoted in Donald Davie, *Ezra Pound: The Poet as Sculptor* (London, 1965), p. 217.
5. Davie, *op cit.*, p. 220.
6. Pound, "Cavalcanti" (1910-34), in *Literary Essays*, ed. T. S. Eliot (London, 1954), pp. 154-155; *Guide to Kulchur* (1938) (London, 1966), p. 152; also "Through Alien Eyes, I," *The New Age* 12 (16 Jan. 1913). The first two extracts quoted and connected in Davie, *op cit.*, p. 219.
7. Davie, *Pound* (London, 1975), pp. 63-64.
8. *Ibid.*, p. 65.

Upward's metaphor for the conception of matter proposed by his contemporary physicists is emphatically endorsed by Davie as an objective guarantee for Pound's practice. But lest this collapse back into its historical and metaphorical moment, he immediately seeks a more up-to-date endorsement along similar lines:

> Upward of course did not live to see this inspired guess "at the first beat" astonishingly confirmed experimentally, when the biophysicists Crick and Watson broke the genetic code to reveal "the double helix" (that is to say, double vortex).[9]

Hugh Kenner's famous explication of Poundian form starts from such a parallel confirmation, backwards through the Fuller knot. He links the central idea—the vortex—with other Poundian notions—the Image, the rose in the steel dust, the ideogram, the fountain/crystal, the act of translation, tradition, the idea of *virtù* and the luminous detail; and he finally explicates and justifies the Poundian form in terms of a fundamental and real world of scientific validation—working back (or around) to Einstein, Marconi, Mendel and the Curies, as in the following example:

> Luminous Details, then, are "patterned integrities" which transferred out of their context of origin retain their power to enlighten us. They have this power because, as men came to understand early in the 20th Century, all realities whatever are patterned energies. If mass is energy (Einstein) then all matter exemplifies knottings, the self-interference inhibiting radiant expansion at the speed of light. Like a slip-knot, a radioactive substance expends itself. Elsewhere patterns weave, unweave, reweave: light becomes leaf becomes coal becomes light.[10]

Professors Kenner and Davie, telling us what reality/matter is, both propose a Poundian base founded in modern science—a reference that cannot help but pass beyond explication or illustration to validation.

Pound cannot be explained in terms of traditional categories because he has indeed contacted something which itself has invalidated the outmoded and partial categories of previous dualistic philosophy. One assumes a radical rupture between the real world and its reflection in traditional mainstream discourse; hence there is no case to answer from the latter paradigm. We in fact need such another paradigm as Pound offers as a way out of reductive dualisms through a new trans-discursive reality—or rather a reality which has always been there, but which had been "sunken" by those dualisms. The new paradigm gestures to this scientific reality at the same time as it recuperates the neglected/marginalized

---
9. *Ibid.*, p. 66.
10. Hugh Kenner, *The Pound Era* (London, 1972), p. 153; and the chapter *passim*.

traditions, and synthesises the two, the lost radiant world found again by modern science and rendered by Pound.

This process of explication thus escapes the self-reference of the Poundian discourse by means of its extra-discursive endorsement. The "mainstream" question is answered from somewhere else—the world of scientific reality—justifying its practice against the so-called dualist paradigms without having to confront them on their own ground.

By this appeal, the explication necessarily implies that the *forma* is objective and real. "The magnetic lines of force—to use the poet's own metaphor—already exist."[11] But the case is clearly not that simple; we cannot neglect Pound's emphasis on the shaping force of the artist and the problems of De Born and Sordello, for example.[12] A myth is "an impersonal or objective story," an "equation," but it is "woven out of his own emotion"; and "Our only measure of truth is, however, our own perception of truth."[13] That is to say that there appear to be two series of *forma*: the form inherent in nature, and the shaping force of the artist/hero/statesman.[14] The question is always: how do they relate? There are various complementary ways in which the two series may be theoretically related. Apart from a simple affirmation of faith, we might choose to endorse Pound's own categories as they develop through the career/work—leading to Heydon's signatures or Richard St. Victor's "contemplatio," for example.[15] There are

---

11. Eva Hesse, introduction to *New Approaches to Ezra Pound* (London, 1969), p. 24. *Cf* (for the use of the poet's own metaphor) Max Nänny, *Ezra Pound: Poetics for an Electric Age* (Berne, 1973)—e.g.: "The 'circuit' of facts that, provided an adequate mental energy is applied to it, generates instant illumination—so vital in the electric age."
  Davie is unambiguous:

  For Pound, colour inheres in the coloured object, it is of its nature; just as the carved or hewn shape inheres in the stone block before it has been touched; just as words inhere, in the natures they name, not in the minds that do the naming. Not in painting any more than in poetry will Pound agree that "it all depends how you look at it." Nature exists as other, bodied against us, with real attributes and her own laws which it is our duty to observe.
  "The Poet as Sculptor," in Hesse, *op cit.*, p. 201.

12. *Cf* "Near Perigord" and Canto 2.
13. Pound, "Arnold Dolmetsch" (1915), *Literary Essays*, p. 431; *cf* "Psychology and Troubadours" (1912) in *The Spirit of Romance* (New York, 1968), p. 92; and:

  Poetry is a sort of inspired mathematics, which gives us equations, not for abstract figures, triangles, spheres, and the like, but for human emotions. If one have a mind which inclines to magic rather than to science, one will prefer to speak of these equations as spells or incantations; it sounds more arcane, mysterious, recondite.
  Ibid., p. 14.

14. "The serious artist is scientific in that he presents the image of his desire, of his hate, of his indifference as precisely that, as precisely the image of his own desire, hate or indifference," "The Serious Artist" (1913), *Literary Essays, ed cit.*, p. 46.
15. *Viz*, for example, Walter Baumann, "Secretary of Nature, J. Heydon," in *New Approaches*. . . .

proximate idealist analogues, such as Emerson or Goethe.[16] And/or one might construct a parallel instance, such as Daniel Pearlman's use of Jan Smuts' "holism."[17] Or finally, the realist justification by metaphors from science.

Professors Kenner and Davie tend ultimately towards the latter, and thereby testify to the basic consistency, however expressed: emotion causes pattern to arise, but the pattern is determined in the structures of the natural world; the sentence reflects a process in nature.[18] In the end, I feel that Pound, without abdicating the conceiving function, certainly intends us to believe that the form held in the mind, the trace in the air, can and must finally reflect a form that is inherent in nature. Not only

> "From the colour the nature
> & by the nature the sign!" [90/605]

but also

> i.e. it coheres all right
> even if my notes do not cohere [116/797].

It is not "a" rose possible in the dust, but, *ex stare*, "*the* rose"— despite the fact that

> This liquid is certainly a
> property of the mind [74/449].

Whilst objective and real, the pattern is not independent of the subject—but neither is it purely subjective and idealist.

The *forma* is therefore either the locus of synthesis or the threat of contradiction, depending on one's "point-of-view," or rather, one's relation to the Poundian paradigm in which these things cohere. But one senses a crisis even within the paradigm when Christine Brooke-Rose confronts Donald Davie's basically objectivist argument with her own account of Pound's basically subjectivist organization. She acknowledges our possible confusion, but reassures us that "there is no real contradiction" in "this paradox, as in all great art, of impersonality and the highly personal voice, the absence and the presence."[19]

It remains however a problem: do the lines of force, after all, exist in nature, or only in the conceiving mind? Do they exist in

---

16. For example, Eva Hesse: "the poet's deep-rooted conviction that there is, as Goethe has it, 'an unchartered pattern' in objective things that corresponds to the unchartered pattern within the subjective being" (*New Approaches . . .*, p. 19). See also, Ian F. A. Bell, "Pound, Emerson and 'Subject-Rhyme,'" *Paideuma*, 8-2, pp. 237-239.
17. Daniel Pearlman, *The Barb of Time* (New York, 1969), p. 42. Pearlman includes a footnote indicating that Pound had told him that he had not read Smuts.
18. Pound, "As for Imagisme," in *Selected Prose*, ed. William Cookson, (London, 1973), p. 344; *The Chinese Written Character as a Medium for Poetry* (1920) (San Francisco, 1969), p. 10.
19. Christine Brooke-Rose, *A ZBC of Ezra Pound* (London, 1971), pp. 186-187.

parallel, or in an interaction? In which case, under what process of parallelism or what process of interaction? The problem is felt acutely at the level of history, in terms of the status of the patterns perceived and inscribed in the poem. Professor Davie feels that the project is undertaken with "a genuine scientific humility," but that it collapses into an "absurdly, even insanely, presumptuous" vision.[20] How are we to avoid reducing history to a merely personal myth?

Christine Brooke-Rose resolves the general formal problem to a large extent in traditionally Poundian terms, making use of both Davie's and Kenner's arguments, and the appeal to science. But she includes a gesture back towards a mainstream:

> If philosophy must be dragged in, Pound seems to me much closer, in some, not all, respects, to Husserl's Phenomenology.... Phenomenology eliminated the old dichotomy between realism and idealism by reducing a world, once regarded as transcendental, to its manifestations within consciousness.[21]

from which she rapidly invokes Jakobson, Kristeva and Lacan.

Despite Brooke-Rose's reluctance, it seems to me that philosophy, in one sense or another, can finally hardly be kept out when a poet seeks to write a "poem including history," or asserts that "poetry is a science," or that the gods exist, or that it coheres all right. These categories—history, science, gods and nature—are theoretical signifiers and realities of a particularly prior and public order, whose theoretical history cannot be ignored in their appropriation, except by a totalitarian act of global ideological redefinition.

The proposal to read Pound phenomenologically is hence tempting, and has been taken up again recently by Eric Mottram.[22] Phenomenology offers a seductive framework of coherence and a more public support, inasmuch as it answers the mainstream on its own ground, without collapsing back into a dualism whose rejection likewise defines it as a philosophical moment; it does so furthermore with all the force of the apparent support of anthropology and modern science—which figure large in its own evidences and supports. Or, as Eric Mottram writes: "it seems at least

---

20. Davie, *Ezra Pound: Poet as Sculptor*, ed. cit., p. 204.
21. Brooke-Rose, *op cit*, pp. 123-124.
22. Eric Mottram, "Pound, Merleau-Ponty and the Phenomenology of Poetry"—(forthcoming, based on a paper given at the Pound Conference in 1981). It is curious that it has taken so long for this possibility to be pursued; it may have offered a theoretical support (and a way of reading) a long time ago, and the parallel might well have looked at first sight more tenable in relation to Heidegger than, say, to the later Sartre. Does the delay in attempting the connection say something about its feasibility—is it merely part of the general refusal of the paradigm, or does it indicate a symptomatic unease about its suitability?

possible that Pound's phenomenological interchanges between nature and human nature are nearer modern scientific practice than reversion to some simplistic, nineteenth century separation of the two."[23]

The "phenomenological interchange" would hence explicate the *forma* in terms of a specific interactive relation between the subject and the object, the individual and history. "The shape occurs," writes Pound; "That is, it occurs phenomenologically," writes Eric Mottram:

> Mind both affects and is transmuted. . . . Pound maintained a physical sense of interface with the universe through the phenomenology of perception. But, as this present essay is attempting to show, this is a twentieth-century condition rather than his uniqueness. Its presence in Olson, Ginsberg, Enslin and others is, of course, in part due to his particular formulations. But in Europe, too, contemporaneously, Merleau-Ponty gives this necessity in "Eye and Mind."[24]

Phenomenology is *par excellence* a discourse of interaction, which Eric Mottram hence seeks to privilege within the "twentieth-century condition," in a parallel to Pound's "interface," both of which have their "bases" in modern science.

There is undoubtedly a "rhyme" here, so to say; but, as is notorious with the "rhyme" model, it tends to conceal more difference than it indicates real similarity. For, clearly, Phenomenology, although privileged, is not the only discourse to respond to this "condition." On the contrary, the very generality of the condition makes the differences between one response and another more important than the similarities. A commitment to the interactive nature of reality is not necessarily a commitment to Phenomenology, any more than it is necessarily a commitment to Poundian process.

It is furthermore not adequate to relate one or another particular discourse to a self-evident scientific truth, for most models of response to the "twentieth-century condition"—unitary,

---

23. *Op cit.*
24. *Literary Essays,* ed cit., p. 152; quoted by Mottram. In this paper, Eric Mottram takes issue with a number of things I argue in my thesis, *Ezra Pound and the Phantasy of Science* (University of York, 1978)—basically my contention that Pound lacks a category of fiction, due precisely to his use of a "scientific" model and the technique which that model underwrites. Eric Mottram's argument is worthy of a more careful reply than this footnote, let alone this paper, can provide. But equally well, it is not enough to say that "Perhaps such arguments can be best confronted here by suggesting that they point towards the difference between Merleau-Ponty's philosophical discourse and Pound's poetic discourse." It seems to me that the differences between Pound and Merleau-Ponty are not reducible to the difference between philosophic logic and "poetry"—*The Cantos* are not that sort of poem, and Pound's whole career refuses the privilege of a poetry that is not answerable to its action.

interactive or dialectical—base themselves, to some extent or other, in modern science. The significance of science is not, and never can be self-evident and transparent—no more for Phenomenology than for Pound. There is always a process of mediation in which the "fact" is transformed, and Science provides validation not by "bases" but by metaphors.

Hence, to take a possibly more significant example for Pound than, say, radium: the earlier proposition by Clark Maxwell, which was confirmed by experiment in 1888 by Heinrich Hertz, as to the electromagnetic nature of light (and which led, amongst other things, to wireless technology), from which come the rose in the steel dust, the coherer, and the light tensile. For Clark Maxwell, the theory has the status neither of a philosophy nor a natural event, but of a hypothetical *equation*; for Hertz, it is an experimental *instrument*. For Oliver Lodge and Marconi, it is a *technology*.[25]

For the founding mathematical relation to grant significance to the orders of phenomena involved—light, magnetism, electricity—it has to be applied materially in both a commercialized technology—a phenomenology of commodities—and in discourse; a process in which it is obviously transformed. Two modes of discursive production are involved: an *epistemological reflection* and a *popularization of science*, in both of which pseudo-science and science fiction play their part.

Phenomenology is one such discourse by which the revolutions of modern science were mediated into popular thought. But it is far from the only one, and it too has its history of production. If we look at Phenomenology thematically, we are bound to find sufficient similarity to generate a possible "rhyme." But in the context of the generality of the "condition" it is rather in terms of a differential history than of a unifying thematic rhyme that we

---

25. As Gaston Bachelard writes: "Une telle soudure de deux phénoménologies aussi diverses que l'électricité et l'optique suggère des significations nouvelles. Autrement dit, les phénomènes immédiats, soit optiques, soit électriques, prennent de nouveaus sens" [*Le Rationalisme appliqué* (1949) (Paris, 1975), p. 153]. But Bachelard is careful to distinguish between a "rational" and a "phenomenalist" reading of the process:

> Pour comprendre la valeur épistémologique de cette corrélation (de Maxwell) il suffira de comparer ce rapprochement *rationaliste* de deux domaines: électricité et optique et le rapprochement *phénomeniste* des mêmes domaines pour comprendre l'infirmité d'une étude philosophique directe des phénomènes.
> —*loc cit.*

Bachelard's point—and I think it is entirely born out in the case of Pound—is that the phenomenalist "intuition" conceals the subject within a world of objects: an "irrational" concealment, however "authentic," which will work out its contradictions when it re-enters the world of theory or material reality.

The different process of signification of science are finely illustrated between the two technicians of the wireless, Marconi and Lodge: the difference between an entirely commercial and a strangely mystical reading of the same technology.

will best understand the relation between the two interactive models. Whereas there is no direct historical contact between Pound and Phenomenology, there is, on the other hand, a specific contemporary model for Pound's science, whose discourse can be traced in his own—as has been argued elsewhere by Ian Bell and by myself.[26]

The epistemological model is, in sum, that of empirio-criticism, or "reductionism"—as in Ernst Mach, Henri Poincaré and Karl Pearson. It is my sense that the existence of this contemporary and concrete model, which itself maintains historical relations of similarity *and* difference with elements of Phenomenology, makes the appeal of the latter redundant and misleading. At the same time, the empirio-critical model does succeed in answering Yvor Winters' criticism, without the need to confine oneself solely to the self-validating Poundian paradigm.

Many of the supports for Pound's poetics come from a series of discoveries made by physics towards the end of the century that were putting radically in question the basic principles of physics itself and, moreover, its place as the privileged center of mechanicist materialism.[27] In lieu of a reunifying theory (Einstein *et seq.*), in order to save science from vitalist, idealist and spiritualist opportunism, a new epistemology was required.[28] The most popular was the theory of empirio-criticism, by means of which

---

26. Ian Bell, *op cit.*; and "The Phantasmagoria of *Hugh Selwyn Mauberley*," *Paideuma*, 5-3, pp. 361-385, and "Mauberley's Barrier of Style," in Philip Grover, ed., *Ezra Pound: The London Years* (New York, 1978). There are other models also present in Pound, which have been studied by Ian Bell. My thesis emphasises empirio-criticism, but it also deals with other popularized discourses, such as that of the *Society for Psychical Research* and Bernard Hart (a follower, in fact, of Karl Pearson). See my *Alguns dos nossos melhores poetas são fascistas* (Coimbra, 1981) and "Ezra Pound: A Model for His Use of 'Science,'" *Biblos* (Coimbra), LVII (1981).

27. See Henri Poincaré, *The Value of Science* (1905) (New York, 1958), chapter 8, where he confesses that the six basic principles of physics (as he sees them) were currently under threat from physics itself.

28. Thomas Szasz writes:

> Until the turn of the century . . . it was thought that the proper aim of "science" was to produce "objective descriptions" of nature and to formulate these economically by theories which are "true." Mach challenged this illusory security of "science" and "truth" which was associated with Newtonian physics.
> See the introduction to Ernst Mach, *The Analysis of Sensations* (1897) (New York, 1959), p. ix.

In his obituary on Mach, Einstein acknowledged a great debt to the man "who shook this dogmatic faith . . . [in] mechanics as the final basis of all physical thinking." He also remarks that Mach "was not very far from requiring a general theory of relativity." But then in his *Autobiographical Notes*, he writes: "in my younger days, however, Mach's epistemological position also influenced me to be essentially untenable." [Quoted in *op cit.*, pp. xiii-xiv]. In this way, Einstein locates Mach precisely within the space between the collapse of one paradigm and the emergence of a new one, which points to the characteristic contradiction of the Machist holding operation: it has to defend science without yet having the theory with which to do so. Hence empirio-criticism is not a theory so much as a rhetoric.

"Mach sought to reformulate Newtonian mechanics from a phenomenalist standpoint."[29]

The revelation of the incorrectness of Newtonian categories suggested that they were not physical truths, but rather *fictions* — *meta*physical assumptions organizing our *perception* of the world. Empirio-criticism therefore first proposed itself as the self-conscious critique of those subjective assumptions, based in a science of perception.

Mach significantly applied himself firstly to the nature of the object: the idea of *substance*. Starting from the again newly-popular Heracletian truth, he concluded that the object was a *construct*:

> Nature exists once only. Our schematic mental station alone produces like events. Only in the mind, therefore, does the mutual dependence of certain features exist.
> All our efforts to mirror the world in thought would be futile if we found nothing permanent in the varied changes of things. It is this that impels us to form the notion of substance.[30]

The fictive construct represents the permanency of the world as determined by our *experience* of that world: the central category of "elements of sensation" — "Of what is beyond . . . 'things-in-themselves,' as the metaphysicians term them, we can know but one characteristic, and this we can only describe as a capacity for producing sense-impressions, for sending messages along the sensory nerves to the brain."[31]

From this empirical base a substitute for the object is generated: "Any group of immediate sense-impressions we project outside ourselves and hold to be a part of the external world. As such we call it a *phenomenon*, and in practical life term it *real*."[32] The phenomenon is a constructed fiction of the real based in the concrete reality of sensation and mediated by processes of association. Hence we come to the central correction of the revealed pseudo-objectivity of Newtonian science:

> It thus comes to pass that we form the notion of a substance distinct from its attributes, of a thing-in-itself, whilst our sensations are regarded merely as symbols or indications of the properties of this thing-in-itself. But it would be better to say that bodies or things are compendious mental symbols for groups of sensations — symbols that do not exist outside of thought.[33]

---

29. John Losee, *A Historical Introduction to the Philosophy of Science* (London: Oxford University Press, 1972), p. 169.
30. Mach, *Popular Scientific Lectures* [1894-98] (La Salle, Illinois: Open Court, 1943), p. 199.
31. Karl Pearson, *The Grammar of Science* (London: Walter Scott, 1892), p. 81.
32. *Ibid.*, p. 77.
33. Mach, *op cit.*, pp. 200-201.

A crucial inversion in the language of science thus takes place. Instead of "real things" being signified by sensations (materialism), sensations are represented by constructed "things" or "substances." In short, the "object" is shifted from the level of the signified to that of the signifier.

But empirio-criticism is not a simple empiricism, since it concerns itself as much with the constructivism of "the creative imagination"[34] as with the physics of perception. It "proceeds from the direct—what might perhaps be termed the physical—association of memory, to the indirect or mental association; it passes from *perceiving* to *conceiving*."[35] It moves from description to a discourse of *formula and law*.

Demystifying Newtonian absolutes by the recognition that science is a language, empirio-criticism proposes that it is a special kind of language: mathematical, and specifically algebraic:

> The aim of research is the discovery of the equations which subsist between the elements of phenomena. The equation of an ellipse expresses the universal *conceivable* relation between its co-ordinates, of which only the real values have *geometrical* significance. Similarly, the equations between the elements of *phenomena* express a universal, mathematically conceivable relation.[36]

On this basis, Mach constructs a theory of *relational analogy*—"an effective means of mastering heterogeneous fields of facts in unitary comprehension" which is a pathway to "a *universal physical phenomenology* embracing all domains."[37]

Empirio-criticism thus proposes a global system of *formal conceived relations, drawn from phenomena, which may be signified by objects, but which signify concrete active experience*. The problem is once again to avoid the theory collapsing back into subjectivism on the basis of the constructive and empirical components. It creates necessity and objectivity for itself by asserting, basically, four things.

---

34. Pearson, *op cit.*, p. 44.
35. *Ibid.*, p. 56. Compare Pound's account of Imagisme in relation to Ford's Impressionism. He admired its "objectivity," but accused it of "laps[ing] into description," because of the "passivity" of its "receptive" attitude: "The *conception* of poetry is a process more intense than the *reception* of an impression. Poetry is in some odd way concerned with the specific gravity of things, with their nature . . . and no impression . . . can, recorded, convey that feeling of sudden light which works of art can and must convey" (Review of Ford, *High Germany, Poetry Review*: March 1912). *Cf* also "Vorticism" (1914) *Gaudier-Brzeska* (New York, 1970), p. 89 and following note.
36. Mach, *op cit.*, p. 205; *cf.* Poincaré, *op cit.*, pp. 76-77. For Pound's model of constructive relational form, expressed in terms of mathematics, see "The Wisdom of Poetry" (1912) in *Selected Prose* and "Vorticism" in *Gaudier-Brzeska*. Through the essays of this period, Pound constructs a model of the poet as psychologist-mathematician, a model linked closely to myth and magic. See also, for its consequences, Walter Baumann, "Ezra Pound and Magic: Old World Tricks in a New World Poem," *Paideuma*, 10-2, pp. 209-224.
37. Mach, *op cit.*, p. 250.

Firstly, the necessity in perception: "The order in which we arrange conscious phenomena does not admit of any arbitrariness. It is imposed upon us."[38] Secondly, the objectivity of formal relation itself: "all that is objective is devoid of all quality and is only pure relation."[39] In the third place, it raises the intersubjectivity of perception and conception to the level of universality:

> It will be said that science is only a classification and that a classification can not be true, but convenient. But it is true that it is convenient, it is true that it is so not only for me, but for all men; it is true that it will remain convenient for our descendants; it is true finally that this cannot be by chance.
> In sum, the sole objective reality consists in the relation of things whence results the universal harmony . . . they are . . . objective because they are, will become, will remain, common to all thinking beings.[40]

But the fourth assertion is perhaps the most important, and expresses the interaction between the world of nature and the subject that experiences that world in terms of the manner in which he conceives it (the "continuum"). Thus Poincaré generated the characteristic empirio-critical sentence: "It is the external world which has imposed the continuum upon us, which we doubtless have invented, but which it has forced us to invent,"[41] and this sentence in turn makes possible the radical synthesis of Mach: "From our standpoint, the antithesis of subject and object, in the ordinary sense, does not exist."[42]

There is clearly not time to demonstrate the extent to which this model informs much of Pound's scientific discourse, from "The Serious Artist," through "The Wisdom of Poetry," "As for Imagisme," "Vorticism," "Arnold Dolmetsch," to (especially) *The Chinese Written Character . . .* ; nor its use in Hudson Maxim, William James, the Society for Psychical Research, and Bernard Hart, for example; nor its parallels with Remy de Gourmont. But I hope that enough will have been suggested, and can be born out in Pound's actual poetic technique of formal sensational analogy, signified by object signifiers.[43]

---

38. Poincaré, *op cit.*, p. 26.
39. *Ibid.*, p. 136.
40. *Ibid.*, p. 140.
41. *Ibid.*, p. 80.
42. Mach, *The Analysis of Sensations*, p. 341. The statement follows the following assertion: "The science of psychology is auxiliary to physics. The two mutually support each other, and it is only when they are united that a complete science is formed. . . ." The logic depends firstly on the ambiguity of "sensation" and "phenomena" (subjective/objective) and the proposition that science is a matter of language (a construct). Psychology and physics are then symmetrical ways of looking at the same ambiguous object. This is characteristic of the empirio-critical pitch, and of important consequences for the evolution of the new psychologies.
43. See Canto 74/449; plus, for example:

In brief, I am proposing that the model of relation of subject to object is not Phenomenological, but what might be called, in the empirio-critical sense, "phenomenalist." And I am proposing moreover that subtle as it may at first sight appear, this does make a difference.

Firstly it interposes a specific popularizing discourse of science, at a specific historical moment, between the phenomena (radium, wireless, etc.) and their "evident" significance. Pound's use of science would not then be related to a "permanent world," but to a concrete *history of discourses*. Hence the direct appeal to modern science, and still more the endorsement of the metaphors drawn from it by Pound or Upward, is not an adequate extra-paradigmatic validation for Pound's practice. The model rather suggests that Pound's use of science indeed passes through another paradigm which is surprisingly "mainstream" in modern popularized science.[44] This point then requires us to confront the historical partialities of empirio-criticism, like the fact that it offered itself historically as the great alternative to the other dominant reading of interactive scientific reality, dialectical materialism.[45] There are definite ideological conclusions to be drawn from this fact.

We would likewise have to consider the relations between Phenomenology and empirio-criticism which, if it fails to invalidate the Phenomenological reading, would at least radically qualify it. Phenomenology clearly in some sense emerges out of empirio-criticism—and indeed there are strains in Phenomenology which have little to do with the Machists. However, inasmuch as there are relations between the two theories, there are also major and significant differences.

>   Tyro,
>   Twisted arms of the sea god,
> Lithe sinews of water, gripping her, cross-hold,
> And the blue-gray glass of the wave tents them,
> Glare azure of water, cold-welter, close cover [2/6]

and

>   void air taking pelt.
>   Lifeless air become sinewed [2/8]

to "Gods float in the azure air" [3/11]. All of which may be read, as technique, through Fenollosa; but it also makes admirable sense within the empirio-critical model.

44. Empirio-critical assumptions are frequently to be found in contemporary popularized science—even in Pound critics [see, for example, Brooke-Rose, p. 123]. More respectably, one finds a more refined model in Karl Popper's epistemology; but here we find precisely the importance of the superficially subtle distinctions—as when we compare Popper with Gaston Bachelard.

45. As testified by Lenin's *Materialism and Empirio-Criticism* (1908; 1920) (Moscow, 1970), which demonstrates the prevalence of the model, the ease with which it could be, and was, recuperated by "mysticism"—as in elements of the Society for Psychical Research—and the urgency felt by materialists to answer it.

Empirio-criticism characterizes itself by its alternation: when attacking mechanicist or metaphysical materialism, it is frankly idealist; but when defending science from the vitalists, it reads objectively. This is its "verbal synthesis," as Lenin describes it, and its ideological contradiction.[46] On the other hand, Phenomenology *tends* to declare its idealist tendency, especially in its relations with Existentialism. But as it has developed, partly out of empirio-criticism, Phenomenology has found itself, especially recently, encountering the limiting crisis of its subjectivism. At this point, it has found itself confronting the very problem which, in its origins, it set out in a sense to avoid: in Sartre's return to Marx and Lacan's reading of Freud (against Merleau-Ponty).[47] In this sense, Phenomenology represents another postponement, especially a postponement of an encounter with dialectical materialism, which will no longer wait.

In short, in considering this question in terms of a concrete history of discourses, we find ourselves in a world of differences, not in a world of "rhymes"—that is to say, back in a history which escapes subjective control. In this way, the paradigm, far from having to be "dragged in," refuses to keep out. Pound's "alternative" paradigm cannot—any more than Pound himself—forever postpone its encounter with history—not his conception of history, but rather real history: the history which produces Pound, rather than the history that Pound produces. This history is a narrative of differences and conflicts, of which one might say, as Basil Bunting so rightly says of *The Cantos*: "you will have to go a long way round/if you want to avoid them."[48]

---

46. Empirico-criticism enjoys this possibility thanks to the ambiguous status of "sensation," "phenomenon" and "language." As Lenin says: "On the one hand, Poincaré's theory lends itself to the support of philosophical idealism; on the other hand, it is compatible with the objective interpretation of the word 'experience.'" [*Ibid.*, p. 285]. See also pp. 112-113.
47. Or indeed, Claude Lévi-Strauss' fear that he may have reinvented God: see Jacques Lacan, *Le Séminaire, II* (Paris, 1978), p. 48.
48. Basil Bunting, "On the Fly-Leaf of Pound's *Cantos*."

DENNIS BROWN

THE TRANSLATION OF HISTORY IN THE EARLY CANTOS

I should like to begin this paper with a quotation from a note on John Buchan's *Cromwell*, which Pound published in *The New English Weekly* on 6th June, 1935:

> Buchan has a little mislaid the real reason for writing and reading history, namely that the past should be a light for the future. That the purpose of history is instruction, that is to make people think and to guide their thought toward what will elucidate today and tomorrow.
> ... This mustn't be taken extremely. But we should distinguish between historic study having purposeful focus on life as we know it, and a sort of extension of books of reference, "mines" as they are called, for those who want to collect matter which can be so focused. "Purposeful focus" does not mean distortion.[1]

I start with this—for Pound—relatively cautious and circumspect rationale of "writing and reading history" because it seems specifically pertinent to any understanding of *The Cantos*, Pound's "tale of the tribe" which is a long poem "including history." The kind of history we find in *The Cantos* is not "a sort of extension of books of reference," but a "light for the future" whose purpose is "instruction"—"to make people think and to guide their thought. . . ." History in *The Cantos*, in short, is focussed on an assessment of the needs of the present and future. One is reminded of Eliot's view of the "monuments" of tradition, whose significance and order is altered by the poetry of the present. From the Poundian point of view, poets are uniquely qualified to assess the needs of the present and future in their role as "antennae of the race," "barometers," "seismographs," "litmus papers," "voltometers," "steam gauges," etc. But whether or not this is so, the method clearly takes us rather far from the writing of history as it is normally understood. Pound's focus is not on the pastness of the past, but on the needs of the present and future. In this

---

1. *Ezra Pound: Selected Prose, 1907-1965*, ed. W. Cookson (London, 1973), p. 236.

sense, history in *The Cantos* is a carrying forward, a trans-lation. The method is essentially poetic and hence is on a par with Pound's translation of past litérature into the newly-minted language of his day.

What then becomes of Pound's often-repeated appeal to facticity, the "gristly resilient facts" on the plane of history? Here, I think, we must distinguish between historical event and documented discourse. The fidelity of *The Cantos* is less to historical events than to specific discourses, whether historical or not. Past events, after all, are not like Agassiz' fish: they are not present to be inspected. Discourses are, however, and *The Cantos* specialize in collating and "translating" a rich variety of world discourses. Hence Pound's frequent invocation of authorities: "Lie quiet, Divus"; "Lo Sordels si fo di Mantovana"; "As Poggio has remarked." However, while such fragments of discourse are there to be inspected, the early cantos do not make much attempt to sift fact from fiction in the manner of "Near Perigord." At the same time, many of the discourses favored in the early cantos are of dubious historical veracity. The *Poema de Mio Cid*, for instance, is scarcely a factual record of its hero's career. As Colin Smith has pointed out in his recent edition of the poem, the material about Raquel and Vidas is very likely an addition from the Arab tradition of tales about cheating.[2] But for Pound's purpose, this scarcely matters: whatever the real events in Roderigo Diaz' life, the *Poema* represents a significant discourse in its own right and of its own genre. It is a poem itself "translated" from the past to a later Medieval "present" and "future"—an assertion of values which Pound, in his turn, "re-cycles" in terms of a twentieth-century context.

The example of the "poema" may be borne in mind in an approach to the most apparently historical part of the early Cantos—the rendering of Sigismundo Malatesta. At first glance, stubborn facticity is insisted upon, especially in the case of the letters in the post bag. But Daniel Bornstein makes some interesting comments on Pound's material in "The Poet as Historian: Researching the Malatesta Cantos," observing that Pound "generally seems to have relied on the documents published by Yriarte and others rather than seeking out the originals."[3] For instance, all the letters used are in Yriarte's nineteenth century history. One further source which Pound particularly relied on was Broglio di Tangelia's *Cronaca Universale*, and Bornstein suggests that he used

---
2. *Poema de mio Cid,* ed. Colin Smith (Oxford, 1972), p. xxiii.
3. Daniel Bornstein, "The Poet as Historian: Researching the Malatesta Cantos," *Paideuma*, 10-2, pp. 283-291.

this as a model for both the "matter and manner" of *The Cantos* as a whole—"the jumble of materials and the mix of languages bear a marked resemblance." Far from Pound attempting to assert a modern, analytically-historical style, he deliberately "translates" the Renaissance mode of discourse—paratactical rhythms, bizarre collocations of facts, opinions and poems, side allusions to ravelled-up intrigues, and so forth. There is here no clear separation of event from opinion, no analysis of the motives behind the intrigues, no operation of cause and effect—and hence no attempt at an explanation. The whole consists of a "translation" of discourses about discourses (the original documents) into a new discourse, these cantos. The "factive" allegiance of Pound, then, is less to putative events in the life of Malatesta than to the chronicle's positive assertion of the importance of energy, resilience, love and the cultivation of art. It is not wholly facetious to suggest that the real hero of these cantos is Broglio, a chronicler whose *virtù* renders his subject a "light" for the present and future.

If my emphasis is correct, then we are in a better position to see the real plane of unity in *The Cantos*. Truth and Calliope may slang each other in Canto 8, but they are both united on the plane of discourse. Pound is little interested in abstracting event from the mode of telling, or myth from the poetry which has expressed it, or in privileging "factual" history over other modes. *The Cantos* do not insist on transcendent realities somehow outside of writing. On the contrary, their basic material consists of discourses of varying kinds, interwoven into a new fabric of inscription. Mythology is "translated" from previous poems—Homer, Ovid, Dante, etc.; history is "translated" from previous chronicles—Varchi, Poggio, Broglio, etc. Thus, the deeds of Malatesta, El Cid, Confucius, Dionysus and Odysseus are all on one unified plane, that of fruitful discourse. Historical character and event are essentially signifiers which establish an ideology for the world to come.

This is not to suggest that Pound "distorts." In a letter to John Quinn about his research on Malatesta, Pound stated that he wished to "avoid a few historic idiocies, or impossibilities," and to find those "*minor* points that might aid one in forming an historic rather than a fanciful idea of [Malatesta's] character."[4] Pound of course was writing out of an intellectual climate which would expect historical credibility. "Historical idiocies or impossibilities" would mar any twentieth century poem or novel which included an historical dimension. But the emphasis in this letter is

---
4. Quoted by Bornstein, pp. 287-288.

that of a writer, not an historian. Pound's research is essentially concerned to create a persuasive discourse. So even the Malatesta letters may be seen chiefly as rhetorical devices to give the stamp of veracity to the canto. And in this Pound is still continuing the tradition of a certain kind of epic. In his introduction to the *Poema de Mio Cid*, Colin Smith writes:

> The P.M.C. is full of details of counting the booty, of feeding the horses, and of journeys by way of a day's stages which can be traced on the modern map; the numbers of enemies slain are more or less credible, there is only one brief divine apparition, and the Cid dies humanly rather than heroically. Our definition of *historicidad* in epic should therefore be not "the accurate representation or preservation of history" but "the use of historical or pseudo-historical detail for purposes of artistic verisimilitude.[5]

This applies fairly directly to Pound's case in the early cantos and helps explain the fact that while most parts of Malatesta's letters are translated into rough-and-ready English, others are left in the original, thereby proclaiming their "authenticity."

If the material content of the cantos, then, is not fully researched events but discourses which point forward to the future, what is the nature of the "translation" process which mediates the chain of discourses into renewed signification? There are, I think, three stages of the process that should be described here, the first of which is the act of selection. While *The Cantos* is surely the most monumentally allusive poem in English, it still constitutes a selection of fragments out of the virtually infinite reservoir of world writing. History here is expressed as a collage of specifically-chosen instances or *exampla*. At the stage of selection the "translator" is looking in each case for the ideogram which will illuminate the present by means of the voices of the past. For instance, the discursive fragment from the *Poema* does not attempt to do justice either to the career of the real Cid or to the epic poem. The particular details are selected for "translation" because they signify courage, persistence, craftiness, etc.—qualities particularly relevant to post-war Europe. El Cid becomes the signifier of what Europe lacks, just as Pound's selection of "The Seafarer" for translation, out of the entire canon of Old English poetry, signals the connection he sees between the early English adventurer and the Bohemian poet in Edwardian London among the "wine-flushed" burghers.

In poetic practice, the "luminous detail" is such because it particularly illuminates the present. The reality of this is evident

---

5. *Poema*, p. xxii.

in the case of Pound's famous early example taken from Burckhardt's *The Civilization of the Renaissance in Italy*:

> When in Burckhardt we come upon a passage: "In this year the Venetians refused to make war upon the Milanese because they held that any war between buyer and seller must prove profitable to neither," we come upon a portent, the old order changes . . . commercial sense is sapping [the old] regime.[6]

For Pound—the thinker *outside* the poem—this fragment is seen very much in terms of his developing opposition to the commercial spirit of contemporary London, an opposition that would result in his attack on usury and all that went with it. Here, in embryo, he sees the deathly spirit of "made to sell and sell quickly" triumphing over the notion of the just war, the ban on interest, etc. Here is the beginning of the "thickening of the line." It comes as rather a shock, then, when we go to Burckhardt and find that in his context the detail means something quite different.[7] It is in fact one of several instances adduced to illustrate the rise of "modern statistics" which is seen as a progressive development in a city (Venice) where "the supreme objects were the enjoyment of life and power." It is not that Burckhardt denies the rising commercial interests—on the contrary he emphasises them—but that, lacking Pound's opposition to present practices, he sees this movement towards "modern political life" as a basically good thing with its emphasis on individual lives (*"anime"*) as opposed to "hearths," etc., its commitment to accurate recording (something Pound would approve in a different context), and its preference for peaceful trade over despotic war (Frederick II is his example of the latter). Pound, in fact, has wrenched this detail out of the content and purport of Burckhardt's history in order to make it ideogrammic of his view about the rise of usury. The point is not so much whether Pound or Burckhardt are correct in their interpretations but whether this kind of detail can, in itself, abstracted from the general historical context, give one "a sudden insight into circumjacent conditions, into their causes, their effects, into sequence and law." Historical discourse would have to weigh this detail with all other available evidence in order to reach a conclusion. The poet on the other hand is looking for rhetorical force. He selects this detail because it interprets the poet's present.

This helps to explain the quirkiness of many of Pound's selections. Why is the cheating of Raquel and Vidas highlighted in

---

6. Pound, *Selected Prose*, p. 22.
7. Jacob Burckhardt, *The Civilization of the Renaissance in Italy*, trans. S. G. C. Middlemore, revised edition (New York, 1960), p. 84.

the short *El Cid* fragment? Why is the "bathing" of John Borgia focussed on in Canto 5, out of the great wealth of information we have about the Borgias? Why, indeed, is John Quinn's bawdy tale to the bankers given two pages in Canto 12? In each case the selection is made less with concern for the historical context than with an eye to its telling power *vis-à-vis* the present and future.

Which brings us to the second aspect of "translation"—the structuring of the selected fragments in relation to each other, so as to point up their illuminating function. Here we may note immediately that, unlike Browning in *The Ring and the Book*, for instance, Pound makes almost no attempt to simulate, at points, such touchstones of modern historical discourse as causal argument, sequential narration, impartial weighing of accounts, or even rhetorical connectives. On the contrary, the relationship between the "luminous details" in the early cantos is essentially one of montage—a discursive practice of modern artists in strong contrast to traditional modes of connection. Fragments from more conventional discourses are here "translated" into a semi-patterned aesthetic resonance where they illuminate by frictional comparison and contrast.

Canto 3 provides a conveniently short model of the method. The canto begins with a personal "clip" about Venice, partially echoing fragments of Browning in *Sordello* and lines of Dante and d'Annunzio. At line 7 this is "spliced" into an expanded "translation" of the Ur-Canto 1, lines 9-11—a pastoral, dawn scene "bright" with gods, in strong contrast to the earlier Venetian richness and bustle. The Lake Garda scene is here held within the bounds of self-conscious signification by a reference to Catullus through Poggio Bracciolini. The steps in line 19 then lead us to a major montage juxtaposition, signalled typographically, after which we have the *Cid* paraphrase which takes us to line 37, with two phrases left in Spanish to provide verisimilitude. A brief "clip" on Ignez da Castro's murder then merges into a description of the walls of the Ducal Palace at Mantua, capped by the motto "Nec Spe Nec Metu" which speaks for Pound in Venice, and for El Cid, as well as for Isabella d'Este. By montage, then, Pound has brought together various fragments from the past to illuminate the near-present of his Venice arrival and hence the future of *The Cantos*—as well as the reader's present and future.

We may note one particular effect of this method. Lacking the usual rhetorical connectives, the cantos also lack discrimination and subordination between types of discourse. As we noted earlier, fragments of "history" are rendered, by montage, on the same plane as myths, personal interpolations, bawdy anecdotes and so forth. Far from highlighting the relative veracity of chronicle, the montage method renders it on a par with the fanciful and fantastic. None of the "luminous details" carries real status from its relation to actual event. But all, whatever their modes of discourse, are united, through juxtaposition, and significant in terms of their power to speak to the twentieth century and beyond. In the montage technique we experience a total democratization of discourses which is the reverse of the hierarchical method of the "scientific" archivist who privileges historical veracity over any other mode of writing.

The third stage of "translation" is that actual provision of the new Poundian language—translation as the word is most frequently used. Of course, as we have seen, Pound sometimes leaves fragments of the original for the sake of verisimilitude. However Pound's basic project as poet is to "translate" past discourse into a "language to think in"—to "make it new" in a style which points to the present and future. And in this, as in his translations of Latin, Anglo-Saxon, Chinese, Provençal and Italian poetry, he may take liberties with the discourse of the past to obtain telling power and significance in the present. Thus, just as he offends language specialists in "The Seafarer" and "Homage to Sextus Propertius," so he may well offend historians when he renders the Rimini carpenter's son's letter in the following way:

> Sense to-day I am recommanded that I have to tel you my father's opinium that he has shode to Mr Genare about the valts of the cherch ... etc....
> Giovane of Master alwise P.S. I think it advisabl that I shud go to rome to talk to mister Albert so as I can no what he thinks about it rite.

"Translation" indeed! A subtler problem is represented in this rendering of Varchi:

> If when the foot slipped, when death came upon him,
> Lest cousin Duke Alessandro think he had fallen alone,
> No friend to aid him in falling.

The chronicler's prosaic enquiry into "the facts" has here been translated into . . . poetry. The carefully-chosen Anglo-Saxon diction, the "dying fall" of the cadences ("when death came upon him"; "No friend to aid him in falling"), the general "*melopoeia*," all detract from the fragment's status as historical discourse as such. Similarly phrases such as "Siggy, darlint" or "young pullets make thin soup" speak a contemporary idiom which tends to sever their connection with the original. Once again, Pound is more concerned to speak to the present than to evidence the alien pastness of the past. Discourses are "made new" and pointed toward the future.

All three aspects of "translation," then, are concerned with presenting (in both senses) the past in the context of the poem's date-lines, and just as the past is the product of selection and contextualization, so too is the present. In this sense the poet invents the present and future he addresses: or put another way, the present here is itself a "translation" of contemporary discourses—those for example of Sir James Frazer, Remy de Gourmont, Ernest Fenollosa, Allen Upward, T. E. Hulme, Major Douglas and Leo Frobenius. The present in the early part of the poem is very much that of the War years and their aftermath, seen through an idiosyncratic ideology itself partly based on the discourses of certain writers and friends. The present is largely that of a fallen world needing redemption into a brighter future by chosen fragments of past writing. Hence the strategic importance of the Hell Cantos coming just after the example of El Cid, Malatesta and Confucius. It is to *this* hellish world that the fragments of discourse must bring illumination—a world where scholars (including no doubt "scientific" historians as well as philologists) sit on "piles of stone books," their writing not being of the kind that can enlighten the future. So too it is the poets—Blake, Peire Cardinal, Dante and Sordello—who in particular are shown fleeing "hell mouth" and essaying the purgatorial road to refinement. But just as Pound's selection from the past may well offend historians, so too must his depiction of the First World War in terms of details about friends in trenches, anecdotes, and pastiche foreign accents. Such "translation" of contemporary history should warn us not to expect a specifically historical version of the past.

But my emphasis on the process of selection is not intended to refer everything in the poem to the choice and control of the author. If Pound chooses among discourses (past and present), the nature of his choice will also be largely determined by the particular discourses he has read. For instance, his discriminations in history as in literature are clearly explicable in terms of his absorption with Homer, Dante, Confucius and Scotus Erigena. So we might borrow Eliot's simile to suggest that the poet's mind is a catalytic chamber where discourses impact on and merge with each other—the stronger selecting out the weaker—to produce further discourse (e.g. *The Cantos*) without the interposition of an entity called "personality." However, more important than the putative mental action of the poet is the structural evidence of the poem itself. For *The Cantos* speak not as one single voice but as an echo-chamber of disparate discourses. Granted the invisible "translation" of Pound, an individual with views, outside of the poem, the voices of the cantos are seen to proceed not from an authorial center but from previous writings. "Ego scriptor," when he appears, is not a "final author" but a linguistic posture from borrowed Latin—a second-hand signifier thrown up by and within the chain of discourses. Here I agree with Marianne Korn when she writes in "Truth Near Perigord": "The poem is discourse, and the words constantly disappoint any expectation of an *individualized* authorial being, an intention separate from the text."[8]

We have to tread a fine line here—as we do in distinguishing between historical event and discourse about event: on the one hand the Poundian "*virtù*," on the other, those discourses that yet fresh discourses beget. But the nature of the new emphasis *The Cantos* enforces becomes clearer if we consider the reader's role. Wherever authorial perspective is omitted—where the poetry does not postulate a fixed viewpoint determining the discourse, as judge, philosopher, historian or whatever—there the reader's mind is automatically brought into free play. It reminds one of the Rorschach test, where the point of the ink blot is not to express the psychiatrist's fixations but to elicit the patient's. Much of Pound's criticism, including his anthologies and translations (which are other forms of criticism), is designed to stimulate the reader's active intelligence—as opposed to passive registration. Similarly *The Cantos* with their specific appeals to the reader— "O voi che siete in picciolette barca," "You who expect to get through hell lightly"—their syntactical breakages that cry out for completion—"So that—" at the end of Canto 1, or "And . . ." at the end of 2—make their total denial of the familiar authorial perspective in the Babel of masks, styles, and genres, finally force the reader to assess and complete the meaning for himself. The enlightenment of the present and future is not, then, didactic in the old sense, because the reader is not directed as to precisely what to think. On the contrary, "the purpose of history is instruction, that is to make people think." This is a far cry from "justifying the ways of God to man or anything else," which Pound denounced in Milton. What the tone and structure of the early cantos signals is that the present and future reside in the readers. Pound "translates" the past according to his lights: he carries forward the discourses he sees as relevant to ongoing action and discourse. But at the same time the montage method he employs allows—indeed enforces—wide divergencies of response. The historical fragments, in particular, entice the reader to further

---

8. Marianne Korn, "Truth Near Perigord," *Paideuma*, 10-3, p. 578.

research, force him to consider them in relation to other types of discourse, lead him to evaluate their meaning in terms of his own sense of the past, present and future.

I suggest in conclusion, then, that we should not look to *The Cantos* for history in the usual sense of the word, and certainly not for an inclusive historian—or a historian somehow outside the text—who will weigh all the evidence, assert a hierarchy of factive texts or mount an explanation as to the meaning of events. The subject of *The Cantos* is discourse—a word I have over-used here because it applies to both written and spoken language, because it avoids the usual naive distinctions between fact and fiction, history and mythology, etc., and because much recent work by Barthes, Derrida and Foucault, in particular, give it a specific explanatory power in terms of the puzzling but fascinating project which is *The Cantos*. Pound has "translated" his discursive material by radical selection, re-contextualization and "making it new" in new words. His poem is an energy field where meaning is endlessly re-processed in terms of specific eras and voices. As such, it implicitly calls into question the meaning of historical analysis within the context of other discursive practices, probing the assumption of the fixed viewpoint from which events can be impartially judged, and the adoption of a neutral "objective" discourse whereby history can be expressed and explained. *The Cantos* insist on a multiplicity of discourses and suggests that meaning in culture is kept alive by an active inter-relationship between the past and present, through the "re-cycling" of key instances of enlightenment. Finally, it demonstrates that "illumination" is not a matter of some view pinned down in immoveable generalization on the page, but arises from a reciprocity between the "*virtù*" of both writer and reader through the medium of the ideogram.

STEPHEN WILSON

A TENTATIVE INTERVENTION
IN THE ARGUMENT "SOUS LES LAURIERS"

These fragments you have shelved (shored).
"Slut!" "Bitch!" Truth and Calliope
Slanging each other sous les lauriers: . . . [8/28]

The Malatesta cantos, which these lines introduce, are the poem's first sustained attempt to "include history," and it is in them that we first encounter many of the techniques we have learned to recognize as characteristic of historical narrative in *The Cantos* (an obvious example being the insertion into the text on a large scale of documents, fragments of documents, letters, etc.). A recent study of *The Cantos*, that of Michael Bernstein, describes the opening lines of the Malatesta sequence as a "decisive turning point."[1] Further, the quality of the Malatesta cantos has been as widely attested as their innovatory and positional significance, and they have come to be regarded as a *locus classicus* of how Pound's poem can successfully "include history": a view to which Pound himself lent his authority by instancing them, in *Guide to Kulchur*,[2] as a justification of his attempt to write an "epic." We could say that the Malatesta cantos mark the point at which the text announces its epic intentions, and generates a new order of discourse and a new set of controlling conventions and strategies designed to meet Pound's specifications for what an epic should be, which can perhaps best briefly be conveyed by quoting two of his maxims: "An epic is a poem containing history," and "Poetry asserts a positive."[3]

The opening lines of Canto 8 play an important role in this process; they can be seen as the equivalent of the formal invocation of the Muse with which traditional epics begin: their position

---
1. Michael André Bernstein, *The Tale of the Tribe: Ezra Pound and the Modern Verse Epic* (Princeton, N.J., 1980), p. 40.
2. *Guide to Kulchur* (1938) (London, repr. 1966), p. 194.
3. *The Literary Essays of Ezra Pound*, ed. T. S. Eliot (London, repr. 1960), pp. 86, 324.

in the canto, the space they seek to occupy—"sous les lauriers"—and the allusion to Calliope seem to support this. This is a useful way of reading these lines, provided we remember that the "traditional epic" had privileged access to certain areas of experience, and to a range of procedures of textual organization agreed upon as being characteristic and appropriate to itself, and recognized as requiring from the reader a particular order of submission to the text. For the "modern epic"—for *The Cantos*—no such state of affairs exists, and thus it cannot begin by simply announcing itself, by sounding the appropriate note, and assume the appropriate responses. Rather, it must begin by making a space for itself, by recognizing the claims and merits of other ways of handling the same material—in Pound's case "history"—by distinguishing itself from them and by asserting the value of its own mode of access to the past. This, I would argue, is exactly what the opening lines of Canto 8 do for the Malatesta cantos; hence their importance to any discussion of history in *The Cantos*.

The Malatesta cantos are also a useful starting point for a discussion of Pound's attempt to write a "poem including history," because they have been so well read, both qualitatively and quantitatively. In other words, most of the proper names, references, allusions, etc., have been identified, glossed, traced to their sources and elucidated in various ways; consequently, this section of the poem has ceased to be "difficult" (in the somewhat limited sense the word usually has when applied to *The Cantos*): has, indeed, become highly accessible, highly visible. The Malatesta cantos, however, have not ceased to be problematic and complex, and any serious encounter with the text quickly moves into areas of difficulty in which the indexes and companions are of little help; for instance, determining the nature of Pound's historical discourse, how it "contains history," how it can be validated either as history or poetry.

At this point, I would like to return to the opening lines of Canto 8, quoted earlier, and to attempt a reading of them, also looking at some of the ways in which they have been read. This, I hope, will both illustrate my last point, that *The Cantos* remain difficult even when they have been comprehensively annotated, and afford a useful insight into what we might expect from the poem's attempts to "include history." As I have said, the essential function of these lines is to distinguish Pound's mode of perceiving and mediating the world from other available modes, and in doing so to create a space for the epic historiography of *The Cantos*. A strong reading of these three lines is, therefore, important if we wish to understand the nature of the "history" that follows them.

In the light of our present concerns, the significant and problematic elements in the lines are the allusion to T. S. Eliot's *The Waste Land*, and the Truth/Calliope quarrel.

We instantly recognize, and can readily re-contextualize, the quotation (or mis-quotation) from *The Waste Land*; but what point is being made? Is it, as Carroll Terrell seems to suggest— stressing the word "fragments" and pointing out that both *The Waste Land* and *The Cantos* are poems made up of fragments[4] —an acknowledgement by Pound of a sense of community of concern and method with Eliot? Or is it, as Dekker and others have argued, an attempt on Pound's part to make a clear distinction between his own and Eliot's practice, thus making the reference a critical, even hostile one (Eliot is "shelving" the past, denying the possibility of meaningful access to it[5])? Both these readings have something to be said for them, and we should begin by acknowledging that Pound and Eliot shared a number of beliefs and assumptions about the nature of history. Both had a strong sense of the importance of the past, and believed that the present should stand in some sort of significant relationship to it, and, further, would have agreed that no such state of affairs existed *circa* 1920. They also shared a view of history, particularly recent history, as decline following an historically locatable "fall" (whether it be the "dissociation of sensibility," or the founding of the Bank of England). Granting this much, we must however finally recognize that the differences between the two are in this context more significant. Crudely, we could say that for Eliot the past could be evoked elegiacally, or adduced as a standing rebuke to the present, but could not be made available, as Pound believed it could and should be, as a source of revitalization in the lapsed world, or made to serve as a dynamic example. For Eliot, not only is what is lost unrecoverable, but what remains is subject to a constant, and ultimately unstoppable and irreversible, process of attrition, and he is engaged in a doomed holding action against the forces of erosion and decay (in the terms of the line, he is "shoring up" the fragments). This may be an heroic attitude, but it is a form of heroism that is inimical to Pound's epic ambitions. I would therefore agree with those who read the line as being concerned to make a distinction, but disagree with the consensus view of the nature of the distinction being made; I believe it is the parenthetically-offered correction, "shored," that refers to Eliot's practice,

---

4. Carroll F. Terrell, *A Companion to The Cantos of Ezra Pound* (Berkeley, Los Angeles and London, 1980), pp. 36-37.
5. George Dekker, *Sailing After Knowledge: The Cantos of Ezra Pound, a Critical Appraisal* (London, 1963), p. 31.

and that it, and not Pound's misquotation, is the negatively connotated form in the line. "Shelved," in this context, should be read not as meaning put to one side, or abandoned, but as made more easily and readily available—as we shelve our books in order to be able to get at them quickly and conveniently when we need to. "Shelving," in this sense of the ordering of information so that it becomes more accessible and hence more useful, is a distinctly Poundian activity. In his 1918 essay on Henry James, Pound defines "honest criticism" as "saying to one's reader exactly what one would say to the friend who approaches one's bookshelf asking: 'What the deuce shall I read?'"[6] This makes explicit a dramatic situation, an assumed relationship with its audience, that is characteristic of a great deal of Pound's prose (and is not uncommon in *The Cantos*); and it is one in which the bookshelf plays a central role, not only as a record and a repository, but also as a potential source of remedy, or dynamic example. It could even be said that the cantos which follow this line (8 to 11), consisting as they do partly of a row of historical documents, letters and other texts, resemble a bookshelf.

This reading is, I believe, reinforced if we look at the line in the context of the canto that precedes it. Canto 7 has been described as Pound's "Waste Land"—a description that is only useful insofar as it conveys a sense of the distinctly Eliotic note struck at points in that canto: for example, "Life to make mock of motion:/ For the husks, before me, move,/The words rattle: shells given out by shells"; or "Lift up their spoons to mouths, put forks in cutlets,/And make sound like the sound of voices. . ." [7/27]. More usefully, Canto 7 should be read as an extended essay in pastiche in which Pound depicts contemporary (i.e., immediately post-World War I) society, assuming the styles of some of the then-available modes of perceiving and writing about the modern world (Eliot's, for instance, and—perhaps more importantly—that of the modern novel, particularly the Jamesian variation of it). A careful reading of this canto reveals that it is as much a critique of the discourses it assumes, and of the views of the world they imply, as it is a straightforward condemnation of the superficiality and sordidness of modern life; it recognizes the justice of the "beer bottle on the statue's pediment" view of modernity, but at the same time frets at the limitations of a discourse seemingly impotent in the face of it, unable to do more than register distaste. This impatience, apparent from the beginning ("Sceptic against all this one seeks the living,/Stubborn against the fact," and a few lines later,

---
6. *Literary Essays*, ed cit., p. 306.

"Damn the partition!" [7/25]), increases until towards the end, "seeking the living," the canto moves away from the "dry" modern world to the Italy of Lorenzaccio and Alessandro de Medici—in terms of the famous line from the canto, away from "rooms" to "chronicles"—where he finds more life:

> Lorenzaccio
> Being more live than they, more full of flames and voices [7/27].

Read in this way, Canto 7 prepares the reader for the poem's announcement of its epic intention in the opening lines of Canto 8, and affords an insight into how the epic history of *The Cantos* will differ from Eliot's "shored fragments"; Pound's poem will "seek the living," it will—to return to the maxim quoted earlier—"assert a positive."

My reading of Canto 7 also provides a useful insight into the second problem raised by the lines under discussion: the Truth/Calliope slanging-match. Calliope is comparatively straightforward: the muse of epic poetry, we may assume, is also the muse of Pound's "poem including history," and represents the narrative values and qualities that we will find embodied in the account of Sigismundo that follows. What "Truth" might signify in this context, and why the two should be so violently at odds, is more problematic. The usual reading of this line assumes an irony and glosses "Truth" as something like "official history" or "received opinion." The usefulness of such a reading, to a large extent, depends on whether or not the criticism of history implicit in the line is seen as having a local and specific application to the "official history" of Sigismundo Malatesta, or as having a more general application to all such histories; and on whether or not Calliope is perceived as offering a somehow "truer" (i.e., more accurate) History, or as being ultimately concerned with some ahistorical order of meaning or truth. The latter position seems to me to deny the value or place of history in *The Cantos*; for Pearlman,[7] for example, the Malatesta cantos are essentially a mythopoeic exercise, the recreation in historical space of an archetypal figure (Odysseus Polumetis), and history (even Sigismundo) can only enter the poem by becoming mythologized. In such a reading, Calliope becomes not the muse of a "poem including history," but of a poem that essentially *excludes* history. Limiting the range of reference of the line avoids these problems, and can generate a far stronger reading of the four cantos that follow: readings that

---
7. Daniel S. Pearlman, *The Barb of Time* (London and New York, 1969). Pearlman argues the thesis that Pound is concerned to transcend or "escape from" history into the timeless, eternal world of permanent values.

acknowledge their specificity and concern with historical accuracy (I am thinking in particular of Michael Harper's excellent essay[8]). Such a reading renders the ironic identification of "Truth" with "official history" particularly telling us, as it would seem that many historians have taken uncritically the partisan *Commentaries* of Pius II (an inveterate enemy and political opponent of Malatesta) as their principal source when writing of Sigismundo. The second alternative must, as I have said, be given credit for recognizing the text's concern with historical accuracy, and Pound's characteristic urge to "set the record straight," broadly, the concern to "include history"; finally, however, I do not believe that the Malatesta cantos are, or could ever be, "a transparent account of the recognisable world,"[9] or that they can be, adequately, dealt with critically in terms of the accuracy or otherwise of the account of Sigismundo Malatesta which they offer. A strong reading of our three lines, and of the whole of the Malatesta cantos, must acknowledge not simply the concern to "include history," but also the larger aspiration to write a "poem including history." This seems to me to suggest a more useful reading of the "Truth/Calliope" argument.

The attempt, in the twentieth century, to write an epic ("a poem including history"), to make history, and hence the modern world, accessible to verse, does not bring the poet into conflict or competition with the historian but (as Lukács would suggest) with the novelist. To see "Truth" as representing the mode of access to the past and to contemporary history, afforded by the novel, and so to read the argument *"sous les lauriers"* as referring to the rival claims of the novel and the verse epic as fictional modes of understanding history, seems to me the most useful reading of these lines.

The terms of this argument can be more fully understood if we read these lines, as suggested, in the context of the canto that immediately precedes them. Canto 7 is partly a critique of the capacity of the novel to deal adequately with contemporary history. Pound's brilliant pastiche implicitly recognizes and concedes this mode of writing's ability to record adequately, to render the surface, while finding it finally unsatisfactory, lacking in that quality he terms the "living." For instance, in the lines quoted earlier—

---

8. Michael F. Harper, "Truth and Calliope: Ezra Pound's Malatesta," *PMLA*, XCVI, 1 (Jan. 1981), 80-103.
9. Frank Kermode, *The Genesis of Secrecy* (Cambridge, Mass., and London, 1979), p. 101.

> Sceptic against all this one seeks the living,
> Stubborn against the fact [7/25].

"all this" and "the fact" are contemporary history as mediated in prose fiction ("the wilted flowers," "the empty rooms," "the flimsy and damned partition," etc.); Pound does not deny that this is an accurate reflection of the surface of the modern world, but is "stubborn against" it in the belief that there is something else, "the living," a positive value not given in prose but which, we may infer, is accessible to poetry. Pound discusses this question in similar terms in his 1918 essay on Henry James,[10] which must have been written at about the same time as Canto 7, sharing many of its themes and concerns and being, I believe, usefully read as a source for and commentary on it. In a long footnote to the essay, Pound offers the following account of the "root difference" between poetry and prose:

> Most good prose arises, perhaps, from an instinct of negation; is the detailed, convincing analysis of something detestable; of something which one wants to eliminate. Poetry is the assertion of a positive, i.e. of desire, and endures for a longer period. . . .
> Most good poetry asserts something to be worthwhile, or damns a contrary; at any rate asserts emotional values. The best prose is, has been a presentation (complicated and elaborate as you like) of circumstances, of conditions, for the most part abominable or, at the mildest, amendable. . . .
> Poetry = Emotional synthesis, *quite as real, quite as realist as any prose* (or intellectual) analysis.[11]

Here Pound is explicitly claiming for poetry (by reason of its ability to "assert a positive," to achieve a synthesis in contrast to the purely analytical—in Pound's terms, negative—capability of prose) that it can express the "living" element (enduring emotion) that escapes prose, and that it can do so not only in a "real" way but in a "realist" way. This last point is significant because it brings Pound into direct conflict with the then-prevailing critical orthodoxy which held that the novel had "replaced" the verse epic precisely because of its greater capacity for "realism"; in Lukács' terms, its greater capacity to render a world ". . . in which the extensive totality of life is no longer directly given . . .", a world in which ". . . meaning in life . . ." is "immanent."[12] I do not know whether or not Pound was familiar with the work of Lukács, but

---

10. First published in *The Little Review* (London, August 1918), reprinted in *Literary Essays*.
11. *Literary Essays*, p. 324; my italics.
12. Georg Lukács, *The Theory of the Novel*, trans. Anna Bostock (London, 1978), p. 56. *The Theory of the Novel* was written in 1914-1915, but not published until 1920, so is virtually contemporary with Pound's essay on James and the Malatesta cantos.

he was certainly aware of, and strongly objected to, the orthodoxy that proscribed the verse epic (there was a mass of evidence to support this, in his prose, letters, the "Ur-Cantos" and in *The Cantos* themselves). Pound would have conceded that during the nineteenth century poetry had "fallen behind" prose (for instance, in *How to Read* he writes that with Stendhal ". . . the serious art of writing 'went over to prose' . . ."[13]), but he believed that this loss of prestige or status was temporary and reversible and held poetry to be potentially the "higher form." Verse, Pound believed, could and should be "as well written as prose," and at its best it could not only embody the "prose virtues" and deal directly, "realistically," with a complex world, but, by reason of its capacity for "positive assertion" of that which "endures for a longer period," could surpass prose. It is of such poetry that the Calliope of Canto 8 is the Muse, and, as such, it is she and not "truth" (the muse of prose) who is most fitted to tell the "openly volitionist" story of Sigismundo, "the factive personality, the entire man."[14]

II

I have been attempting to demonstrate how the opening lines of Canto 8 fulfil the functions I ascribed to them earlier; to distinguish *The Cantos'* discourse of history from other available discourses, to assert the value of that discourse—and in doing so to create a space for the history that follows. The next step—determining more exactly what fills that space—is beyond the scope of this short paper. I would, however, like to close with some observations on the narrative strategy most commonly associated with history in *The Cantos*, of which the Malatesta cantos are often cited as a particularly successful example. Pound, it is well known, rejected conventional narrative strategies and logically integrated discourse in favor of what is variously known as the "scientific method," the "method of luminous detail," the "inductive method" or the "ideogrammic method." Which of these terms we use does not seem to me to make a great deal of difference; my own preference is for the third alternative. By now, what this method is or how it works needs no explanation from me, and I will confine my comments to a consideration of it as narrative strategy; this, I think, is useful if only to make the point that, contrary to the claims sometimes made for them, *The Cantos* are a narrative poem.

---

13. *Literary Essays*, p. 31.
14. *Guide to Kulchur*, p. 194.

In theory, Pound's narrative method does not seek to impose meaning or significance on the material it presents (as does, say, logical exposition or argument that subordinates certain elements and foregrounds others according to a syntax of causation), but rather seeks to present the elements without privileging any particular one, allowing the meaning or significance inherent in them to emerge by a process of induction. Thus, Pound argues (and many of his critics have agreed), is the "objectivity" of modern science conferred upon the study of history or literature.

This model of how narrative in *The Cantos* works, deriving from Pound himself, is difficult to reconcile with Pound's claim that the Malatesta cantos are "openly volitionist" (i.e., intentionalist) and that they "establish clearly the effect of the factive personality," or for that matter with his larger claim that "poetry asserts a positive," unless we assume that the text is totally transparent upon history, and that the patterns of meaning and significance that historical events assume in *The Cantos* are inherent in the events themselves (this may well be what Pound would like us to believe, but that is a very different matter). Similarly, if Pound had simply presented the "facts in the case of Sigismundo Malatesta" and left the rest to the reader, we would expect the cantos dealing with Sigismundo to have generated readings as diverse as the judgments passed on Malatesta himself by historians and commentators. This however has not been the case; there is some measure of disagreement about the accuracy or justice of Pound's account of Malatesta, but very little about what he is actually saying. If we discount, as I believe we must, the naive theory of the total transparency of the text, and the motion that only Pound was in possession of the "facts," and that they admit of only one interpretation, then we are forced to the conclusion that, on the level of narrative organization, the "Malatesta cantos" do not operate in the way indicated by the model outlined earlier. Rather, Pound's "inductive method," like any other form of narrative, is essentially interpretative and necessarily imposes significance, order and meaning on its constituent elements in accordance with the ideology of the subject. In fact, the Malatesta cantos are peculiarly impatient of this interpretation, "exigent" to use Pound's own word ("the text is somewhat exigent" [98/691]); on the basis of the information given only one conclusion is possible—Pound's—and to reach any other the reader would have to bring to the text knowledge, or a perspective on events, that Pound has deliberately excluded, and which the text resists: the presentation of the figure of Pius II, particularly in Canto 10 ("that monstrous swollen, swelling s.o.b." [10/44]) is a good example of this. Whatever its application in other fields, in historical narrative (in *The Cantos*) the "inductive method" can only be a rhetorical device intended to produce an illusion of objectivity and so enhance the plausibility of the interpretation offered, and close off other possible interpretations to the reader.

A brief examination of one of the several theoretical accounts Pound offers of his narrative method may help to clarify this. One such occurs in "Date Line,"[15] an essay published some years after the Malatesta cantos but nonetheless useful for our present purposes. Here Pound offers the analogous model of the experimental biologist to explain or illustrate his method. The biologist, Pound says, proceeds by the examination of specifics (". . . he expects to explore a limited field . . .") and by this method hopes ". . . to improve the knowledge of certain details and, if lucky, to clarify the relations of that field, both in regard to the field itself, and to its exterior reference."[16] He will not expect to gain this end through the perception of logical or causal relationships, but through induction:

> You don't necessarily expect the bacilli in one test tube to "lead to" those in another by a mere logical or syllogistic line. The good scientist now and then discovers similarities, he discovers family groups, similar behaviour in presence of like reagents, etc.[17]

A row of test tubes conveys a vivid impression of the series of discrete elements that comprise Pound's narrative, and the perception of "family groups," similarities, common patterns, etc., is important in reading *The Cantos*. One of the ways in which we are made aware of what is important or significant in a particular canto is by recognizing that certain elements "repeat," or exhibit a common pattern with, other discrete elements that the text has already indicated are important or significant. Thus far, the analogy holds and is of some value, but beyond this it begins to break down. Discrete historical occasions may or may not form "family groups," but the discrete elements of a narrative only do so if the narrative itself has so organized them, if they have been "emplotted" in such a manner as to emphasize their similarities rather than their differences, and this necessarily involves interpretation from an ideological perspective. Some of the "family groups" Pound perceives (Jefferson and Mussolini, or Malatesta and Pound's own grandfather, for instance) clearly illustrate this.

Such "family groups" tell us more about the subject, Pound, then they do about Jefferson, Mussolini or Malatesta. This may

---
15. First published in *Make It New* (London, 1934); reprinted in *Literary Essays*.
16. *Literary Essays*, p. 76.
17. *Ibid.*

seem obvious, but the point is worth making because this is precisely the conclusion that Pound did not want, or intend, the reader to reach. The narrative strategy of *The Cantos*, and the theory Pound elaborated around it, is specifically designed to disguise this, to present the subjective and ideological as the objective and "scientific." If Pound's "history" is considered only in its own terms, this is obscured as Pound intended it should be. It is, therefore, important to attempt to describe and analyze Pound's historiography in terms other than its own. I cannot, I am afraid, undertake to provide anything like a conclusive demonstration of the value of such an exercise, but I will offer a necessarily-brief illustration.

The historical narrative found in Cantos 8 to 11 may, I believe, be most usefully described as "pseudo-chronicle," taking chronicle to mean "a conjunction of non-causal singular statements which expressly mention the subject,"[18] but also including the sense of chronicle as something anterior to history, the totality of events from which the historian must select and reorganize certain elements in order to produce a history.[19] Pound's narrative is pseudo-chronicle because it does contain causal statements, and because the selection and organization—what Hayden White would term the process of "emplotment"[20]—necessary to produce a history has taken place but has been disguised. This reading clearly reveals Pound's basic strategy: characteristically, he is attempting to validate his history by denying that it is a "history" (i.e. a subjective interpretation of events); and the chronicle-like surface of the narrative is intended to produce the illusion of objectivity.

In all of this, I am not trying to suggest that Pound is doing anything wrong, in the sense of being unethical. I am not even concerned with the historical accuracy of his account of Malatesta. Pound is a political writer (I am thinking of Orwell's definition of "political purpose" in a writer as the "desire to push the world in a certain direction, to alter other people's ideas of the kind of society that they should strive after"[21]) and as such is entitled

---

18. Morton White, *The Foundations of Historical Knowledge* (New York, 1965), quoted in Kermode, p.103.
19. The above account is deeply endebted to Frank Kermode's discussion of the problems of these aspects of historiography in *The Genesis of Secrecy*, particularly Chapter V, "What Precisely Are the Facts," pp. 101-123.
20. Hayden White, *Metahistory: the Historical Imagination in Nineteenth Century Europe* (Baltimore and London, 1973), p. 7: "Emplotment is the way by which a sequence of events fashioned into a story is gradually revealed to be a story of a particular kind. . . . such as the Epic. . . ."
21. George Orwell, "Why I Write," in *Collected Essays, Journalism and Letters*, 4 vols. (Harmondsworth, Middx., 1975), I, 26.

to use all the rhetorical means at his disposal to persuade, seduce or coerce the reader into agreement. Nor am I principally concerned with establishing the value of the particular approach to narrative in *The Cantos* which I have so inadequately sketched out. My point is simply this: that the critical encounter with Pound's text can only usefully take place in terms other than Pound's own. Not to attempt this, to surrender to the seductive and elegant totalitarianism of Pound's text and the theoretical context he provided for it, is a serious dereliction of our primary duty as critics and scholars of *The Cantos*.

IAN F. A. BELL

THE PARALYZED HISTORY OF CANTO XXXI

To begin again, the practice of the entire sequence is foregrounded by the field of Canto 31 as the reader is shifted form the Renaissance of Malatesta to the "Nuevo Mundo" of Jefferson and Adams; a shift that is mimed by the ceremony of the ancient language in its opening and closing lines, and the new possibilities of 1776. We are presented with a strategy of construction in two senses; in the initial figuration of Jefferson himself not as a politician but as a temperament alert to the possibilities of reconstruction in technological progress, and in the array of ready-made linguistic objects in the form of the quotations Pound chose as *The Cantos'* programme. It is in the latter sense that we witness the ludic *joissance* of Pound's concern with the tactics of beginning during the early 1930s, particularly since, to note *The Cantos'* most obvious characteristic, so few of its lines "originate," as it were, in Pound himself. Indeed, the myth of origination constitutes the very fulcrum of Pound's play. If nothing else, the ready-made objects strike us by precisely their own objectivity, their status of having been made, and by their signification of an overwhelmingly concrete world. They operate as items of material and mechanical notation both in the themes they offer on behalf of an Enlightenment sensibility and in their immediate roles as semantic occasions. Such solidity, employed for the first time in the sequence (an expressive feature of its willingness to interrogate the problem of origination) cannot be innocent of the paralyzed solidity characteristic of the world of technology and commodity that was advanced capitalism's valorized configuration of Enlightenment materialism.[1] Paradoxically, it was to resist such a world that Pound invoked its own scientific and technological precepts

---

1. See Theodor Adorno and Max Horkheimer, *Dialectic of Enlightenment* (1947), trans. John Cumming (London, 1979) and Alfred Sohn-Rethel, *Intellectual and Manual Labour: a Critique of Epistemology* (London, 1978).

to sustain his own poetics,[2] and it is within this paradox that we may determine the condition of disablement which is the province of the poem.

By the vocabulary of literary criticism, Pound's composition of Canto 31 was metonymic, and recent work by Herbert Schneidau[3] and Max Nänny[4] has displayed how metonymy may be seen as a decisive component of much of Pound's innovatory procedure. Here, however, metonymy projects itself to such an extent that we have to consider it not merely as a compositional feature, but as a part of the poem's very theme. It is, indeed, the major articulation of the poem's autoreferentiality, its display of its own technology. Nänny has noted that Pound "tends to prefer icons and indices to verbal symbols,"[5] and this is exactly the effect of Pound's metonymy; to use his "indices" his "luminous details" as icons, not to claim sacred or metaphysical values, but as a means of refusing such values by the seeming objectivity of his "particulars." Part of the office of this objectivity is to attempt to engage an impossible authenticity: Nänny claims that Pound's habit of quoting "original" words "is above all an attempt at assuring ear-witness, first-hand *authenticity of statement.*"[6] Such a claim relies on the myth of the priority or reality of the oral in opposition to the written, but Pound's seeking of his material from correspondence (sited, as it were, *between* the oral and the written) and not from public papers does suggest that it was a myth he could use in his play with the question of origination. And, of course, Canto 31 opens with speech, but it is in a language no longer spoken and, furthermore, is deliberately ceremonial.

We may note here how any spontaneity that may accrue to the oral is heavily modified by the ontology of quotations as ready-mades and by their initial thematic concern with the technological re-making of nature by Enlightenment science. Schneidau, in arguing for Pound's ideogrammic method as metonymic, has stressed that it "cannot *depend* on analogy" since it is a

---

2. I have tried to elaborate Pound's discourse in this area in *Critic as Scientist: the Modernist Poetics of Ezra Pound* (London, 1981). Adjacent and invaluable work has been performed by Martin A. Kayman in his unpublished D.Phil. thesis, "Ezra Pound and the Phantasy of Science" (University of York, 1978), part of which has emerged in print as "Ezra Pound: a Model for his Use of 'Science,'" *Biblos*, LVII (1981), pp. 505-526, and *Alguns dos nossos Melhores Poetas São Fasçistas (Uma Introduçao a Ezra Pound)* (Coimbra, 1981), Chapter IV.
3. Herbert Schneidau, "Pound, Olson & Objective Verse," *Paideuma*, 5-1, pp. 15-29.
4. Max Nänny, "The Oral Roots of Ezra Pound's Methods of Quotation and Abbreviation," *Paideuma*, 8-3, pp. 381-387; and "Context, Contiguity and Contact in Ezra Pound's *Personae*," *English Literary History*, XLVII, 2 (Summer 1980), pp. 386-398.
5. Nänny, "Context, Contiguity and Contact...," *loc cit.*, p. 389.
6. Nänny, "The Oral Roots...," *loc cit.*, p. 382.

practice of one "who grasps words literally but not metaphorically."[7] Such literalness would seem to propose a further mode of authenticity whereby objects and words are perceived and offered exactly for what they are: their literalness makes no further (symbolical, metaphorical or allegorical) demands. What Schneidau fails to account for here is the function of the reader: which is to say, he refuses to locate that function as part of the closed system of *The Cantos*' tactics. The syntheses effected by Pound's technological poetics are designed, as Paul Smith and Alan Durant have argued, as a "defusing of the threat that dialectical process poses to monosemy," and the consequence is a paradoxical insertion into the world of commodities that they intend to resist. Smith and Durant point illuminatingly to the reductive function of the reader here:

> ... in the sort of writing that Pound undertakes, meaning becomes a given object, to be handed on by the writer; and manufactured by the writer, not by the reader. Meaning is merely a commodity which can supposedly be passed on, traditionally.[8]

So we need to recognize that the proposed authenticity of Pound's literalness is reductively operational at the level of the poem's practice of presentation. Frederic Jameson has shown how the machine-like metonomy of Wyndham Lewis serves not so much to displace metaphor but to conceal it in order to demystify the process of creation (which has always relied on the Aristotelian of metaphor) by an "unnatural or artificial redoubling of "nature" by its expression, or by language."[9] The redoubling process is particularly apparent in Canto 31 where the poem is

---

7. Schneidau, *op cit.*, p. 19. Pound's literalness lends further weight to the insistently objective, factual tissue of the poem (figures most explicitly in the tobacco stanza), and we see here the contradiction of his materialism. Schneidau, in the later essay, has commented on behalf of Joyce's Dublin that "It goes beyond those rationales for realism that were produced by the insinuation of scientific method into narrative techniques. On the other hand, it may have to do with the development of a renewed sense of the reality of history." But this "reality" is inevitably paradoxical; Schneidau continues by noting Joyce's irony: "Far from implying a guarantee of metaphysical 'truth' behind the work, the germs of fact opened vistas of disparity between event and representation." ("Style and Sacrament in Modernist Writing," *The Georgia Review*, XXXI, 2 (Summer 1977), pp. 435-436.) To see the "disparity between event and representation" as a play of irony for Joyce cannot be transferred to the case of Canto 31 where the very solidity of its world disables its language as Pound struggled to refute the false materiality of a commodity society with the allied materiality of his own practice. His methods of constructive precision and economy, designed to stress the reality of things, were exactly those of capitalist production itself and its consequences in reification that he so hated.
8. P. H. Smith and A. E. Durant, "Pound's Metonymy: Revisiting Canto 47," *Paideuma*, 8-2, p. 331.
9. Frederic Jameson, *Fables of Aggression: Wyndham Lewis, the Modernist as Fascist* (Berkeley, Los Angeles, London, 1979), pp. 28-29. Jameson obliquely reminds us of the liberation promised by technology (particularly by the Enlightenment ideology) when he notes that "the mechanical, the machinelike, knows an exaltation peculiarly its own" (p. 25), where a machine is "less a thing than a center of radiant energy" (p. 82).

constructed wholly by a series of synecdoches themselves extracted from material that is already written. We attend to the mechanics of creation as the machine which is Thomas Jefferson is jerked through his dislocated routine (the extracted quotations which, on the page, form no identifiable text of their own) by Pound in the role of artisanal engineer.[10] Pound elaborated this demystification: the natural world suggested by the opening tag from *Ecclesiastes* was not only resisted (in its cyclical form) and re-made by Jefferson's mechanical constructivism, but it also posited a source of plenitude no longer available in that re-made world. Words themselves could no longer seek a resource of richness, fecundity and organic guarantees from the metaphors of a world that, in truth, had never existed: they would have to content themselves, through the doubled contradiction of their own insistent solidity whereby they exhibit the disparity between event and presentation, with an acknowledgement of their secondariness. Jameson has well expressed the characteristic of this secondariness in the case of Lewis:

> Since there exists no adequate language for "rendering" the object, all that is left to the writer is to tell us how he would have rendered it had he had such a language in the first place.
> There thus comes into being a language beyond language, shot through with the jerry-built shoddiness of modern industrial civilization, brittle and impermanent, yet full of a mechanic's enthusiasm. Lewis's style is thus a violent and exemplary figure for the birth of all living speech and turns to its own advantage the discovery that all language is a second-best, the merest substitute for the impossible plenitude of a primary language that has never existed. In this sense all speech must settle its accounts with the optical illusion of a natural language if it is to be delivered from a terrorized reduction to silence.[11]

Pound plays explicitly with this secondariness in his opening to the poem:

Tempus loquendi,
Tempus tacendi.
Said Mr Jefferson: It wd. have given us time.

---

10. Pound's project here was in part a continuation of the programme of his London years which adopted the vocabulary of technology to offer the artist's constructions as commensurate with any other comparable system of work or production, allying the artist to the ordinary business of practical living. (See my *Critic as Scientist, ed cit.*, p. 74.) It was not accidental that the composition of Canto 31 which insisted on the scientific interests of Jefferson belonged to the period of his first public acclamation of Agassiz and his designation of Mussolini as "Artifex."
11. Jameson, *op cit.*, p. 86. I should make it clear that I do not consider Lewis' exercise to be exactly comparable to Pound's. Lewis presents an extreme case, but, while considering Canto 31, I think it necessary to point out the general features shared by their respective ideologies of language.

His reversal of the original order of the Latin, his deliberate translation of two of its words ("Tempus" and "loquendi") and his equally deliberate refusal to translate its final word ("tacendi"), a refusal which is emphasized by the visual "silence" of the typographical space where "time" floats freely, demonstrate a humorous awareness of his play. Not only had Mr. Jefferson never "said" anything of the kind,[12] but the "It" is given no reference and, within the humor of Pound's refusal to translate "tacendi" silently inscribes the vacant place for its meaning, its context for what might have been. The silence of "It" mimes the virtual silence of Pound's own speaking voice for the rest of the poem: the origination of speech, sanctioned by the seasonal fecundity that is celebrated in the fuller text of *Ecclesiastes*, is thus turned back on itself.

Translation inevitably displays the doubleness of its function, the doubleness that enables Pound's game in these opening lines. In the penultimate stanza, he points to its more debilitating aspect in "A tiels leis... en ancien scripture, and this/they have translated *Holy Scripture*...." Pound's source, Jefferson's letter to Adams of 24 January 1814, was a lengthy diatribe against those who "extend the coercions of municipal law to the dogmas of their religion, by declaring that these make a part of the law of the land." Jefferson selected Finch's mistranslation of Prisot's *"ancien scripture"* as "holy scripture" (further perpetuated by a lengthy and impressive list of the legal misreadings which followed) to point the fraudulent way whereby the principles of religion were invoked on behalf of the common law. The activity of mistranslation demonstrates vividly the secondariness of language, and acquires its particular potency here in a context so central to the distrust of monotheism shared by Jefferson and Pound.[13] Pound

---

12. That is to say that I, in company with those commentators who have substantially annotated the poem by means of Jefferson's correspondence [Robert M. Knight, "Thomas Jefferson in Canto XXXI," *Paideuma*, 5-1, pp. 79-93; Stephen Fender, *The American Long Poem* (London, 1977), pp. 94-109; George Kearns, *Guide to Ezra Pound's Selected Cantos* (Folkestone, 1980), pp. 80-92] have been unable to locate its source. In a poem so constructed, the absence of this source in the context of the other absences in these opening lines is a matter of more germane importance than merely the incompleteness of a scholar's list, of faulty memory on the part of Pound.

13. *The Adams-Jefferson Letters*, ed. Lester J. Cappon, 2 vols. (Chapel Hill, 1959), II, pp. 421-425. Jefferson's attack on the tyranny of lawyers who so perverted civic justice by invoking faked relitious sanctions (pp. 422-423) was followed by an equally violent diatribe against that other monotheistic institution, the bank (pp. 424-425). The letter concluded with a postscript admiring William Barton's recent biography of "our good and really great Rittenhouse" who "as a mechanician . . . certainly has not been equalled" (p. 425). The range and strength of this configuration of interests—by no means, of course, rare in Jefferson's correspondence—informs the weight of Pound's concern with translation in the poem itself and, I would suggest, enables us to see his selection from this particular letter as an especially vibrant moment in the field of Canto XXXI.

adds to its potency by inserting one of the rare lines of his own after the quotation: "and they continue this error." His point is to be taken literally in two senses; referring to the repetitions of the original mistranslation listed in Jefferson's letter, and to Pound's notion that they continue in his own time; yet a further prison for the contemporary world. This is a prison both of words and ideas: meaning suffers both from perversion in the example of mistranslation and from the immobility of silence in the absence of any reference for Jefferson's "It"—inevitable consequences of the problems of evaluation in the "instability and uncertainty" that the Russian linguist V. N. Volosinov detected as characteristics of contemporary language in 1930.[14]

We witness Pound's attention to the question of meaning as part of his play with language's secondariness in the cipher he quotes from Jefferson's letter to Madison of 2 August 1787: "This country is really supposed to be on the eve of a XTZBK49HT." The secrecy of the cipher, at one level, matches the secrecy of Jefferson's reiteration of Adams' proposal for repaying America's debt to France by borrowing from Holland.[15] But as a linguistic event, it further incorporates the meaninglessness of its arithmetical status (in which its figuration as "O" signifies the silence of its nothingness) and of its status as an arbitrary collection of characters. A cipher bears, of course, a close resemblance to a hieroglyph. Joseph Riddel has demystified the notion of poet as Egyptologist to characterize one who "descends into the crypts in order to read the secret language of hieroglyphs" not to "retrieve a meaning lost or buried in past forms" but to "effect a new writing, a pro-jecting

---

14. Volosinov insisted on the inadmissability of a disjuncture between referential meaning and evaluation: "The separation of word meaning from evaluation inevitably deprives meaning of its place in the living social process (where meaning is always permeated with value judgement) to its being ontologized and transformed into ideal Being divorced from the historical process of Becoming." This, in part, proposes again a problem of authenticity, since by "evaluation" Volosinov intends "the expression of a speaker's individual attitude toward the subject matter of his discourse." [*Marxism and the Philosophy of Language* (1930), trans. Ladislav Matejka and I. R. Titunik (New York and London, 1973), pp. 57-58.] In other words, authenticity may only be gauged in the context assumed by an exchange between two or more voices, a condition of interchange, through the generative powers of language's indirection and ambiguity, which offers the socially hazardous possibility of revision of dialectical insertion. In the third line of Canto 31, the condition of such exchange is explicitly a non-dialogic moment (figured by the absence of its context) which responds to the enclosure suggested by the preceding ceremonial language from *Ecclesiastes*. (I am appreciative of a conversation with my colleague Richard Godden on this point.)

15. *The Papers of Thomas Jefferson*, ed. Julian P. Boyd, 19 vols. (Princeton, 1955), XI, pp. 662-664. The cipher itself is used on p. 664 and belongs to a code which Jefferson used extensively at the end of the letter. The early correspondence between Jefferson and Adams also contained occasional coded passages. The secrecy of a cipher, whereby its reference is available only to those who know the code, suggests ciphers as the most appropriate expressions of the privatization consequent upon technology.

of old signs that is the 'beginning' of writing."[16] It is through their very secrecy and initial meaninglessness that ciphers draw attention to themselves as pieces of writing since they are wholly free from the determinants of organized grammar. In this sense they claim a paradoxical naturalness, of a chaotic kind, for their arbitrariness declares itself unbounded by any law. Their event is thus a contorted reminder of the technological liberation that was so powerfully maintained by Enlightenment thought in general and by Jefferson in particular.

The arbitrariness of the cipher also recognizes itself as a doubled displacement: as with any signifier, it displaces what it signifies which itself (some more organized word; in this case, "bankruptcy"[17]) has already displaced its object of signification. Pound stresses this doubleness by a further act of translation. In the Lipscomb and Bergh edition of Jefferson's *Writings* that he consulted, no cipher as such was given: it offered a row of asterisks in place of the "unintelligible" cipher that Jefferson had originally used.[18] We have here a pure case of constructing something out of nothing, which took the form of a nonsensical filling of the gap in Jefferson's text. Indeed, it was doubly nonsensical because Pound did not possess the code whereby the cipher could be translated back into a communal language. The cipher's alphabetical and numerical jumble inscribes it as both metonymic and mechanical, presenting a visible typography to the technique and subject of Canto 31. As a wholly displaced event (having, in Pound's expression, no possible area of signification) it disperses the questions of origination and secondariness with which *Nuevo Mundo* prepares itself to be reconstructed.

Metonymy, as the literary trope which matches the poem's invocation of technology, marks a mechanical inventory; in Jameson's phrase, "a step-by-step dismantling of the body's gestural machine."[19] It is a means of deconstructing the world, but incorporating the danger of providing its synecdoches with a larger burden of meaning than they were designed to carry. As with any machine, too great an overloading instigates break-down, an explosion of energy. The cipher is the ultimate paradigm for this process: its arbitrariness literally dismantles organized language to display in naked form the displacement and secondariness that characterize language's translations, removing words entirely

---

16. Joseph N. Riddell, "Decentering the Image: the 'Project' of 'American' Poetics," *Boundary 2*, VIII, 1 (Fall 1979), p. 163.
17. See *The Papers of Thomas Jefferson, ed cit.*, XI, pp. 664 and 668n.
18. See Fender, *op cit.*, pp. 98 and 99.
19. Jameson, *op cit.*, p. 31.

from the community of communication. Its energy is foregrounded as the joy of playing freely with the keys of a typewriter expresses itself in a typographical dazzle, a cacophony of characters, paradoxically to snub the paralysis of the world as market-place, a world which sought its beginnings in the libertarian promise of Enlightenment mechanics in order to begin again, to re-translate and re-make. The random distribution which characterizes the field of the cipher renders it the appropriate expression of the voice offering the interrupted commencement of *The Cantos* as a whole: the voice of the con-man, the joker, of Odysseus in the non-originating persona of "No-man," the paradoxical silence which, at the risk of non-sense, exploits and deconstructs the confinement of communal discourse.

ALAN J. PEACOCK

POUND AND PROPERTIUS:
THE LIMITATIONS OF AN HISTORICAL PERSONA

I

Critical views on Pound's *Homage to Sextus Propertius* tend to be divergent and partisan. Notoriously the poem inhabits a critical no-man's-land between specialists in modern English literature and their counterparts in the Classics; and historically, to state the matter as briefly as possible, the "ancient" camp has tended towards outrage at the poem's shortcomings as a translation of Propertius (which it clearly is not), while the "modern" camp, though generally fairer and more enthusiastic, has not always been fully alive to the important verbal and thematic interplay between Pound's text and that of Propertius. Many of the problems surrounding the poem seem attributable not so much to the text itself as to limitations of approach in its exponents.[1] So I should say straight away that no grand synthesis is attempted in what I have to offer today. I will be looking at Pound's poem primarily in relation to Propertius rather than attempting to do justice to it as a piece of twentieth century literature.

If there is a critical predisposition in what follows, it will probably stem from an interest in the seventeenth- and eighteenth-century neo-classical "imitation": it seems to me that many of the difficulties associated with Pound's *Propertius* fall away if it is approached in the light of the combination of sensitivity to an original "model" and commitment to up-dating and re-fashioning which is expected in the traditional imitation. In the *Imitations of Horace* Pope takes quite drastic liberties with the Latin text; and revisions of authorial tone and *persona* boldly

---

[1]. One obvious exception to this generalization is of course J. P. Sullivan, whose contribution to the study of Roman love elegy and Pound is available in various places and, notably for the present topic, in *Ezra Pound and Sextus Propertius: A Study in Creative Translation* (London, 1965). I quote from his text of the *Homage*.

accommodate his temperamental needs. So with Pound's *Propertius*: in the normal neo-classical way, he presents some of his concerns in 1917 "largely but not entirely"[2] in Propertian terms. There is, it seems to me, very little in the form or even the techniques of the poem which is problematic—if it is read in the light of the practice of such as Ben Jonson, Donne, Pope, Samuel Johnson, etc., in their re-working of classical texts. The old arid debate as to whether the *Homage* is a translation or an original poem need never have taken place.

Beyond this, however, there remains something troublesome. The permissive conventions of the "imitation" are so apposite for a consideration of the form and technique of Pound's poem that it is difficult not to feel that there must be some reason why classicist critics in particular have not seen the poem within this tradition—a tradition moreover which, over the centuries, has played a prime role in preserving the classical legacy as a vital element in our literature. It is not simply a matter of narrowness of approach. There is, I think, a dimension to Pound's projection of Propertian *persona* which may account for the failure of many critics to occupy what seems the obvious common ground. A brief glance at what may be expected in the neo-classical imitation may be useful here.

Traditionally, the model in an imitative exercise may be fastened upon for a variety of aesthetic, prudential or strategic reasons. Pope's successful imitation of Horace *Satires* 2,i in "To Fortescue" is generated initially by prudential considerations: Pope's own satirical writings are under attack and, as his *Advertisement* indicates, he sees the value of enrolling the authority of Horace in his reply. The oblique nature of Horace's ironic *apologia* with its easy-going, non-pugnacious tone, is perhaps not an entirely comfortable mode for Pope's temperament. Ultimately, therefore, Pope's more aggressive character emerges and towards the end of the poem, where Horace mentions his famous predecessor Lucilius as a model of satiric fearlessness, Pope takes the bold step of assuming this mantle himself, and takes leave of his Horatian *persona* with the much more assertive section beginning:

> What? arm'd for Virtue when I point the pen,
> Brand the bold front of shameless, guilty men. . . . [105-106]

The point I want to make is that the adoption and manipulation of a particular classical model in this type of imitation is a matter of literary calculation: there needs to be no special temperamental

---

2. *The Letters of Ezra Pound, 1907-1941*, ed. D. D. Paige (London, 1951), p. 310.

affinity between the imitator and the imitated: the adopted *persona* is neither sacrosanct nor stable.

In Pound's case, however, the adoption of a Propertian *persona* is presented as much more than a matter of literary convenience or strategy. Pound comments on his fellow-feeling with the Latin poet in terms which have a strong historical resonance: attitudes to war, empire and the poetry that celebrates them are at issue; and behind the *Homage* is the dramatic historical backdrop of the First World War. We seem to be confronted with a pair of embattled poets, individuals under pressure from the jingoistic and militaristic forces of their historical times whose poetry as a result takes on the significance of a political gesture. Hence the vein of critical comment where Propertius is seen as "the mask through which Pound registered his protest at what he thought was the monstrous state of society and culture in which he found himself living."[3] The *Homage*, that is, takes on a penumbra of historical significance stemming from Pound's stark twinning of his own historical circumstance with that of Propertius: "it [the *Homage*] presents certain emotions as vital to me in 1917, faced with the infinite and ineffable imbecility of the British Empire, as they were to Propertius some centuries earlier, when faced with the infinite and ineffable imbecility of the Roman Empire. These emotions are defined largely, but not entirely, in Propertius' own terms."[4] The parallelism between Pound's situation and that of Propertius is insisted upon and pushed towards the center of the debate: the *persona* is not simply a literary device which may be revised, elaborated or even dropped (as we saw in Pope). Something more is at stake: Pound is insisting on certain truths concerning his own times *and* those of Propertius; and it is perhaps this level of historical insistence that precluded a *laissez-faire* attitude to the poem on the part of some critics. Pope's Horace is essentially a literary *persona*; Pound's Propertius is to some considerable extent presented as an historical one.

It is precisely here, however, that I want to stop, take stock, and then begin to re-align comment in a literary direction. I want to attempt to show how Pound's identification with Propertius involves in many ways a mis-reading of Propertius; and one which has led criticism away from certain important areas of engagement with Propertius' work in the *Homage*.

---

3. Sullivan, *op. cit.*, p. 27.
4. *Letters, op. cit.*, p. 310.

I put the focus on the *work*, therefore, rather than the man: for the Propertius with whom Pound identifies exists essentially only as he emerges for him from the four books of elegies. Pound's apprehension of Propertius becomes now a literary-critical question. (For the moment I shelve the historical question, but will come back to it at another tangent.)

II

We move, then, to the question of Pound's ability, so to speak, to "get under the skin" of a Latin poet by scholarly or intuitional means (i.e., as a fellow-poet); and his activities leading up to the *Propertius* provide some pointers. Obviously the studies which produced *The Spirit of Romance* (1910) led him into Latin areas, though he relies very much upon received authority in that book; but it seems that as early as 1907 Pound was already involved in the study of such as Martial and Catullus. In 1916 he was turning over the idea of providing a "decent"[5] translation of Catullus and Propertius. The impression given is of a sustained and serious contact with these poets.

Catullus emerges from the prose criticism as Pound's prime enthusiasm in this area, and perhaps I may use him to make a couple of points at this stage. Peter Whigham has commented on how Pound found a useful stylistic model here in the volume *Lustra*.[6] It is notable however that there is little sympathetic engagement with Catullus in terms of translation or imitation. Rather we have the more tangential approach to the Latin poet as seen in "'Blandula, Tenulla, Vagula.'"[7] This is a celebration of Sirmio and Lake Garda which Pound visited in 1910 and 1911 (the poem was written in 1911) and by which, as letters of the time and later references indicate, he was entranced. Obviously we have to keep in mind Catullus' 31st poem in which, after lengthy duties and travel abroad, he greets his longed-for Sirmio warmly and humanly, like an old friend or retainer ("*salve, o venusta Sirmio*," 12), and relishes the pleasure of arriving home and sinking into his own bed. In Pound's poem, the journey is now life's journey, and Sirmio is envisaged as the ideal spiritual locale beyond which the soul will not want to travel. There is a hint of the same idea of well-deserved rest as in Catullus' poem

---
5. *Ibid.*, p. 142.
6. Peter Whigham, "Ezra Pound and Catullus," in *Ezra Pound: Perspectives*, ed. Noel Stock (Chicago, 1965).
7. *Personae: Collected Shorter Poems of Ezra Pound* (London, 1952), p. 53.

in Pound's "when our freedom's won," and the same stress on the welcoming topography of Sirmio and the waves of Lake Garda; but the effect is entirely different:

> What hast thou, O my soul, with paradise;
> Will we not rather, when our freedom's won,
> Get us to some clear place wherein the sun
> Lets drift in on us through the olive leaves
> A liquid glory? If at Sirmio,
> My soul, I meet thee, when this life's outrun,
> Will we not find some headland consecrated
> By aery apostles of terrene delight,
> Will not our cult be founded on the waves,
> Clear sapphire, cobalt cyanine,
> On triume azures, the impalpable
> Mirrors unstill of the eternal change?
>
> Soul, if She meet us there, will any rumour
> Of havens more high and courts desirable
> Lure us beyond the cloudy peak of Riva?

Catullus' warm and affectionate salute to Sirmio is quite transformed when meshed in, as in the case, with the more metaphysical ideas of Hadrian, whose famous "Animula, blandula, vagula" is presumably the prompt for Pound's title: "'Blandula, Tenulla, Vagula.'"

Catullus' lyric then provides the jumping-off ground for a Poundian poem rather than an imitative challenge and in particular we do not find the kind of special insight which a more direct imitative exercise or translation might provide. This category of criticism is given importance by Pound himself in "Date Line"; and R. P. Blackmur many years ago suggested that "in verse and when directly handling the fabric of verse perhaps our most acute critic, he is in his general prose our least responsible."[8] In terms of Pound's dealings with ancient poetry the distinction holds good, though I would say that the prose criticism is sometimes desultory rather than irresponsible: that is, it does not represent the sum total of what Pound may have to offer. To try to clinch his notion in positive terms I will simply quote Pound's translation of Catullus' famous 85th poem:

> I have and love. Why? You may ask but
> It beats me. I feel it done to me, and ache.

Here, where Pound is directly engaging with the Latin of Catullus, we are presented with a fine version of a poem which has been done less than justice by translators over the years. In Pound's

---
8. R. P. Blackmur, "Masks of Ezra Pound," *Hound and Horn*, VII, 2 (1934), p. 179.

version there is considerable critical insight in his preservation of the tentative, un-pat tone of Catullus' epigram:

Odi et amo, quare id faciam, fortasse requiris?
nescio, sed fieri sentio et excrucior.

Pound avoids the mistake of reading later developments of a well-worn topos back into the first century B.C.; and he does this by reacting to the language.

To begin to make an approach to Propertius, then, I want to keep very much in mind this notion that Pound may perceive or intuit that, so to speak, something is "going on" in a Latin poem—while he is directly engaged with the text; whereas his conscious rationalizations will not necessarily be at the same level. To be more specific for the present purpose, a limited appreciation of the conventions of Roman love-elegy may compromise Pound's interpretation of certain effects which he senses in Propertius. There is no question as to whether Pound is "right" or "wrong" about Propertius. The relevant question is: does he, in his engagement with Propertius' text, provide anything which is of real value for our reading of Propertius?

The kind of answer which it is possible to give to this question can be demonstrated by reference to the issues which our topic today naturally raises—that is, the political implications of the *Homage*.

The political dimension has regularly been seen as the fulcrum of Pound's identification with the Roman poet's concerns; though I have earlier begun to question certain aspects of the identification. It is nevertheless an area where Pound has specifically claimed a critical value for the *Homage* in indicating "the *way* in which Propertius is using Latin" as a means of "tying blue ribbon in the tails of Virgil and Horace."[9] What he means by this can be seen from the following well-known passage in the *Homage*, where Virgil's efforts in the field of epic are treated:

> Make way, ye Roman authors,
>   clear the street, O ye Greeks,
> For a much larger Iliad is in the course of construction
>   (and to Imperial order)
> Clear the street, O ye Greeks [Section XII]

The presentation of the *Aeneid* as some sort of lumbering edifice, coupled with the explicit "and to Imperial order," amounts to a heavy satire on Virgil's subscription to an officially encouraged literature of national importance; but the Latin that Pound is glossing is simply:

---

9. *Letters, op. cit.,* p. 246.

> *Cedite Romani scriptores, cedite Grai!*
> *nescio quid maius nascitur Iliade.*
>
> (Yield Roman writers, yield Greeks!
> Something greater than the Iliad is being born.)
>
> [2, 34B, 65-66]

Pound obviously thinks that the tribute is inflated a shade beyond the limits of seriousness, and is thus a subtle deflation. He is also perhaps bearing in mind the context in which the lines occur, where Propertius has been lecturing the love-struck Lyceus on the value of elegiac love-poetry. Philosophy, didactic poetry, epic and drama are of no use to the man who wishes to charm a beautiful girl [46]; only the love-elegist has this gift. Lyceus must take his cue from the experienced Propertius [55-60]. Since it is at this moment that Propertius sees fit to praise Virgil's enterprise in the epic field it is easy to appreciate the way in which Pound's mind may be working in interpreting the Homeric comparison. The reading obviously merits consideration, though the explicitness and emphasis of Pound's version are disproportionate to any possible irony in the original. What is, at most, a wryly ambivalent obeisance from the "mere" elegist in the direction of official poetry in the epic vein becomes a pointed attack upon Virgil as a political time-server. The animus is not warranted in this particular context; nor (as will be argued later) is it necessarily a true reflection of more generalized elegiac or Propertian attitudes. There then is a crucial consideration in the present exercise. Pound unequivocally feels that he is reacting to discernible attitudes in Propertius' work with which he feels a particular sympathy; though I have begun to suggest the limitations of his view. Let us however at this point look at the positive side of things, the extent to which Pound may, so to speak, be "on to something" even if his overall view may need qualification.

Although I resisted earlier Pound's implicit case for a politically anti-Virgilian point in the couplet quoted, I do not by any means rule out the possibility of an equivocal note in the elegist's salute to the "higher" literary project of his fellow-poet. As we will see later, it is part of the elegiac pose to be calculatedly less than respectful towards established proprieties, and Pound is acute in his suspicion of declarations of this sort in the work of Propertius.

On the subject of ironic praise for epic aspiration, one poem which immediately suggests itself is I, 7, where Propertius introduces a flattering Homeric comparison into what must be an ironic context. Propertius' friend Ponticus is engaged in composing a *Thebiad* and is offered a self-deprecating salute by the elegist:

> *Dum tibi Cadmeae dicuntur, Pontice, Thebae*
>   *armaque fraternae tristia militiae,*
> *atque, ita sim felix, primo contendis Homero*
>   *(sint modo fata tuis mollia carminibus:)*
> *nos, ut consuemus, nostros agitamus amores,*
>   *atque aliquid duram quaerimus in dominam* [1-6].

[while you, Ponticus, tell of the city of Cadmus-
Of Thebes, and the dolorous clash of fraternal arms,
And contend—so may I be happy!—with Homer the champion
(If only Fate deals gently with your songs!),
I urge my usual theme of love, and look
For a way to prevail with the cruel girl.][10]

However, the respectful tone of this passage and Propertius' apologetic reference to his own line of poetry have to be read in the light of the change of roles that Propertius envisages in the second half of the poem, where he warns that Ponticus too may fall in love one day and find himself unable to compose the appropriate *mollem versum* [19]. In these circumstances, suggests Propertius, their roles would be quite reversed; and the final lines of the poem envisage Ponticus as a literary novice in need of instruction from Propertius, the recognized expert in love poetry [21-26]. The opening lines, with their flattering Homeric comparison, were obviously written in ironic anticipation of this final section—in a way which is still to be capped by the stage-management of I, 9. Here we find Ponticus not only helplessly in love as predicted, but with a common prostitute or, perhaps, slave [*quaevis . . . empta modo*]. In this context where an Homeric comparison is made, then, Propertius' irony turns upon an opposition of "mere" love-elegy and "serious" poetry; and I am suggesting that the Virgil sally which we were looking at earlier in Propertius, with its Homeric reference, contains much of the same attitude. If there is irony in it, it is in this area of elegiac banter rather than in the sphere of political comment. We have seen enough, however, to consider that Pound is perhaps on the scent of something very interesting; and it turns on the question of irony.

The key term in Pound's exegesis of Propertian irony is "logopoeia." In his correspondence Pound describes it as "the dance of the intellect among words" and then goes on to define it in more precise terms: "it employs words not only for their direct meaning, but it takes count in a special way of habits of

---
10. *The Poems of Propertius*, trans. Ronald Musker (London, 1972), p. 54.

usage, of the context we *expect* to find with the word, its usual concomitants, of its known acceptances, and of ironical play."[11] In this connection the "Ponticus" elegy which we were just now looking at is interesting. In the lines we quoted there is an effect which depends precisely on "the context we *expect* to find" with a particular word. Ponticus, exclaims Propertius, will rival Homer "*sint modo fata tuis* mollia *carminibus*"; whereas Propertius is content to seek "*aliquid* duram . . . *in dominam*." Now since the terms *durus* and *mollis* are regularly used in Propertius to typify epic and elegiac poetry respectively, his reversal of their normal context [12] begins to sound much like logopoeia in Pound's definition of the term: he is making play precisely with "the context we *expect* to find with the word" and exploiting "habits of usage."

This is not of course a poem on which Pound comments. He makes it clear, however, that we are not to look for one-for-one correspondences in his elucidation of Propertius' tone, explaining how his version of a particular poem may be governed by "implications derivable from other writings of Propertius, as, for example the 'Ride to Lanuvium' from which I have taken a color or tone but no direct or entire *expression*."[13] By the "Ride to Lanuvium" Pound means the splendidly rumbustious IV, 8, where in a scene likened to the sack of a city the enraged Cynthia routs the two girls with whom the poet is being unfaithful, exults in her victory and imposes her *imperium* on the poet with harsh conditions; the poet at one point considers "pitching his camp" elsewhere. It is easy to see what Pound is getting at: the suggestive imposition of terminology drawn from one sphere of activity aptly, but with a witty sense of incongruity, on another. It might seem too that by this sort of analogy we could begin to legitimize the irony which he reads into the Virgilian couplet quoted earlier. Here, however, I think we should proceed to some important distinctions.

In particular, IV, 8 is emphatically a love poem, and as such cannot directly sanction Pound's underlining of what he clearly sees as a political dimension in Propertius which, during the First World War, he found particularly cogent: he says how the *Homage* "presents certain emotions as vital to men faced with the infinite and ineffable imbecility of the British Empire as they were to

---
11. *Literary Essays of Ezra Pound*, ed. T. S. Eliot (London, 1954), p. 25.
12. See e.g. Kenneth Quinn, *Latin Explorations: Critical Studies in Roman Literature* (London, 1963), p. 133.
13. *Letters,op. cit.*, p. 311.

Propertius some centuries earlier, when faced with the infinite and ineffable imbecility of the Roman Empire. These emotions are given largely, but not entirely, in Propertius' own terms."[14] It is just after this point that he mentions the "implications derivable from other writings," instancing the "Ride to Lanuvium." It is this shift between love and politics that I want to call into question: the fact is that Propertius is above all a love-elegist rather than a political writer. To realize why Pound sees Propertius as the latter we have to consider some conventional aspects of Roman love-elegy.

III

The elegiac attitude to war, empire and the literature that celebrates them certainly trades in what may be termed political attitudes—but not necessarily for pointed political reasons. The rejection of political or military values may be part of a gesture essentially divorced from political preoccupations. It is not the subject-matter but the calculation which is important; and in this sense elegiac "politics," if they deserve the name, are essentially anodyne. It is difficult to show in the elegists any unequivocal anti-militarism or adverse political comment amounting to the sort of root questioning of Rome's imperial status and military activities that Pound divines in Propertius. The debate is the far more trivial one of "who does the fighting?" Elegiac dissent is social rather than ideological in emphasis, and also literary rather than real. (Tibullus does his military service and praises the successful general; Propertius does eventually turn his hand to nationalistic themes.) Within the literary conventions of love-elegy of course the fighting is assigned to the military rather than the elegists who present themselves as a different breed of men altogether from the coarse and materialistic soldier: the sensitive elegist, in his obsessive amatory concern, must thus caricature any group which threatens his standing with his mistress with such vulgarities as hard cash from the real world.

Crucial to all this however is the fact that it is all safely located within the elegiac ethos: what is at issue is the status of the soldier in the demi-monde which the elegist portrays as his own natural preserve: the soldier, like the "rich rival" is fair game as a representative of the conventional social world that the elegists reject in favor of their own studiedly nonconformist scheme of values.

---

14. *Ibid*, p. 310.

In their literary pursuit of their less-than-respectable love-affairs the elegists disregard normal Roman standards of behavior. Demeaningly enthralled as they are by their partners, they are quite willing to confess to idleness, cowardice and seemingly any unmanly humiliation according to an inverted code of values which gives love and its literary celebration a quite un-Roman priority. It is though, essentially, a shared pose. We are dealing with a literary "system" of love with its own specialized amatory rhetoric; and it is because they are part of a known rhetoric, calculatedly at odds with normal standards, that the alternative values that the elegists cultivate are without political bite. They erect, for instance, a system of "anti-virtues"[15] such as *ignavia*, *inertia* and *nequitia*, flagrantly countering the corresponding Roman qualities of *virtus*, *industria* etc.; but since these depend upon an awareness of an orthodoxy for their Bohemian impact, they may even be seen as confirming, to this extent, established proprieties: the fact that conventional values are turned so precisely on their head is an indication that we are dealing with rhetoric rather than revolt.

It is this inverse system of values of course, where soldiering for instance is rejected in favor of a more pacific and sensitive life of love and poetry, which leads the elegiac lover perversely to present himself as a "soldier" of love pursuing the "wars" of Venus. This is a regular motif in elegy, and there is a calculated outrageousness in the proposition;[16] and it is in this light that elegiac reference to politics and national affairs should be viewed. Antimilitarism, moral unorthodoxy, indifference to the ideal of a normal Roman career—all these can be ascribed to the "Bohemian" pose of the elegists, as can their position vis-à-vis the more nationally committed types of literature which they decline to involve themselves in through the conventional *recusatio* or refusal-poem. Pound, on the other hand, seems to read these elements as he finds them in Propertius as a protest against empire and the poetry that celebrates empire. Hence the primary focus of his indentification with Propertius is questionable.

Oddly enough, the aspects of the elegists' code that have just been touched on—their bravado, their insistence on their own alternative values, their subscription to a doctrine of individual experience in a world of Art for Art's sake—are the sort which in many ways might be thought to have provided an obvious point of contact for Pound in his earlier years as a colorful character

---
15. *Cf*, e.g., Jean-Paul Boucher, *Etudes sur Properce* (Paris, 1965), pp. 13-39.
16. Ovid of course capitalizes on this aspect in his well-known *Amores* I, 9: "*Militat omnis amans*. . . ."

about London and literary *enfant terrible*. Donald Davie comments how Pound in his London years, perhaps socially uneasy or uncertain as an American, "over-compensated with aggressive affectations of dress and behaviour, a calculated outrageousness which he seems to have concocted on Whistler's model."[17] The phrase "calculated outrageousness" would be a good one for suggesting the sense of elegiac *nequitia*; and some further comments by Davie seems to me to make interesting correspondences with the essentially anodyne nature of elegiac revolt: "Bohemianism was what English bourgeois society expected of its artists; as long as the self-styled artists indulged Bohemian antics, the solid citizen knew where he stood with them, and could extend an amused tolerance. Their manifestos and exhibitions were part of the London scene; part of what Tommy Atkins came home to on leave. . . ."[18] Without wishing to trivialize what Pound has to say about his concerns about empire, etc., in 1917, and remembering that he lost personal friends in the war, I suspect that Pound's identification with Propertius in the actual poem (conscious or otherwise) is to be found in these areas, and once again I insist on the distinction between what is happening in Pound's close involvement with an ancient poet and his interpretative pronouncements. There is some glimmering of support for this from Pound himself in some second thoughts on the poem communicated to Thomas Hardy, where he says flatly that "the Propertius is confused."[19] In a subsequent letter concerned with the use of the word "homage" in the title Pound continues in the following terms: "I ought to have concentrated on the subject—(I did so long as I forgot my existence for the sake of the lines)—and I tack on a title relating to the treatment—in a fit of nerves—fearing the reader won't sufficiently see the super-position (?) the doubling of me and Propertius, England today and Rome under Augustus. . . ." This is not completely clear; it has some interest for what we have been saying earlier about the angling of the poem and Pound's determined identification of his own situation with that of Propertius. Interesting too is Pound's stress on the special value of his immediate response to the text where "I forgot my existence for the sake of the lines." My view is that Pound was indeed, especially in the prose comments, over-anxious to stress the Pound/Propertius, London/Rome historical twinning; and that he did to a considerable extent in the actual text of the *Propertius* react to "the lines," especially in the more amatory sections of the

---
17. Donald Davie, *Pound* (Fontana Modern Masters, 1975), p. 32.
18. *Ibid.*, pp. 33-34.
19. This and the following quotation are from Davie, *op. cit.*, pp. 46, 49.

poem. Propertius' stance as a love-poet offered considerable purchase for the Pound of the London period to come to grips with, and it is in this area, the area of the "young turk"[20] flamboyantly rubbing up against certain aspects of conventional wisdom and behavior, that I would begin to look for historical parallels. Rome offered something of the same license to the elegist.

I should say that I am not simply referring to trivialities of dress and behavior (sombrero hats, corduroy suits, tulip eating, etc.) though these are symptomatic of the attitudes I am concerned with: I am referring to the poetically acceptable (but in many quarters socially unacceptable) determination of the poet to go his own way, if needs be in the teeth of society—or, where society is annoyingly tolerant, by creating the necessary friction himself by certain sorts of literary and social behavior.

In 1916, Pound brought the young Iris Barry down from Birmingham to London, where she found herself intimidated to be "striding along beside the Spirit of Revolt itself."[21] Subsequently he wrote to her recommending Catullus, Propertius, Horace and Ovid, and warning her against his twin *bêtes-noires* Virgil and Pindar "the prize wind-bag of all ages. *The* 'brass-drum'. . . ."[22] Remembering Pindar's drum, and the "loud-mouthed" Virgilian-style product that Pound refuses to produce in the *Homage*, it is interesting to look at Pound's entry in the poetry competition organized to celebrate the 250th anniversary of Newark, New Jersey. The last stanza of "To a City Sending Him Advertisements"[23] goes:

> If your professors, mayors, judges . . . ?
>   Reader, we think not . . .
> Some more *loud-mouthed* fellow,
>   *slamming a bigger drum*,
> Some fellow rhyming and roaring,
>   Some more obsequious back,
> Will receive their purple,
>   be the town's bard, . . .

The phraseology of the *Homage* is there, but who are the targets? Not martial or imperialist figures, but civic and academic dignitaries; and what Pound argues for in the poem is poetic quietism and licensed idleness:

> Will you let quiet men
>   live and continue among you,
> Making, this one, a fane,

---
20. *Ibid.*, p. 35.
21. Charles Norman, *Ezra Pound*, 2nd edn. (London, 1969), p. 193.
22. *Letters, op. cit.*, p. 138.
23. Norman, *op. cit.*, pp. 187-189. Italics mine.

> This one, a building;
> Or this *bedevilled, casual, sluggish fellow*
> Do, once in a life, the single perfect poem,
> And let him go unstoned?

The protestation is very reminiscent of the elegists' flaunted lack of *industria*, their willingness to live a feckless life in pursuit of their amatory and aesthetic priorities.

My suggestion is that Pound had a ready-made instinctive entrée to this ethos which does not register in his political prose readings of Propertius or the junctures in the *Homage* where the politics are heavily sign-posted. The emphasis on these political projections has, I suggest, provided something of a critical red herring in diverting attention away from what emerges in Pound's line-by-line response to Propertius' text.

IV

The aggregate loser in this process has been the straight amatory content of the *Homage*. If the poem is read with an eye to themes like anti-militarism and anti-imperialism, the amatory sections will tend to be problematic. They will appear peripheral to the poem's assumed central concerns—even though they comprise the major part of the poem.

I would like to reclaim the whole of the poem, and suggest that it is more of a piece when read in terms of the attitudes which I have stated for Propertius the love-elegist and which Pound, as I have argued, may have been especially well placed to tune in to. What emerges from such a reading is a jauntier, more frivolous, but also more entertaining and rounded poem. For the sections comprising the elegiac demurral at the prospect of writing the "higher" kind of poetry *can* be assimilated into the complex attitudinizing that is part and parcel of the elegiac *persona*.

Pound's response to Propertius in the actual text of the *Homage* is on a wide base, of which the sections with "political" content form a part, as is the case with Propertius himself; and both Pound and Propertius show a sophisticated complication of attitude to the disaffiliated-lover role in all its projections. This thematic complexity and sophistication registers from line to line in the text:

> Shades of Callimachus, Coan ghosts of Philetas,
> It is in your grove I would walk,
> I who come first from the clear font
> Bringing the Grecian orgies into Italy,

and the dance into Italy.
Who hath taught you so subtle a measure
          in what hall have you heard it?
What foot beat out your time-bar,
          what water has mellowed your whistles?
                    [Section I]

I had been seen in the shade, recumbent on cushioned
   Helicon,
The water dripping from Bellerophon's horse,
Alba, your king, and the realm your folk
          have reconstructed with such industry
Shall be yawned out on my lyre—with such industry.
My little mouth shall gobble in such great fountains
"Wherefrom father Ennius, sitting before I came, hath drunk."
                    [Section II]

If any man would be a lover
          he may walk on the Scythian coast,
No barbarism would go to the extent of doing him harm,
The moon will carry his candle,
          the stars will point out the stumbles,
Cupid will carry lighted torches before him
          and keep made dogs off his ankles.
Thus all roads are perfectly safe
          and at any hour;
Who so indecorous as to shed the pure gore of a suitor?!
   Cypris is his cicerone.
                    [Section III]

There is a characteristic off-key quality evident in these lines: an aliveness to the possible suggestions of phraseology in responding to a Latin text, and an ironic reserve which is endemic in the poem. We have a unique Poundian argot formed of Latinate polysyllables, puns, translationese, stray associations, archaic English phraseology and modern slang. The verbal texture of the poem is paramount, and this is the product of Pound's close contact with Propertius' text. It is a line-to-line quality which will not necessarily be adequately dealt with in Pound's prose generalizations on the *Homage*.

We come back again then to logopoeia. Pound noted that it cannot be rendered "locally" but might pass through a paraphrase so that "having determined the original author's state of mind, you may or may not be able to find a derivative or an equivalent."[24] My suggestion is that the whole of the *Homage* is shot through with equivalents for this elusive quality which he finds in Propertius. Pound's ability to tune in to Propertius in these terms seems

---

24. *Literary Essays, op. cit.*, p. 25.

to me far more interesting, historically and otherwise, than Pound's ruminations on ancient Rome *vis-à-vis* modern London.

If there were time, I would argue that some of the most extreme-seeming techniques in the poem such as the mistranslations and misspellings are part of Pound's attempt to communicate Propertius' cultivated and sometimes humorous double-take on both his role as an elegiac lover and the specialized and in many ways over-worked language which he brings to this role—or, to put it another way, on the problem of being part of the next generation or so of romantic lover-poets *after* Catullus.

Elegiac criticism has moved on considerably since Pound wrote the *Homage*, and the approach has swung round entirely. Tibullus, Propertius' fellow elegist, is no longer seen (as he was for so long) as a sweet and ingenuous sentimentalist but, increasingly, as a sometimes witty manipulator of a store of stock themes and attitudes: similarly with Propertius. It is becoming clear that there is a cultivated "knowingness" about the tone of elegy. None of this would have been obvious to Pound from the critical literature available to him, and symbolized for him in the figure of Mackail. One thinks, for instance, of Sellar dutifully recording Propertius' "wastage in love" as a biographical fact, or finding a special feeling for nature in this notably urban poet.[25] Pound was remarkably perceptive, in 1917, in distrusting all this sort of dilute Romanticism and persevering in attempting to isolate the special qualities which he saw in Propertius. A glance at recent editions of Propertius and Tibullus will show how much their poetry depends upon such things as irony and verbal association.[26]

I would like to stress then that the qualities that Pound brings out in Propertius are not merely Propertian but, in a way that he could hardly have suspected, generic. This is another dimension which I feel could usefully be explored.

I have had time only to give a brief indication of alternative foci of interest to the kind of generalization I have been questioning. Basically, what I am suggesting *vis-à-vis* these politico-historical emphases is that they do not take us very far into Propertius (in the way that the line-to-line tenor of the *Homage* does); but also that they do not take us very deeply into the Pound of this period either.

---

25. W. Y. Sellar, *The Roman Poets of the Augustan Age* (Oxford, 1892), pp. 281, 316 et seq.
26. *Cf.* R. I. V. Hodge and R. A. Buttimore, *The "Monobiblos" of Propertius* (Cambridge, 1977) and M. J. C. Putnam, *Tibullus: A Commentary* (Oklahoma, 1973).

JOHN J. NOLDE

EZRA POUND AND CHINESE HISTORY

I

Ezra Pound "discovered" China soon after his arrival in London in the autumn of 1908. A few months after settling in he met Laurence Binyon, Victorian poet of some standing and a member of the Department of Oriental Prints and Drawings of the British Museum.[1] Binyon, apparently, gave Pound a ticket to his lecture on "Oriental and European Art" which, in later years, EP remembers in Canto 87.[2] By 1910-11 he had become something of a protegé of Binyon and was impressed by the latter's *The Flight of the Dragon: An Essay on the Theory and Practice of Arts in China and Japan*, published in 1911 by L. Cranmer-Byng as part of the *Wisdom of the East* series.[3]

Other influences came from Allen Upward. Upward had been introduced to China by Cranmer-Byng about the turn of the century,[4] and in 1904 his slim volume entitled *The Sayings of Kung The Master* was published in the *Wisdom of the East* series. Pound seems to have met Upward in 1911[5] and saw to the publication of excerpts from *The Sayings of Kung The Master* in *The New Freewoman* in November and December, 1913.[6] Upward's "Scented Leaves from a Chinese Jar," a series of poems in the Chinese vein were placed by Pound in Harriet Monroe's *Poetry: A*

---
1. Noel Stock, *The Life of Ezra Pound* (New York, 1970), p. 60.
2. *Ibid.*, p. 61. Carroll Terrell, "The Na-Khi Documents," *Paideuma*, 3-1, p. 95.
3. Pound reviewed the book enthusiastically in the second number of *BLAST* (1915), p. 86.
4. See Upward's autobiographical poem, "Discarded Imagist," in *The Egoist* (June 1915), p. 98.
5. Herbert Schneidau, *Ezra Pound: the Image and the Real* (Baton Rouge, 1969), p. 118.
6. November 1, November 15, and December 1, 1913. Pound reviewed Upward's *Divine Mystery* (1911) in the same magazine of November 15. His review of Upward's earlier book, *The New Word* (1908), appeared in *The New Age* (April 1914). Reprints of both reviews are published in *Ezra Pound: Selected Prose, 1905-1965*, ed. William Cookson (New York, 1973), pp. 403-412.

Magazine of Verse in September, 1913.[7] It was Upward who pointed Pound toward Chinese philosophy, for EP wrote his parents in October, 1913, that Upward had got him to read "Confucius and Mencius in French translation."[8] This must have been Pauthier's *Confucius et Mencius: Les Quatre Livres de Philosophie Morale et Politique de la Chine*, Paris, 1852, which was to become the primary source for Canto 13.[9]

By this time Pound had run across Herbert Giles, *A History of Chinese Literature*, New York, 1901,[10] and he used Giles' translations of two short poems by Li Po and Fu I in the first edition of *BLAST* in 1914.[11]

But it was the discovery of the papers of Ernest Fenollosa in 1913 that was decisive in bringing about his lasting interest in China and its culture. Pound had met Fenollosa's wife Mary in London in the late winter or early spring of that year, and she had agreed to turn over to the young poet her late husband's papers and notebooks. Fenollosa, at the time of his death in 1908, had been one of the foremost western students of Chinese and Japanese art.[12] He had been appointed, freshly out of Harvard, to the chair of philosophy in the newly created University of Tokyo in 1877 and soon developed a deep interest in Japanese art, which at the time was looked down upon by the Japanese themselves as primitive and inferior. Almost single-handedly, he had launched a campaign to re-introduce Japan to her own cultural heritage and was so successful in his effort that the Emperor appointed him to an Imperial Commission to tour the West in search of ways to improve art and art education. In 1890 Fenollosa returned briefly to America as Curator of the Japanese Department of the Boston Museum of Fine Arts. After returning to Japan in 1896, he turned his attention to Chinese poetry, Buddhism, and Noh Drama.

---

7. Pound reported to Monroe that Upward's poems "were not paraphrases, but were made up": *Selected Letters of Ezra Pound, 1907-1914*, ed. D. D. Paige (New York, 1971), p. 22. Upward relates in his "Discarded Imagist" poem that he had been led to China by Cranmer-Byng, who "gave him a book of Chinese gems by Professor Giles."
8. See Robert Schultz, "A Detailed Chronology of Ezra Pound's London Years, 1908-1920," *Paideuma*, 11-3, p. 466.
9. It was at this point that Pound must have learned of Pauthier's *Chine, ou description historique, géographique et Littéraire de ce vaste Empire, d'après des documents Chinois* (Paris, 1837), which seems to have been his introduction to Chinese history.
10. Schultz, *op cit.*, p. 466.
11. *BLAST* (1914), p. 48. Herbert Giles' translations of Li Po and Fu I appear on pages 135 and 153 of his *A History*.... In the 1915 edition of *BLAST* (p. 22), Pound also inserted a poem concerning the story of Chuang Tzu and the butterfly. Here Chuang Tzu becomes, in Pound's poem, "So-Shu," probably from the Japanese transliteration of the notes of Ernest Fenollosa. It was not until the publication of Pound's 1926 *Personae* (1971 edn., p. 118) that the name was corrected.
12. Details from the life of Fenollosa are taken from Laurence W. Chisolm, *Fenollosa: the Far East and American Culture* (Westport, 1976).

John J. Nolde

The Fenollosas left Japan in 1900, and Ernest spent the remaining years of his life working on his pioneering study *Epochs of Chinese and Japanese Art* and lecturing on the importance of understanding the civilizations of East Asia. In 1908 they sailed for London, where Ernest spent the summer working in the British Museum. Early in September he suffered a severe heart-attack and died on September 21st.

After her husband's death his wife devoted her efforts to the completion and publication of *Epochs*. . . . She travelled to Japan for final checking and returned to England in 1912 to consult material in the British Museum. Her husband's two volume work was published by Heineman in October, 1912.

Just how Pound and Mary Fenollosa met is unclear. Many years later Pound recalled that he had met Mary in London at the home of Sarojini Naidu, an Indian poetess.[13] T. S. Eliot believed in 1917 that it was Mrs. Fenollosa's reading of Pound's poems in *Poetry* that prompted her to send her husband's papers to Pound.[14] Fenollosa's biographer has concluded that "Pound met Mrs. Fenollosa probably through Heineman or Laurence Binyon. . . . Pound was so enthusiastic about Fenollosa's literary researches that Mrs. Fenollosa promised on her return to America to send him whatever translations and notes she had."[15]

The material consisted of large notebooks of cribs and comments on the work of Li Po, pages of notes on Noh Drama, a draft of a series of lectures on the Chinese written language, and miscellaneous additional material.[16] Ezra apparently received this material in December, 1913 and was soon at work.[17] His translations from the Noh were sent to Harriet Monroe's *Poetry* in January, 1914. *The Quarterly Review* published his "Classic Drama of Japan" in October, 1914. In November, 1914, he wrote his parents that he had begun work on Fenollosa's Chinese notes,[18] and the results, translations of 16 poems (including 12 by Li Po), were published as *Cathay* in 1915. In Hugh Kenner's words:

> So it came about that the opportunity to invent Chinese poetry for our time fell not to some random modernist but to a master. The 14 poems in the original *Cathay* . . . were the first *vers-libre* translations not derived from other translations but from detailed notes on the Chinese text.[19]

---

13. *Ibid.*, p. 222.
14. *Ibid.*
15. *Ibid.*
16. Hugh Kenner, *The Pound Era* (Berkeley, 1971), p. 198.
17. Schulz, *op cit.*, p. 467.
18. *Ibid.*, p. 472.
19. Kenner, *op cit.*, p. 198.

This discovery of Fenollosa's notebooks and the publication of *Cathay* did more than "invent Chinese poetry for our time." It was also the gate through which Pound entered the garden of Chinese philosophy and history. It opened to him an entirely new world which, he often said in later years, was closed to young men in the schools and universities of America. The "discovery of China" seems to have had the same effect on Pound as it must have had upon Leibnitz or Voltaire in the eighteenth century. Their knowledge of the Middle Kingdom was sketchy indeed, but all three sensed the existence of a culture, a civilization, which had all the attributes of the ideal society: government by philosophers-kings, a gorgeous art, a system of morality unconnected with the institutionalized religions (which Pound had come to abhor), a universal, social consciousness, the kind of society of which men often talked but rarely achieved.

There was another consequence of the "discovery." Pound had already concluded that the Western world was on the verge of a new Renaissance, especially America. In August 1912, he expressed in the magazine *New Age* his belief in the possibility of an American Renaissance, and in a letter to Harriet Monroe about the same time he spoke of an "awakening [in America] that will make the Italian Renaissance look like a tempest in a teapot."[20] By 1915 he began to emphasize the role of a "comparative" approach as a means of achieving intellectual and cultural change:

> The first step of a renaissance, or awakening, is the importation of models for painting, sculpture or writing. We have had many "movements," movements stimulated by "comparison." ... The romantic awakening dates from the production of *Ossian*. The last century rediscovered the middle ages. It is possible that this century may find *a new Greece in China*.[21]

An important find among Fenollosa's material was, of course, the draft of the essay *The Chinese Written Character as a Medium for Poetry*, which was to form the basic stuff of EP's "ideogramic method." For the purposes of the present article, Fenollosa's essay was important for another reason. It kindled in Pound the missionary zeal about China and its culture which was to pervade his later writings. Fenollosa had written:

> It is unfortunate that England and America have so long ignored or mistaken the deeper problems of Oriental culture. We have

---

20. Harriet Monroe, *A Poet's Life* (New York, 1938), p. 260; Stock, *op cit.*, pp. 120-121.
21. *Poetry: a Magazine of Verse* (February, 1915), p. 228 (italics added). Reprinted in *Literary Essays of Ezra Pound*, ed. T. S. Eliot (New York, 1968), pp. 214-215.

misconceived the Chinese for a materialistic people, for a debased and worn-out race. . . . We have stupidly assumed that Chinese history affords no glimpse of change in social evolution, no salient epoch or moral and spiritual crisis. We have denied the essential humanity of these people; and we have toyed with their ideas as if they were no better than the comic songs in an "opera bouffe."

The duty that faces us is not to batter down their forts or exploit their markets, but to study and come to sympathize with their humanity and their generous aspirations. . . . We need their best ideals to supplement our own—ideas enshrined in the art, in their literature and in the tragedies of their lives.[22]

Having published *Cathay*, he reworked Fenollosa's essay, and it was first published in serial form in *The Little Review*, beginning in September, 1918. He later included it in *Instigations* in 1920 and published it separately in the Ideogramic Series in 1936.

II

Pound began his study of Confucius soon after *Cathay*. Using the translation of the *Four Books* by M. G. Pauthier, he worked his way through the *Analects* (the *Lun Yu*) and included some of this material in one of his "Imaginary Letters" in 1917-1918.[23]

The Cantos were begun in 1915 and first published in small groups between 1917 and 1924. Hugh Kenner's comments are the most relevant. Describing *The Cantos* as "a poem containing history," Kenner comments:

And history in the Pound Era seemed calling for such a poem, expecting it to make a difference. Whatever enters the mind's ecology makes a difference. . . . Minds are *in* history. To offer men's minds a reading of historical patterns might consolidate or might alter those patterns, and would anyhow affect the mind's sense of being at home. If we believe that good things have been and will return we can manage to live with bad things. If we believe that the human will is efficacious, we shall want to expedite the bad things' passing away. And the grounds for such beliefs was what poets sought in history, writing "poems including history," attentive to that ecology of events in which any detail may be symptomatic to everything else that is happening.[24]

In short, Pound was attempting a history of Western Civilization in poetic form. The poem was to be a morality tale, a mirror

---
22. Fenollosa/Pound, *The Chinese Written Character as a Medium for Poetry* (San Francisco, 1936), p. 4.
23. Reprinted in *Pavannes and Divagations* (1958: New Directions paperback, 1974), pp. 72-73.
24. Kenner, *op cit.*, p. 362.

in which modern man could see reflected what was wrong and right in his past. And all this was to make a difference. It is no coincidence that the early cantos were begun during the terrible events in France. Western civilization seemed on the point of self-destruction. The Armistice and Versailles were to solve nothing. Clearly the politicians and "statesmen" had not "made a difference." Perhaps a poet *could*.

The China influence appears early in *The Cantos*. Canto 13 was published first in Ford's *Transatlantic Review* in January, 1924[25] and later as part of *A Draft of XVI Cantos* in January, 1925. It is a series of excerpts from Pauthier's translations of the *Analects*, taken from the *Quatre Livres* . . ., and a reference to the same author's *Chine*. . . . Pound chose only a few episodes: Confucius asking his disciples what they would do if a ruler asked them for advice; the case of the educated man who refused to serve a corrupt king; a discussion of a ruler's need to control himself before he can control others.

The concluding lines of Canto 13 are most important and tell us much about what Pound is trying to do. He had discovered, presumably from Pauthier's *Chine* . . ., that Confucius often lectured from a small pavillon known as the *Apricot Altar*.[26] It was there that he pointed out to his disciples that the wisdom of the ancient sages never perished (*"les doctrines des anciens rois Wen et ne se sont pas perdues sur la terre; elles se sont maintenues parmi les hommes"*) and charged them with the task of carrying on these doctrines after his death (*"et ce sont eux qu'il chargea son tour du soin de propager cette même doctrine après sa mort"*).[27] Thus Pound, promising to carry on the torch, ends Canto 13:

> The blossoms of the apricot
> > blow from the east to the west,
> And I have tried to keep them from falling.

Pound's first attempt at an entire Confucian Classic was the *Ta Hsueh (The Great Learning)* or, as he would call it, the *Ta Hio*. This was the shortest—only 1750 characters long—of the *Four Books* and included an introduction by Chu Hsi, the 12th century Sung scholar, who had rescued it from obscurity. To Chu Hsi, the *Ta Hsueh* was the key to understanding the rest of the Confucian canon:

---

25. Ronald Bush, *The Genesis of Ezra Pound's Cantos* (Princeton, 1976), pp. xiv-xv.
26. Pauthier, *op cit.*, p. 176. The story of the *Apricot Altar* has its origins in *The Chuang Tzu*, XXXI: see Angela Palandri, *Paideuma*, 3-3, p. 301.
27. Pauthier, *Confucius et Mencius: les quatres livres de philosophie morale et politique de la Chine* (Paris, 1841), p. 216. Pauthier, *Chine* . . ., p. 176.

John J. Nolde

> In learning one must begin with the *Great Learning* and then successively the *Analects, The Book of Mencius*, and the *Doctrine of the Mean*.[28]

A modern scholar elaborates:

> He (Chu Hsi) compared *The Great Learning* to a blue-print, an itinerary and a framework. . . . It is based on the premise that "one must know what is first and what is last," as stated in the text of the *Great Learning*.[29]

Chu Hsi, of course, was a pivotal figure in the rise of the 12th-century neo-Confucian movement in the Sung Dynasty, though it is not clear that Pound in 1928 was aware of his importance or what he meant by assigning an order of priority to the *Four Books*. But there is little doubt that the *Great Learning* had a profound effect upon him. There was nothing mystical or metaphysical about it. Here was a practical, ethical system, divorced from any religion or religious institution. It pointed a way to world peace and harmony which did not require priests and churches and dogma. Some years later T. S. Eliot asked in public: "What does Mr. Pound believe?" E.P. replied: "I believe the *Ta Hio*."[30] The *Ta Hio: The Great Learning* was published by the University of Washington in 1928. Pauthier's *Quatre Livres* . . . was used as the crib.

Meanwhile, *The Cantos* proceeded apace. *A Draft of XXX Cantos* appeared in 1930, *Eleven New Cantos XXX-XLI* in 1934, and *The Fifth Decad of Cantos XLII-LI* in 1937. Chinese culture plays a minor role in these, except for the beautiful "Seven Lakes Canto" (49), which Kenner has described as "one of the pivots of the poem: the emotional still point of the Cantos."[31]

The origins of Canto 49 are clear enough. The first part is a paraphrase of eight Chinese and Japanese poems from a Japanese manuscript book, arranged as a miniature eight-panel folding screen, which had apparently been in the Pound household in America and illustrated eight famous scenes of the Tung Ting Lake district of central China, painted originally by Mu Ch'i, a Buddhist abbot of the Northern Sung era.[32] Other parts of the canto come from the Chinese poems found in the Fenollosa material. Whether Pound was aware of the fact that the "eight scenes" have their

---

28. Quoted by Chan Wing-tsit, in T. W. de Bary, *The Unfolding of Neo-Confucianism* (New York, 1965), p. 558.
29. *Ibid.*, p. 559.
30. Kenner, *op cit.*, pp. 446-447; *The Literary Essays of Ezra Pound, ed cit.*, p. 86.
31. Hugh Kenner, *The Poetry of Ezra Pound* (Norfolk, Conn., 1951), p. 326.
32. Daniel Pearlman, *The Barb of Time* (New York, 1969), pp. 304-311. Sanehide Kodama, "The Eight Scenes of Sho-Sho," *Paideuma* 6-2, pp. 131-145. On Mu Ch'i, see James Cahill, *Treasures of Asia: Chinese Painting* (Cleveland, 1960), pp. 93-99.

origins in a masterpiece by a Buddhist monk will probably never be known.

"Seven Lakes Canto" may have been "an emotional still point," but the 1930s were for Pound anything but quiet. He had migrated from Paris to Rapallo in 1924 and as Europe drifted toward war he became more and more isolated in Mussolini's Italy. His writings reflected his growing concern with economic and political matters, and as the thirties moved toward the disaster of World War II, his style and tone became shrill and strident: diatribes against usury, the Jews, Roosevelt, essays on economic matters, social credit, and the virtues of Mussolini's Italy. Even when he turned to Confucius his efforts had bitter over-tones. An article entitled "Immediate Need of Confucius," published in *The Aryan Path* in August, 1937, is really a long diatribe against western civilization. And in "Mang Tsze (Ethics of Mencius)" in *The Criterion*, July, 1938, he wrote that the "ethic of Confucius and Mencius is a Nordic ethic."[33] Two chapters in *Guide to Kulchur*, published in 1938, are concerned with China: a truncated version of the *Analects* and a chapter entitled "Kung," which is partly an argument in support of a tax structure proposed by Rossoni, the leader of the Italian syndicalist movement, and partly a plea for better understanding on Confucian China.[34]

By the summer of 1937, Pound was seriously involved in the study of the Chinese language. Somewhere he had acquired a copy of the six-volume Chinese-English dictionary compiled by Robert Morrison in the early nineteenth century.[35] Morrison was the first Protestant missionary to venture into Asia, first to the Straits Settlements of Malacca and then to Macao-Canton. His *Dictionary*, published in Malacca between 1815 and 1822 was a pioneering effort and reflected the primitive state of the West's understanding of the Chinese language at that time. Pound also had a copy of Giles' smaller dictionary, which, published in 1912, was more reliable than Morrison. But both Morrison and Giles were rather thin reeds on which to lean, if one were really to attack the massive problem of learning Chinese. He also had James Legge's translation of the *Four Books* complete with Chinese text and elaborate notes:

> During August and the first half of September 1937, I isolated myself with the Chinese text of the three books on Confucius, Ta Hio, Analects, and the Unwavering Middle and that of Mencius,

---
33. *Selected Prose of Ezra Pound, 1905-1965*, ed. W. Cookson (New York, 1975), pp. 75-80, 81-97.
34. Ezra Pound, *Guide to Kulchur* (New York, 1970), pp. 15-21, 272-279.
35. Kenner, *The Pound Era, ed cit.*, pp. 447-448.

together with an enormously learned crib but no dictionary. You can't pack Morrison or Giles in a suitcase.[36]

The last chapter of *Mencius* (the last pages of Legge's work) must have struck Pound with especial effect during those late summer weeks. Here Chapter XXXVIII in full (italics are Legge's):

1. Mencius said: "From Yaou and Shun down to T'ang were five hundred years and more. As to Yu and Kao-yaou, they saw *those earliest stages*, and so knew their doctrines, while T'ang heard their doctrines as *transmitted*, and so knew them.

2. From T'ang to King Wan were five hundred years more. As to E Yin and Lae Choo, they saw T'ang and knew his doctrines, while King Wan heard them as *transmitted* and so knew them.

3. From King Wan to Confucius were five hundred years and more. As to T'ae-kung Wang and San E-sang, they saw Wan, and so knew his doctrines, while Confucius heard them as *transmitted* and so knew them.

4. From Confucius downwards until now, there are only one hundred years and somewhat more. The distance in time from the sage is so far from being remote and so very near at hand was the sage's residence. In these circumstances, is there no one to transmit his doctrines? Yea, is there no one to do so?

The concluding section of *Mencius* must have shown Pound what he had to do and reinforced his conviction that it was the duty of the wise and sensitive man, as we have seen in Canto 13, to pass on the universal truths from one generation to another. He told us then that he was trying "to keep them from falling." Now, having read Mencius' final words: "Is there no one to transmit his doctrines? Yea, is there no one to do so," he must have seen that the duty was his to make such a commitment.[37] And this brought him to Chinese history and the China Cantos.

III

With the publication of *The Fifth Decad of Cantos XLII-LI* in 1937, Pound's poem had reached its mid-point, its "dimension of stillness." Up to this point, the poet had described what he considered to be the decay and disintegration of Western civilization. From Odysseus in Canto 1 to depression-plagued America in Canto 46, with some exceptions such as Canto 13, history seems to be the tale of a lost struggle; as Daniel Pearlman notes:

---
36. *Selected Prose...*, ed cit., p. 82.
37. *Ibid.*, pp. 89-90.

> In the first phase of the poem, which persists up through Canto 46 the time-embattled human spirit struggles against overwhelming odds to achieve order in spite of surrounding chaos. Time and the clock emerge as the crucial symbol of *negation*, of moral disorder, in these cantos. Western history is portrayed by and large in a state of progressive confusion and decay.[38]

Somehow, western-world man has lost his sense of balance. Somewhere European civilization has lost its sense of *Kairos*, the "fulness of time," and has been entrapped by *chronos*, linear "clock" time; i.e., the West has lost its sense of organic wholeness and has become fragmented and atomized. If Western civilization is to be saved, the "balance," the stable center, must be restored. But how?

Pound's answer is that the heart and soul of Western civilization can be recovered and "made new" by finding again that "qualitative" sense of time that had been lost in the accelerated sweep of "quantitive" time. Man must again become one with nature, with beauty, and must create against the organic wholeness which made for the greatness of Greece and of the Renaissance. Some "order" must replace the "chaos," and Pound had a model at hand, the Confucian model which had attracted him for twenty years. He had used it as a quiet counterpoint through the first half of the poem. Now it was time to write on Confucian order in detail, wherein human affairs are governed by a vision of society ordered and regulated by the ethics of Kung and Mencius and the *Four Books*. Thus the decision was made, probably during his "isolation" with Legge during the late summer of 1937, to turn to Chinese history.

But where was he to turn for his "facts"? Up to this point, his knowledge of Chinese history and culture came primarily from English and French translations of the *Four Books*, from Fenollosa's notes on Chinese history, from Herbert Giles' *History of Chinese Literature* and from Pauthier's *Chine.* . . . He also had at hand a copy of Lacharme's *Confucii: Chi-King* . . . , a Latin translation of the *Shih Ching (The Odes*, or *Book of Poetry)*, made originally in the mid-eighteenth century and published in 1830.[39] But the *Shih Ching* is a collection of poems, supposedly anthologized by Confucius, and even if used as history would not carry the reader beyond the early sixth century BC. Up to the autumn of 1937, then, Pound's exposure to a long sweep of Chinese

---

38. Pearlman, *op cit.*, pp. 27-28.
39. P. Lacharme, *Confucii Chi-King: sive Liber Carminum*, ed. Julius Mohl (Stuttgart and Tübingen, 1830). Pound seems also to have unearthed Henry Yule's *The Travels of Marco Polo*, which was reissued with Henry Cordier as editor, as *The Book of Ser Marco Polo* (London, 1921). See *Selected Prose, ed. cit.*, p. 204.

history was rather limited, despite his debt to Fenollosa and his readings into Confucian philosophy.

In the early cantos, Pound's descriptions of historical eras and events were usually based on primary sources and detailed studies of the period under review. Thus his use of *The Writings of Thomas Jefferson* in Canto 31 and Charles Francis Adams' *The Works of John Adams* in Canto 32. By relying on contemporary accounts he was able to look at the past through the eyes of those who were actually there. At the very least his sources were secondary accounts by those who were of the same culture and civilization of which they wrote. But what of China? His language skill was not good enough to go to Chinese sources, which were hard to come by in any case. Western surveys of Chinese history were too brief and superficial, and all suffered from the weakness of being written by those who lived in a different culture. There were some translations of Chinese histories into Western languages. Both Couvreur and Legge had translated the *Tso Chuan*, but this dealt only with the Warring States era, 722-468 BC. Chavannes had translated about one third of Ssu-Ma Ch'ien's *Shih Chi*, which even in its entirety brought the reader only into the first half of the Han Dynasty (1st Century BC). Weiger's two-volume *Textes Historiques* was an unreliable translation of selected passages of the *T'ung-Chien Kang-Mu* (see below) and is marred by a decided bias against Chinese culture.

There was, in fact, only one source which would fit the requirements. This was the thirteen-volume *Histoire Générale de la Chine* by the French Jesuit de Moyriac de Mailla and published in Paris between 1777 and 1783.[40] De Mailla's *Histoire* is a translation of a Manchu version of the most prestigious of all Chinese histories, the *T'ung-Chien Kang-Mu*, or "The Outline and Digest of the Comprehensive Mirror," which was compiled in the mid-twelfth century under the direction of the Sung neo-Confucian scholar Chu Hsi (1130-1200). The *T'ung-Chien Kang-Mu* was, in turn, a condensation of a much more detailed work by a team of scholars led by Ssu-Ma Kuang (1019-1086) in the eleventh century entitled *Tzu-Chih T'ung Chien*, or "A Comprehensive Mirror for the Aid of Government." The *T'ung-Chien Kang-Mu* was revised and up-dated in subsequent centuries, the most recent revision, at the time de Mailla used it, by the Ch'ing scholar Sung Lao (1643-1713) in 1708.[41] It was translated into the Manchu language upon

---

40. Joseph-Ann-Marie de Moyriac de Mailla, *Histoire générale de la Chine, ou Annales de cet Empire: traduites du Tong Kien-Kang-Mou*, 13 tômes. (Paris, 1777-1783).
41. For bibliographical data see W. G. Beasley and E. G. Pulleyblank, *Historians of China and Japan* (London, 1961), pp. 151-166, and Arthur Hummel, ed., *Eminent Chinese of the Ching Period*, 2 vols. (Washington, DC, 1944), II, p. 689.

orders of Emperor K'ang-hsi, and it must have been sometime after he arrived in Peking, probably in the 1720s, that de Mailla began his French version using the Manchu text.[42] The manuscript was sent to France in installments in the early 1730s, and there was talk of it being published under the sponsorship of Nicholas Freret, with royal support. But *"la morte de quelques personnes en place"* and the general anti-Jesuit atmosphere of the times resulted in its lying dormant in the Bibliotheque de Grand College de Lyon for forty years. It was not until 1775 that the manuscript came into the hands of M. l'Abbe Grosier who, with M. le Roux de Hautesrayes as editor, saw to its publication.[43]

The *T'ung-Chien Kang-Mu* is a long detailed account of Chinese history cast in Confucian moral terms. It is really a Guide for Statesmen, a Cautionary Tale, designed to instruct emperor and ministers in the operation of good government. To Chinese historians, especially after Chu Hsi, history was a mirror wherein statesmen could see reflected the models of past, both virtuous and evil, which could guide them in the present. A modern student of such things writes:

> Bare fact was there inshrined as moral judgement, as its very presence . . . put the stamp of praise and blame on the worthy and the ignoble in history. Bad men and wicked trembled before the accusing thrust of the chronicler's brush; they thought twice about their reputations and gave up their unsurpations and rebellions as a bad thing. History, that is, became a preventive weapon against the future as well as a corrective one against the past. . . . [It] sorted out the good from the bad, the right from the wrong, judged the past, and warned the future. The would-be regicide and power seeker, the self-seeking official who would serve two dynastic houses—all were given notice: desist or live in history forever condemned.[44]

By modern, "scientific" standards, this was not history at all. There is no serious attempt to analyze the philosophers other than Confucius. It treated art, literature, and poetry lightly. It "oversimplified" political revolution and rebellion. "Sources" were not

---

42. Why de Mailla chose the Manchu text poses an interesting problem. There is no doubt that he knew Chinese well, though it is possible that he was more familiar with the colloquial Chinese than with the classical language in which *Tung-Chien Kang-Mu* was originally written. The Manchu script, because it was phonetic, may have been easier to handle. It was also more precise, as de Mailla pointed out: ". . . it was less subject to the ambiguities of the Chinese language" (*Histoire*, I, Preface, p. xlvii). There is another interesting point: de Mailla said that he chose the Manchu text because it, in turn, had been designed upon the order of the Emperor Kang-hsi as an instructional manual for the Manchu people into the mysteries of Chinese civilization (*Histoire*, I, Preface, pp. xlvii, xlviii)—exactly what de Mailla was trying to do for eighteenth century Europe, and Pound, for his generation.
43. *Ibid.*, Préliminaire, I, pp. xxv-xxviii.
44. H. L. Kahn, *Monarchy in the Emperor's Eyes: Images and Reality in the Chien Lung Reign* (Cambridge, Mass., 1971), p. 126.

"documented." But that was not the historian's task. His purpose was to pass moral judgment. One senses an affinity with Dante here. Indeed, *The Divine Comedy* and the *T'ung-Chien Kang-Mu* were written only a little more than a century apart.

This was just the kind of history Pound needed. *The Cantos*, too, were a Cautionary Tale, a Tale of the Tribe, in which the good and evil in Western civilization are revealed. Pound had constructed a mirror in which Western man could see his past reflected. Now he was to introduce another mirror, reflecting another civilization's attempt to solve essentially the same problems.

Exactly how the *Histoire* came to Pound's attention is not clear. He may have noticed a comment in Giles' *The History of Chinese Literature* that the *T'ung-Chien Kang-Mu* was "still regarded (1901) as the standard history of China."[45] He may have picked up the title in the footnotes of Pauthier's *Chine*, which relied mainly on Jesuit sources. Indeed, most nineteenth- and twentieth-century surveys of Chinese history acknowledge their debt to de Mailla in one way or another. He simply may have seen an advertisement in a bookstore catalogue. In any case, on November 18, 1937, the Liberia Antiquaria, Umberto Saba, of Trieste billed Pound for a copy of *Histoire Generale de la Chine* at a cost of L.216. It had been listed at item No. 226 in Catalogue 76.[46]

IV

Pound began work on the China Cantos 53-61 soon after receiving the package from Trieste. His notes were written in four notebooks of approximately eighty pages each (forty pages, recto and verso), in the last of which he began his notes for the Adams Cantos which were to follow. The notebooks were arranged as follows:[47]

---

45. Giles, *History*..., pp. 228-229.
46. Beinecke Library (Yale): Ezra Pound collection, Folder "Financial Papers; Bills for Books."
47. The notebooks are in the Beinecke Library at Yale. See also Mary de Rachewiltz, *A Catalogue of the Poetry Notebooks of Ezra Pound* (New Haven, Conn., 1980), pp. 35-38.

Notebook	Canto, page, and line	Histoire, vol., page	Periods of Chinese History
32	LIII-LIV, 282, 31	I-IV entire	Earliest times to the Chin Dynasty, 399 AD
33	LIV, 282, 32- LIV, 306, 15	V-IX, 585	Early fifth century AD to mid-Mongol era, 1347 AD
34	LVI, 306, 19- LX, 331, 22	IX, 585- XI, 325	Mid-Mongol era to Mid-Ch'ing Dynasty, 1717 AD
35	LX, 331, 23- LXI to end	XI, 325- 610	Mid-Ch'ing, 1717 to mid-reign of Ch'ien-Lung 1780 AD

The China Cantos, preceeded by Canto 52 (based in part on the Confucian *Book of Rites*) and followed by the Adams Cantos 62-71, were in "rough typescript" by February, 1939, the proofs ready for correction by September, and final version in order by November, 1939.[48] Faber published the London edition in January, 1940, and the American edition, by New Directions, was published in September of that year.[49]

V

It is clear that E.P. moves through Chinese history much more rapidly than does his source. It took de Mailla about eight and one half of his eleven volumes to reach the late Sung period (1231), or about 75% of the entire work. Pound uses only three of his Cantos (53-55), about 50% of his entire China section, to cover the same period. Six of his Cantos (56-61) are used to cover the last 500 years of the story, a task that de Mailla covers in about two and one half volumes or 25% of his total effort. Clearly, then, at least half of Pound's efforts are concerned with only a small segment (the later part) of Chinese history, and thus it is fair to ask whether or not the China Cantos reflect with any degree of accuracy the *paideuma* of Chinese civilization and culture?

---
48. *The Selected Letters of Ezra Pound, 1907-1941*, ed. D. D. Paige (New York, 1950), p. 322; Stock, *op cit.*, p. 369.
49. Stock, *op cit.*, p. 375.

There is little doubt that this is what he was trying to do. On page 4v of Notebook No. 33, with the names encircled and boxed, there appears a schematic map:

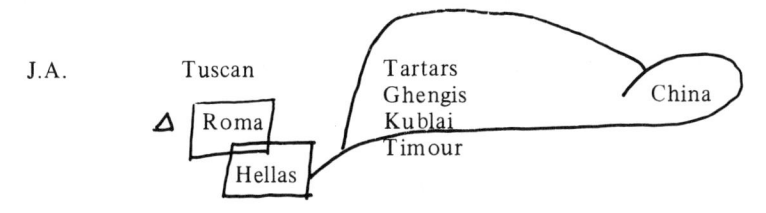

```
J.A.        Tuscan        Tartars
                          Ghengis              China
         △  Roma          Kublai
                          Timour
                Hellas
```

The map appears in a section of his notes devoted to the mid-Mongol period (Canto 56) at the end of the thirteenth century. Students of Chinese history have labelled the Mongol era *Pax Mongolia*, a time when control of China, Central Asia and parts of Eastern Europe by a single power brought relative peace to Eurasia and the first substantial flow of information between China and Europe. The "hordes" of Kublai Khan in China and Batu in Russia acted as a bridge, and Pound's map was an attempt to show how knowledge about China was transmitted from northeast Asia (China) to western Europe (Greece-Rome-Tuscany) and eventually to the American of John Adams (J.A.). Has Pound then, done what he set out to do—has he kept the blossoms from falling?

Through Canto 55 and part of 56, the answer must be "Yes." The story of Chinese history and culture, as transmitted through the *T'ung-Chien Kang-Mu* and de Mailla's translation, emerges clearly from Pound's poem. As we noted above, the *T'ung-Chien Kang-Mu* was a twelfth century condensation of a much larger earlier work and was put together under the direction of Chu Hsi, the dominant figure in the late Sung neo-Confucian movement. It was an historical summary and contained primarily those events which the neo-Confucianists thought would best serve as a moral guide for generations of Chinese rulers and their ministers. It may not have been "accurate" history by modern standards, but it was the history that post-Sung Chinese knew and accepted as the correct version of their own past. The basic themes appear over and over again in Pound's lines: the ancient legends of the invention of agriculture and of writing; the channeling of the floods; the defense of the frontier; the evils of pernicious doctrines, especially Buddhism and Taoism; earth-quakes, eclipses, comets, and the appearance of fabulous animals; the beat-like repetitive recounting of the rise and fall of dynasties.

Above all there was the constant concern for good government. For millennia, the Confucian view held that unless a ruler and his officials were concerned with virtuous rule and the welfare of their people, they and their dynasty were doomed, the "Mandate of Heaven" would be withdrawn, and the mantle of leadership passed on to more vigorous and virtuous leaders. The nexus of the problem was usually economic, and the neo-Confucianists made much of the need for equitable taxes, effective public works, and high agricultural productivity.

These are the things that Pound emphasized, at least in the first half of the China Cantos. For example, beginning with Canto 53 and continuing through Canto 55, over 65% of the episodes discussed are concerned with questions of good and bad governance. In Canto 54 alone, almost 80% of the poem addresses itself to acts of virtuous statesmen, loyalty of subjects to rulers, the fall of evil schemers, and to sound economic policy. For Canto 55 the percentage is about 66% and for Canto 56 Pound devotes over 50% of his time to such matters.

The high point of the first half of the China Cantos is probably the treatment of that great Sung reformer Wang An-shih, of whom we learned in Canto 55. For about a decade in the last quarter of the eleventh century Wang, whom Pound calls "Ngan" took an increasingly ineffective Sung government by the scruff of the neck and tried to shake some sense into it. A series of sweeping reforms, mostly economic, were inaugurated with the approval of a sympathetic emperor. These included a plan to establish a Commission on Financial Planning; a State Loan System for peasants; a price control mechanisms; corvée labor abolished and replaced with a graduated tax; a land-tax based on the productivity of the soil of each region; a State Trading System; and a host of other radical reforms. At first glance, Wang would seem to be a man after Ezra's own heart. Almost two decades earlier (1920) he had written referring to the ideas of Major C. H. Douglas, that it was the duty of the state to lend, not borrow money. "In this respect, . . . the Capitalist usurps the function of the State," and he spoke of government's role in "the administration of credit" and "the fixing of prices on the broad principles of use value."[50] Wang was doing just that, and it is no coincidence that Pound devotes more attention to the great reformer than to any other figure, including Confucius. Thus, from Canto 55:

     and at this time began Ngan
 (or more fully Ouang-Ngan-ché) to demand that they reset
        the market tribunals,
  posting every day what was on sale and what the right price
          of it

---

50. "Probari Ratio," *The Athenaeum* (2 April, 1920), quoted in *Selected Prose, ed cit.*, p. 208.

> posting every day what was on sale and what the right price
> of it
> as had been under TCHEOU emperors
> and that a market tax shd/ go to the emperor from this
> thereby relieving the poor of all douanes
> giving them easy market for merchandise
> and enlivening commerce [55/296]

And on lending money:

> And Ngan saw land lying barren
> because peasants had nowt to sow there
> whence said: Lend 'em grain in the spring time
> that they can pay back in autumn [55/297]

Unfortunately Wang is not treated well in the Chinese histories. He is described as an arrogant, ambitious trouble-maker, with Buddhist and Taoist leanings, and was characterized by the great Confucian scholar Ssu-Ma Kuang as a dreamer whose ideas might have been right in theory but would not work in practice. This is the view reflected in the *Histoire*, and Pound's confusion is evident in his later treatment of Wang in such lines as:

> Students went bhud rather than take Kung via Ngan,
> Flood relief, due to Ngan?
>   joker somewhere?
> came Tsaï King pro-Ngan, probably crooked [55/298-299]

What must have been especially surprising to E.P. was the attitude of Ssu-Ma Kuang, that paragon of Confucian virtue, who proved to be a life-long foe of the Great Reformer and whose death was mourned by the merchants and money lenders of the capital:[51]

> and merchants in Caïfong put up their shutters in mourning
>   for Ssé-kouang
>   [55/298]

Canto 56, most of which is devoted to the Mongol conquest and rule, continues in the same vein, with Kublai Khan playing a hero's role:

> KUBLAI was a bugger for taxes
>
> . . . .
>
> KUBLAI died heavy with years
>   his luck was good ministers, save for the treasury
>   [56/304].

---

51. The editor of the *Histoire* (see VIII, p. 305) does try to save some of Wang An-shih's reputation by pointing out that his reforms did some good for the peasants and were "*odieux aux usuriers qui ne subsistent que de sang des malheureux*" ("hateful for the usurers, who lived only on the blood of the destitute"). Pound notes this in *Notebook 33*, p. 25, but makes no mention of it in Canto 55.

....
> nor had any emperor more care to find men of merit—
> doing what KUBLAI had intended— [56/306]

There are, of course, major gaps in Pound's tale. The usurper Wang Mang and the great historian Ssu-Ma Ch'ien, both of Han times, are not mentioned. Chu Hsi, the driving force behind the Sung neo-Confucian movement and editor of the *T'ung-Chien Kang-Mu*, passes unnoticed. And it is rather surprising that Pound does not mention Li Po, whose poems make up much of *Cathay*. But then, as we have noted, *The Cantos* is a "poem containing history," not history cast in poetic form.

After Canto 56 the tone and thrust of the poem changes. There is much less of the didactic, moralizing emphasis found in the earlier cantos. Less and less are we instructed with tales of corrupt or virtuous rulers, of loyal ministers, or tax reform. We hear much less of the evils of Buddhism and Taoism. Eclipse and comets are rarely mentioned. Whereas in the first four China Cantos well over half of the episodes Pound described are concerned with the Confucian view of good and bad government, the last five cantos seem to be more concerned with the Japanese, the Ming-Ch'ing civil war, the Kaldan Wars of K'ang-hsi, the Jesuit missionaries, and diplomatic negotiations with the Russians at Nerchinsk. In short, there is a different texture to the last half of the China Cantos, and they do not seem to contribute much to Pound's goal of bringing the story of Confucian China to the West.[52] What, then, happened?

The answer is that the *T'ung-Chien Kang-Mu*, of which de Mailla's *Histoire* was a translation, did not go beyond the Mongol period (the middle of Canto 56). In a long footnote at the beginning of Volume X of the *Histoire*, the editor explains: "Because the *T'ung-Chien Kang-Mu*, of which a translation has here been given and which included the history of the first twenty imperial dynasties, does not go beyond those of the Yuan or Mongols, Father de Mailla has seen it necessary, in order to continue his work, to have recourse to contemporary authors in the Ming and Ch'ing dynasties."[53] As for Ch'ing history, de Mailla, again using contemporary sources, carried his work forward to 1722, i.e. the year Yung-cheng came to the throne. At this point the good Father retired from the scene, and the work was continued by the editor, who had to rely largely on sources published in France.[54]

---

52. An exception could be E.P.'s treatment of the Manchu Emperor Yung Cheng. He makes much of Yung Cheng's efforts to play the role of the model Emperor in Canto 61.
53. *Histoire, ed cit.*, X, p. 1.
54. De Mailla chose not to continue the work into the reign of Yung Cheng because to have done so would have involved him in a discussion of affairs of which he himse'

As a consequence, almost one half of the China Cantos, from early Canto 57 to the end, are not based on the standard neo-Confucian *T'ung-Chien Kang-Mu* of Chu Hsi at all. Thus much of the didactic thrust is absent, and we find ourselves involved with missionaries, Russians, and Japanese.

Why, then, did Pound not stop with Canto 56, instead of carrying on into Ming and Ch'ing times? One answer might, quite simply, be "momentum." He set out to cover as much of the sweep of Chinese history as he could, and, in fact, the last lines of Canto 61 come from the last lines of Volume XI, which is the last volume of the historical portions of *Histoire*. In any case, de Mailla's transition from the *T'ung-Chien Kang-Mu* to contemporary sources and the editor's use of sources published in Europe after 1772 are both quite skillful, and unless a reader catches two crucial footnotes, it is quite possible to continue on, thinking one is still reading a translation of the *T'ung-Chien Kang-Mu*. It is not known whether Pound noticed the difference, and I hazard a guess that he did not. But since he was leading his readers toward the American experience, there was much logic continuing the China story to the 1780s and the years of the American Revolution, even though in doing so, he contributes little to a further understanding of Confucian China.

It is possible, of course, that as Pound learned more and more about Chinese history he began to see that the "real" China was not quite the idyllic civilization that he had envisioned. He could not help but realize that the Confucian state, though softened by the Confucian ethic, was still a highly despotic and often brutal structure. As early as 1920, he had explored the "irresistable and impersonal organization [the powerful state], through which the ambition of able men, animated consciously or unconsciously by the lust of domination, may operate to the enslavement of their fellows."[55] Now he was discovering that the Sung State of Wang An-shih may have been precisely that kind of institution. He had written of the importance of human freedom and of the "free exercise of the will."[56] And yet he was seeing that the anti-Buddhist/anti-Taoist policies that de Mailla described were examples of the attempts of the Confucian "establishment" to repress dissent. Worst of all for Pound, was the sight of the great Confucian scholar Ssu-Ma Kuang, poet-historian-statesmen, discrediting the great reformer Wang An-shih and being eulozied for his

---

was a part. To do otherwise might have compromised his position at court, and, perhaps, endangered the Jesuit mission. See *Histoire, ed cit.*, XI, pp. 369, 523.
55. *Selected Prose, ed cit.*, p. 209.
56. *Ibid.*, p. 207.

efforts by, of all people, the merchants and money lenders. It may have been these discoveries that led to a lessening of the didactic, moralizing tone in the last half of the China Cantos.

In a sense, the last five China Cantos served not so much as a "pulpit" but as a "bridge," the bridge implied the Pound's Mongol Map of *Notebook #33*. It was, after all, Marco Polo of Mongol times, the Jesuits of the late Ming and early Ch'ing, and the western merchants and Russian diplomats of mid-Ching through whom the West came to know China with any degree of accuracy, and it may, in the final analysis, make such sense to be concerned with this aspect of the story. Thus, it can be argued that if Cantos 53-56 contain the "blossoms," the later China Cantos tell something of how they were "kept from falling."

LIONEL KELLY

PERSONAL HISTORY IN THE CANTOS

"Pound is not interested in the actuality of the past; he is interested only in its instrumentality,"[1] writes Leon Surette. I assume Surette's view would earn wide assent. I do not seek to corroborate it, but to take up the notion that Pound is interested in the "instrumentality" of the past, and in particular, of that sense of the "past" or "history" which is primarily conditioned by the "authority" of personal history. I choose to illustrate Pound's use of personal history from passages of Cantos 80 and 81.

The composition of the *Pisan Cantos* is a remarkable history: the longest sequence of *The Cantos* composed in the shortest time—a matter of a few months—in the most adverse circumstances. Without access to his own or other libraries, the dynamics of creation are here crucially dependent upon memory, and in particular, the memories of personal history; the poet, his history, his friendships, become—not exclusively but significantly—the subject of his poem. The procedure is consistent with his established practice; statements are proposed, judgments are made, which are then recapitulated, and frequently modified, in later lines in the same canto or a succeeding one: these modifications are affected by shifts of tone. And in his presentation of relationships Pound is engaged with "reputation." What we see is that reputation in the *Pisan Cantos*—as elsewhere, but more successfully here—is used as an index of social and cultural quality. And the subject of "quality" is realized not only through the presentation of Pound's friends and opponents, but also through the arguments about such apparently simple materials such as bread and grain.

I begin then with a quotation from Canto 80, lines of which are repeated in the opening of 81:

---

1. Leon Surette, *A Light from Eleusis* (Oxford, 1979), p. 111.

> that was an era also, and Spanish bread
> > was made out of grain in that era
> > senesco
> > > sed amo
> > Madri', Sevilla, Córdoba,
> > > there was grain equally in the bread of that era
> > > senesco sed amo
> > Gervais must have put milk in his cheese
> > (and the mortal fatigue of action postponed)
> > and Las Meniñas hung in a room by themselves
> > and Philip horsed and not horsed and the dwarfs
> > > and Don Juan of Austria
> > Breda, the Virgin, Los Boracchos
> > > are they all now in the Prado?
> > y Las Hilanderas?
> > Do they sell such old brass still in "Las Américas"
> > > with the wind coming hot off the marsh land
> > > or with death-chill from the mountains [81/493-4494] [2]

This passage takes us back to Pound's visit to Spain in the summer of 1906 when he began work on his M.A. thesis for the University of Pennsylvania. Through the intervention of the American Consul in Madrid he gained admission to the Royal Library there, and was helped in his studies by a young priest, Father José Maria de Elizondo, who, in 1917 visited Pound in London. Pound's friendship with Elizondo receives a retrospective tribute in these lines from Canto 81:

> and he said: "Hay aquí mucho catolicismo—(sounded
> > > > catoli*th*ismo)
> > y muy poco reliHion"
> and he said: "Yo creo que los reyes desaparecen"
> (Kings will, I think, disappear) [81/517].

Now the fullest account of Pound's visit to Spain that year is by Pound himself in the sixteenth section of *Guide to Kulchur*, "Europe or the Setting," which I shall return to later.

What interests me in the passage I have quoted from Canto 80 is the quality of appeal it both makes and possesses. This appeal is determined by two interlocking intentions; one is the exactness of memory; the other is the evocation (and through that—the manifestation) of quality or condition. I will illustrate these intentions as they are realized in the passages I am concerned with. I am also concerned, and this primarily, with the mode of representation or recall of personalities and events, and therefore with the question of "tonalities," the inflections of personal voice which suggest how we should interpret what we are reading. I shall

---

[2]. Ezra Pound, *The Cantos* (London, 1975). All quotations are from the Faber paperback edition, the Revised Collected Edition.

suggest that such a preoccupation raises problematic issues in the recall of Pound's London contemporaries in the later cantos, *Rock-Drill* and *Thrones*, where the question of the gap between "personal truth" and "public status" is clearly evident.

The difficulty of this sort of pursuit in *The Cantos* is illustrated at the start of the verse paragraph from which I have already quoted: if we go to the opening lines of that paragraph we read this:

> Amo ergo sum, and in just that proportion
> And Margot's death will be counted the end of an era.

The reference here to Margot is something of a puzzle; the *Index* suggests Margot Asquith, second wife of Herbert Asquith, the Liberal Prime Minister from 1908 to 1916, and refers us back to Canto 38, which gives us this version of her:

> And Her Ladyship cut down Jenny's allowance
> Because of that bitch Agot Ipswich [38/188].

The 1954 Faber edition of *The Cantos* gives the names Minny Humbolt for Agot Ipswich. Jenny, who is unidentified in the *Index*, is said by Terrell[3] to be a pseudonym for Nancy Cunard, heroine of Michael Arlen's *The Green Hat*, and a figure in Parisian artistic circles in the 20s and 30s, whose Hours Press issued *A Draft of XXX Cantos*; and "her Ladyship" is, according to Terrell, Nancy Cunard's mother, Emerald Cunard. Pound's attitude to Margot Asquith—if indeed it is her—in Canto 38 needs no gloss; but the reference to her in Canto 80 does. "And Margot's death will be counted the end of an era," he writes, and we have to assume that the reference here is ironic, for she died in 1945, and the year is made significant not for the defeat of the Axis powers, but for the death of Margot Asquith.[4] Such a reading of the line in Canto 80 makes sense in the context of the reference to her in Canto 38, but it fits uneasily with what follows in Canto 80, which is an affectionate recall of the German pianist and composer, Walter Rummel, with whom Pound briefly shared rooms in Paris in 1917, and who shared Pound's interest in Provençal songs:

> and dear Walter was sitting amid the spoils of Finlandia
> a good deal of polar white
>   but the gas cut off.
> Debussy preferred his playing
>   that also was an era (Mr. W. Russel) [80/493].

---

3. Carroll F. Terrell, *A Companion to the Cantos of Ezra Pound* (Berkeley, Los Angeles, London, 1980), pp. 155 and 156.
4. According to Professor Terrell, Pound read of Margot Asquith's death in a *Time Magazine* obituary. Copies of *Time* made up the bulk of the library in the D.T.C. at Pisa.

The aggregate effect of these lines illustrates the difficulties we encounter in trying to evaluate the significance of reference in the poem to personalities known to the poet, with the apparently random shift from the use of proper names to the use of pseudonyms. The use of pseudonyms was a lifelong habit with Pound, a matter of temperament one might say, even though the practice appears to go against the grain of his demands for "clarity." References to Uncle William, as to Possum, are simple enough; the pseudonym "Old Vort" certainly irritated Wyndham Lewis. Clearly, in many cases in *The Cantos* the need for a pseudonym or "veiled" naming is determined by the laws of libel; or by some scrupulosity on the poet's part; on the other hand it is often not easy to tell why a pseudonym has been used. Take the case of these two names for the same figure—Minny Humbolt and Agot Ipswich. "Minny" is an acknowledged diminutive for Margaret, and thence also for Margot; the implications of Humbolt are however entirely unspecific "humbug" maybe; perhaps a German or Jewish name is implied. And with Agot Ipswich we are in deeper water. According to the *OED* "agot" is an obsolete form of "agate"; and one of the definitions of agate gives us this figurative usage: "A very diminutive person, in allusion to small figures cut in agates for seals. Obs." It cites an example from *Much Ado About Nothing* [III.i.65 ff.] where Hero is grumbling about Beatrice's capacity to sport with the figure of a man who declares his love:

> Why, you speak truth. I never yet saw man
> How wise, how nobel, young; how rarely featur'd
> But she would spell him backward. If fair-fac'd,
> She would swear the gentleman should be her sister;
> If black, why, Nature, drawing of an antic,
> Made a foul blot; if tall, a lance ill-headed;
> If low, an agate very vilely cut:

If Pound has such an association in mind we are left with the imputation that Margot Asquith, along with her other less admirable qualities, was a small ill-proportioned woman. Her own *Autobiography* seems to corroborate this view of her. This is her own parlor game account of herself, in which the trick was to guess the identity of the figure described and the author of the description:

> In appearance she was small, with rapid, nervous movements; energetic, never wholly ungraceful, but inclined to be restless. Her face did not betray the intelligence she possessed, as her eyes, though clear and well-shaped, were too close together. Her hawky nose was bent over a short upper lip and meaningless

Lionel Kelly

mouth. The chin showed more definite character than her other features, being large, bony and prominent. . . .[5]

None of this, clearly, matters all that much, except that it is characteristic of the difficulties we encounter in pursuing the implications of pseudonymous names in *The Cantos* when their usage appears to be generated by Pound's personal knowledge of the figure concerned. And of course if Pound's animus against Margot Asquith is as convinced as Canto 38 suggests—"That bitch Agot Ipswich"—then she surely features very oddly in Canto 80. For the opening of Canto 80 is principally concerned in the bulk of its lines with an elucidation of a past era, a reverential memory, although its actual beginning is in the present, in the Disciplinary Training Centre at Pisa:

> Ain' committed no federal crime,
> jes a slaight misdemeanor"
> Thus Mr A. Little or perhaps Mr Nelson, or Washington
> reflecting on the vagaries of our rising θεμις

For "Mr A. Little," "Mr Nelson" and "Washington" the *Index* suggests the names of men in prison with Pound: and thus this opening allows Pound to call upon the fortuitous accidentality of history that amongst his prison inmates at Pisa there should have been men whose names were shared with statesmen and generals, thus allowing him the opportunity to use a self-defensive personal comment about the "crime" for which one of them was in there—"jes a slaight misdemeanor" both to affirm his present locus—Pisa—and through it to invoke the relationship between personal corruption and political corruption with which *The Cantos* is so massively preoccupied.

From this point on Canto 80 takes off into a different tonality, of an important kind: "Amo ergo sum, and in just that proportion" he writes, for this canto deals both with conditions of love as revealed in the affectionate recall of Pound's London and Paris contemporaries, and suggests something of the tensions operative within the self of the poet:

> Where memory liveth,
> it takes its state
> Formed like a diafan from light on shade
> Which shadow cometh of Mars and remaineth
> Created, having a name sensate,
> Custom of the soul,
> will from the heart [36/177].

---

5. Margot Asquith, *An Autobiography* (New York, 1920), II, pp. 77-78.

It is unnecessary for me to comment on this passage from Canto 36, except to say that I am sure that Pound's versions of Cavalcanti's poem must have been in his mind, both as he wrote "Amo ergo sum, and in just that proportion" and as the Cavalcanti poem voices the issue of the relationship between memory and love. "Amo ergo sum" is an ethical proposition, validating his procedure of personal recall, and returning him to at least one of his origins, Spain in 1906:

> and Las Meniñas hung in a room by themselves
> and Philip horsed and not horsed and the dwarfs
>   and Don Juan of Austria
> Breda, the Virgin, Los Boracchos
>   are they all now in the Prado?
> y Las Hilanderas [80/493]?

I want now to comment on this recall of the Velásquez paintings in the Prado as he saw them in 1906. This "moment" of Velásquez was one that survived for Pound, intact, for a very long time, and is worth our attention. He writes about Velásquez in a variety of places, using him for example in the review of Eliot's *Prufrock and Other Observations* in *Poetry* of 1917:

> ... let me say that he [Eliot] has used contemporary detail very much as Velasquez used contemporary detail in *Las Meninas*; the cold gray-green tones of the Spanish painter have, it seems to me, an emotional value not unlike the emotional value of Mr. Eliot's rhythms, and of his vocabulary.[6]

Whatever we may think of the usefulness of such a comparison, it has its origin in the "moment" of Velásquez in 1906, for which we have to turn to the *Guide to Kulchur* for a fuller account. There Pound writes this:

> For 31 years I have carried in my mind as a species of rich diagram, the Prado as I saw it, and heaven knows if my readers will see it ever again. In the long gallery you turned after a time to the left. On your left hand in the great room, Las Hilanderas, the spinning girls, with the beamed light, and the duskiness, in the separate smaller room Las Meniñas, the young princesses or court ladies, the mirror with glimpse of Velasquez by the far door painting the picture.
>   On the wall facing the great canvas, alone, his self-portrait. In the great room Don Juan de Austria, the dwarfs, high at the end facing the door, the Virgin enthroned, differing greatly in workmanship, designed shall we say for Church lighting and not for a palace. The Surrender of Breda with the spears, new for the american visitor, only years later in Avignon did one see that this composition was not invented ex nihil and ex novo, but had been in fresco.

---

6. *The Literary Essays of Ezra Pound* (London, 1960, repr), p. 420.

> On the right wall Baldassar Carlos, Philip on foot with his hunting gun, Philip on Horseback, the horse's foot having been done first in a different position. Again by the door Mercury and Argos, and below it the Drinkers.

and finally,

> Our husky young undergraduates may start their quest of Osiris in a search for what was the PRADO....[7]

Of course Pound was very much of his time in this regard for Velásquez, but that matters little; what is relevant to my concerns is the way that passage from *Guide to Kulchur* passes into Canto 80 in a rhythmically modulated recall of the disposition of the paintings in the Prado as they were in 1906: a recall which, through the intonations of a poised nostalgia, registers at once both presence and the anxiety of loss:

> are they all now in the Prado?
> y Las Hilanderas [80/493]?

These intonations of nostalgia, or if you like, of elegiac recall, pass over into the succeeding lines, which are about memory—things as they were—and value—what they cost:

> Do they sell such old brass still in "Las Américas"

and from there into a different tonality again:

> with the wind coming hot off the marsh land
> or with death-chill from the mountains [80/494]?

I was for some time accustomed to read these lines (they are repeated in Canto 81) as referring simply to the local physical atmosphere of Madrid, but of course, bearing in mind the concluding lines of the *Pisan Cantos*, we see that a conjunction is implied between two sets or states of conditions; Madrid 1906/Pisa 1945:

> If the hoar frost grip thy tent
> Thou wilt give thanks when night is spent [84/540].

It is, of course, through such conjunctions that the *Pisan Cantos* are impacted with a resonance of meaning and value, where the locus of his present place, the *situ* of recall, sharply defines the tonality of his "revery."

Velásquez' painting *Las Hilanderas* is, inferentially, recalled in the following lines, as indeed are a number of his other paintings:

> the warp
> and the woof
> with a sky wet as ocean

---
7. Ezra Pound, *Guide to Kulchur* (1938, new edn. 1966), pp. 110-111.

> flowing with liquid slate
> Pétain defended Verdun while Blum . . .
> the red and white stripes
>   cut clearer against the slate
>   than against any other distance
> the blue field melts with the cloud-flow [80/494].

The subject of *Las Hilanderas* is, of course, the fable of Arachne, whose skill in weaving prompted her to challenge Pallas Athena to a competition; when Athena destroys Arachne's web, Arachne hangs herself, and Athena changes her to a spider: the fable is told in *Metamorphoses*, book 6. For Pound in the Disciplinary Training Centre at Pisa the fable of Arachne must have suddenly taken on particular relevance to himself; was he too about to suffer the wrath of the "authorities" for the temerity of his challenge? Pound's Pisan memories of Velásquez' paintings, as he gives them in *Guide to Kulchur*, specifically recalls the image of the artist painting the picture included with the Spanish royal family: Velásquez the artist becomes a part of his own pictorial frame. In the *Pisan Cantos* those moments which reveal Pound in his present situation frame his memory of the friends of the past as Canto 80 unfolds in its great length. I cite as illustration the poise of his realization of his present place in the penultimate page of Canto 80:

> [Only shadows enter my tent
>   as men pass between me and the sunset,]
> beyond the eastern barbed wire
>   a sow with nine boneen
>   matronly as any duchess at Claridge's [80/515].

or, with equal significance:

> That from the gates of death,
>   that from the gates of death: Whitman or Lovelace
>   found on the jo-house seat at that
> in a cheap edition! [and thanks to Professor Speare]
> hast'ou swum in a sea of air strip
>   through an aeon of nothingness,
> when the raft broke and the waters went over me [80/513].

It is a commonplace, but nonetheless important, that it is precisely this sense of the poet as a presence in the poem that gives the *Pisan Cantos* their particular appeal, and makes them accessible to readers for whom many of the other cantos are too remote.

Velasquez then is a primary moment for Pound, in 1906, a moment which survives for him, and presumably, affects his response to the visual arts thereafter. There is hardly a fit language for such an experience as he had in the Prado in 1906, except perhaps the language which registers the emotional significance of the moment. This is what we have in Canto 80 in the recall of Velásquez. It sharply disposes Pound towards the treatment he gives to John Sargent. Sargent was, of course, by 1945, a much denigrated painter; there was a general view of him which proposed that he had sold out on his talent through committing himself to the production of flattering portraits of the occupants of the fashionable world of London high society. In Canto 80 and Canto 81, the proximity of shared experience is called upon by Pound to make comments about Sargent which range between the judgmental and the merely descriptive. In Canto 80 we find this for example:

> and of portraits in our time Cocteau by Marie Laurencin
> and Whistler's Miss Alexander
> (and the three fat ladies by Sargent, adversely)
> and somebody's portrait of Rodenbach
> with a background [80/512].

These portraits are referred to to suggest the different achievements of an era, achievements in which Sargent's portraits are aptly summarized by the descriptive comment "three fat ladies" and "adversely." Yet, in Canto 81, we find Pound back in Spain in 1906, recalling the lines from Canto 80, "come pan, niño," "eat bread, me lad," now ascribed to a particular speaker—Dolores: and then this:

> Sargent had painted her
> before he descended
> (i.e. if he descended
> but in those days he did thumb sketches,
> impressions of the Velázquez in the Museo del Prado
> and books cost a peseta,
> brass candlesticks in proportion,
> hot wind came from the marshes
> and death-chill from the mountains [81/517].

Clearly the references here to Sargent are a good deal less critical than in Canto 80: this derives, I suggest, both from the sense of shared commitment to Velásquez between himself and Sargent—an historical accident after all—and, as a consequence of that, the sense of an afterthought on Pound's part, a willingness to neutralize his earlier judgment of Sargent by here italicizing it, as it were, as though to suggest that that is only one way of seeing Sargent's work:

> Sargent had painted her
> before he descended
> (i.e. if he descended [81/517].

Sargent had been trained in the Paris atelier of Carolus-Duran, who is also—wryly—recalled by Pound in Canto 80:

> "Ah Monsieur" said old Carolus (Durand)
> "vous allez raser une toile?" [80/516].

Richard Ormond's book on Sargent provides the following useful commentary:

> He had set out for Spain in the autumn of 1879 with the primary purpose of studying Velasquez' work in Madrid. . . . Velasquez had been a presiding deity at Carolus-Duran's atelier: "For those who had asked his aid, Carolus-Duran formulated the principles of his own art, and enforced them by an appeal to the practice of others, and, before all, of Velasquez." [R. A. M. Stevenson, *Velasquez*, 1908, p. 107]. There are echoes of Velasquez style in several of Sargent's early works, but actual confrontation with the Spanish artist's major works clearly overwhelmed him. It is not difficult to understand why. . . . To him, as to so many nineteenth century artists, Velasquez was not just another old master, but the messiah of "les valeurs" which, in George Moore's words, "came upon France like a religion." [George Moore, *Modern Painting*, 1906, p. 80]. Sargent might have echoed Manet's words to Fantin-Latour: "How I miss you here, and how you would have loved Velasquez, who would justify the whole trip. . . . He is the painter of painters. I was not taken by surprise, but captivated." [E. Moreau-Nélation, *Manet Raconté par Lui-Même*, I, Paris, 1926, pp. 71-72].[8]

It will surprise no-one, after this, that Manet too gets into Canto 80, in the evocation of past "eras" or moments. In the light of this commentary by Ormond, it is clear that Pound's view of Sargent is, critically, moderated by his knowledge of Sargent's passion for Velásquez; and the implication of the lines

> but in those days he did thumb sketches,
> impressions of the Velázquez in the Museo del Prado [81/517]

becomes, if anything, honorific rather than adversarial. The whole passage from Canto 81 proposes too a quite fascinating other conjunction of experience between Pound and the painter: simply that they had stayed in the same inn in Madrid, the one in 1879 the other in 1906, and that Sargent had painted the woman of the inn; who, in Cantos 80 and 81 is recalled enjoining the young poet to "eat bread, me lad." If my reading is persuasive then one can only lament that the information which might corroborate the details of this fortuitous incident in the young Pound's visit to Spain in 1906 seems now to be beyond the possibility of verification. However, even so slight an incident reinforces my feeling that

---

8. Richard Ormond, *John Singer Sargent* (London, 1970), p. 27.

a much fuller biography of the poet remains to be written, and that one of the primary values of such a biography would be to open up passages in *The Cantos* which are yet obscure.

I shall leave the recall of Velásquez at this point and return now to the opening page of Canto 80 and comment on the references to bread, which, in all conscience, look curious enough because of their insistence.

> an era of croissants
>   then an era of *pains au lait*
> and the eucalyptus bobble is missing
>   "Come pan, niño!"
> that was an era also, and Spanish bread
>   was made out of grain in that era
>   senesco
>   sed amo
> Madri', Sevilla, Córdoba,
>   there was grain equally in the bread of that era
>   senesco sed amo
> Gervais must have put milk in his cheese.

Of course there is much in the preceeding cantos, particularly the *Pisan Cantos*, to prepare us for this sort of discourse, but in Canto 80 it has a peculiarly self-validated quality which arrests the attention. Here it looks to be simply a question of food, the quality of bread, in this case, as the validation of the quality of an era, a time and a place. But we should note the opening of Canto 81 again, signalizing my implicit sense of the intimate relationship of Canto 80 to 81:

> Zeus lies in Ceres' bosom
> Taishan is attended of loves
>   under Cythera, before sunrise [81/517].

This is a collocation of sacred names with mythopoeic resonances; testifying to the syncretic juxtaposition of Greek and Chinese sacred mysteries which the poem invokes, and in such a way as to dignify, along with much else, the expression of sexual love as a symptom/condition of generation.

The references to croissants, pains au lait, and Spanish bread in Canto 80 have been prepared for, however, at a conceptual level in the group of cantos from 45 to 51. In Canto 45 we are told

> with usura, sin against nature
> is thy bread ever more of stale rags
> is thy bread dry as paper,
> with no mountain wheat, no strong flour [45/229]

and Canto 45 concludes with the assertion that

> They have brought whores for Eleusis
> Corpses are set to banquet
> at behest of usura [45/230]

where the reference to Eleusis implies the substitution of a corrupt sexuality in place of the worship of the sacred mysteries of natural generation through which Demeter, the goddess of corn, was celebrated. Framed by the two Usura Cantos (45 and 51), Cantos 47 and 49 pursue the relationship of the mythopoeic and the actual through the recitation of myths of generation—of Adonis, and the redaction of a passage from Hesiod's *Works and Days* in Canto 47; and in The Seven Lakes Canto the penultimate verse paragraph, which I take to celebrate peasant man's organic knowledge of divine power through the circular simplicities of his life serving to displace the effect upon him of imperial power:

> Sun up; work
> sundown; to rest
> dig well and drink of the water
> dig field; eat of the grain
> Imperial power is? and to us what is it?
>
> The fourth; the dimension of stillness.
> And the power over wild beasts [49/245].

In Canto 47, the power over wild beasts is attributed to Adonis, but it is, I would suggest, symbiotically shared by quotidian man in Pound's version of Fenollosa's "earth beating song." It is in the light of these constructions about the significance of Demeter and Adonis in the poem as emblems of man's physical contact with sacred mysteries that the references to the quality of bread in Canto 80 take their meaning, derived from the foregoing conceptual process. They would, otherwise, have a merely idiosyncratic relevance which would be difficult to interpret. But the quality of Spanish bread in that era becomes symptomatic, for Pound, of a moment in his own history—the moment of Velásquez—which has a lasting power for him. Towards the end of Canto 80 he returns to the idea of the sacredness of grain in a manner which calls upon Christian scriptual tradition as well as his own use of the goddess Demeter,

> or remembering Carleton let him celebrate Christ in the grain
> and if the corn cat be beaten
>   Demeter has lain in my furrow
>   This wind is lighter than swansdown
>   the day moves not at all
>   (Zupp, Bufford, and Bohon)
>   men of no fortune and with a name to come[9] [80/513-514].

---
9. Walter Baumann has a note on Mark Alfred Carleton, a pioneering American cerealist, in "Carleton, Paquin and Salzburg," *Paideuma*, 11-3, pp. 442-445.

Lionel Kelly

As far as I am aware, no one has yet made a positive identification of the last named figures, Zupp, Bufford, and Bohun, and perhaps identification is unnecessary. Passages such as these derive their power, absolutely, from the controlling voice of the poet located firmly in the present of the poem.

There is, of course, a whole series of "recalls" in Canto 80, which is a veritable catalogue of names of personalities significant in Pound's personal history, including Hardy, Yeats (repeatedly), Gaudier-Brzeska, Arnold Dolmetsch, Edmund Dulac, Wyndham Lewis, Laurence Binyon, Mabel Beardsley, John Quinn, E. E. Cummings, Ford Madox Ford, A. R. Orage, Aubrey Beardsley, J. Cocteau; there are also Whistler, Sargent and Browning: they constitute for Pound "the tradition" which at the time of writing Canto 80 he thinks of as "waning." The sense of the waning of valuable traditions invokes Pound's parody of Browning's "Home Thoughts from Abroad" and leads into the conclusion of Canto 80 mourning the passing of the tradition of Lawes, and the London which so nourished Pound between 1908 and 1920.

Predominantly, these recalls are determined by Pound's personal "amor," the affections of an aging man—"senesco"—for the places and people of his earlier years: they are frequently honorific, full of understanding and sympathy, as in this passage about Yeats:

> but old William was right in contending
>   that the crumbling of a fine house
> profits no one
>   (Celtic or otherwise)
> nor under Gesell would it happen [ME: scrip money]
>
> As Mabel's red head was a fine sight
> worthy his minstrelsy
> a tongue to the sea-cliffs or "Sligo in Heaven" [80/507].

There are, it would seem, two conflicting tensions at work in the making of this canto. One seeks to celebrate self through the celebration of the past, here wrought to significant meaning by the naming of these "talismanic" names. The other is the insistence upon aging and loss—yet with the determination that his sense of the "tradition" will survive through his own familial acts of "generation":

> before the world was given over to wars
>   Quand vous serez bien vieille
>   remember that I have remembered,
> mia pargoletta,
>   and pass on the tradition [80/506].

"Mia Pargoletta" there must refer to Mary de Rachewiltz, who was back in Rapallo, typing out the *Pisan Cantos* as they came to her in manuscript from her father. What is remarkable about this canto is that within the affectionate recall of his friends there is relatively little sense of anxiety about his present condition, there in the Disciplinary Training Centre at Pisa: indeed, his presentation of himself in the act of composition is remarkably buoyant, though not without a controlled quality of irony: so that even the presentation of aging and loss comes largely as an objective lament.

I think I have written enough about Canto 80—and Canto 81—to fulfill my ambition to assert the centrality of "personal history" as a significant index to the success of the *Pisan Cantos*, and, by implication, to infer the crucial absence of that sense of the self in so many of the other cantos. I am aware that this implies a damaging view of much of the poem, and I don't want to insist upon such a view with any stridency. Pound had shown, after all, as early as *Hugh Selwyn Mauberley*, that a reading of English cultural history in 1920 was perfectly possible whilst the securities of the personal voice in the poem were openly addressed to the reader, even if those securities are given from a paradoxical perspective of self-dismissal, a device, or way of proceeding, which underpins the poem's analytic mode and satiric drive.

I should like to propose too, that it is possible to analyze Cantos 80 and 81 in a way which illuminates their structural length. It is a general problem with *The Cantos* that given the original design of a poem of about 100 or 120 cantos, we are still left with the question of how any one canto is determined in its own structural or narrative space. It is possible to see that in Canto 80, the relationship between personal recall and the presentation of the self in a position of acute danger informs the structure of the canto, so that once the moments of significant recall have all been handled, the canto can properly terminate in that general lament for the loss of vital English culture which it registers. It is the combination of these concerns which organizes the narrative scale of the canto. The relative brevity of Canto 81 depends on the length of Canto 80: 81 reads as an abbreviated recapitulation of its predecessor, but with a significant change of tone in its conclusion, a tone which appropriates scriptural authority. Personal lamentation gives way to a dignified voice transcending the limitations of self.

My view is that the relative withdrawal of the directing personal voice in *Rock-Drill* and *Thrones* supervenes for the reader after the *Pisan Cantos*, and that the references to Pound's London contemporaries in the later cantos become much less secure, and therefore much more difficult to read. The *Pisan Cantos* are justly celebrated for their lyricism, a lyricism which happily contains autobiography, in contrast to the epic mode of the poem as a whole which seeks to contain history.

I take to heart Pound's admonitory lines in *Thrones* which anticipates criticism based on ignorance of the right texts:

>That the books you read shall be
>>cheng
>>king
>>ut supra
>
>And your pals fit to read 'em [98/692]

and acknowledge that there are many occasions in *Rock-Drill* and *Thrones* when the personal voice comes as a welcome relief in the density of those sequences. The voice there, of course, calls upon the whole range of concerns which are the subject of the poem, sometimes to adjure us, as in Canto 99 on the education of children, sometimes to reflect in what appears to be a self-referential way, as in this moment in Canto 93:

>You are tender as a marshmallow, my Love,
>I cannot use you as a fulcrum.
>>You have stirred my mind out of dust [93/632].

We might make an informed guess as to who is the subject of these lines, but it would remain a conjecture. Is the "Love" here referred to a personal love, or that concept of Love referred to earlier in the same canto as the "form" of philosophy and therefore knowledge? Conceivably it is both personal and conceptual here. But what are we to make of this reference in Canto 98, repeated in Canto 102, about Yeats, Eliot and Lewis?

>But the lot of 'em, Yeats, Possum and Wyndham
>>had no ground beneath 'em [98/685]

—a quality of comment that is at odds with the personal value of those friendships elsewhere elegiacally celebrated, and at odds with the public sense of the achievement of these men as it exists outside *The Cantos*. These judgments about his old London friends, those who "made it new," seem to me in *Thrones* curiously unplaced, as though they are part of an argument which is not fully articulated. Perhaps that is the trouble, that their names are here called upon simply as evidence in an argument which has nothing to do with them. In Pisa, memory is what matters and what, crucially, determines the tone of his recall:

>>nothing matters but the quality
>of the affection—
>in the end—that has carved the trace in the mind
>dove sta memoria [76/457].

MOHAMMAD Y. SHAHEEN

THE STORY OF ABD-EL-MELIK'S MONEY IN CANTO 96 AND 97

In a conversation with Daniel Cory in 1963, Pound said, "It is a botch. . . . I knew too little about so many things. . . . I picked out this and that thing that interested me, and then jumbled them into a bag. But that's not the way to make . . . a work of art."[1] Like Cory, we may be tempted to dismiss such a statement as the whim of the moment. However, Pound was often aware of certain shortcomings, at least in the source material of his poetry. In 1955 he wrote to Agresti:

> I have sent Itrat another letter, as Del Mar dug up the one really good bit of Koran that I have ever seen quoted, namely that the Government shd/NOT take in taxes in good money, and pay its expenses in bad or inferior money.
> Del Mar's Hist. Monetary SYSTEMS, really tremendous, I did not get the full power of it when I first read it, done in 1895 when he had been over a lot of ground, and corrects minor errors in earlier works and ends with TREMENDOUS summary which I was too tired or distracted to read 7 years ago.
> Also correlated with Paul the Deacon our Habdimelich and SATANICE stimulatus/i.e. his lucidity.[2]

The point in question is not that Pound was too tired to have a full grasp of Del Mar's history, but rather that he gave Del Mar's history more credit than it actually deserves. For example, Del Mar's section on Islamic history is full of inaccuracy and misrepresentation. Pound's admiration for Del Mar as an historian of monetary systems seems to have led him to believe that Del Mar was reliable enough to render further research unnecessary. Whether the blame rests with Del Mar or with Pound, the result is that the Islamic elements which are used in Cantos 96 and 97 are misunderstood.

---
1. Quoted by Peter Ackroyd, *Ezra Pound and His World* (London, 1980), p. 107.
2. Ezra Pound to Agresti, August 19, 1955, Ezra Pound Papers, Yale University Library, New Haven. Here and in Canto 96 Pound uses a different spelling for Abd-el-Melik

First "the only really good bit of Koran that I have ever seen quoted" appears in Del Mar as follows:

> "There are some who if thou entrust them with a talent (quintar) give it back to you; and some if thou entrust them with a dinar will not return it" [Imran's Family, iii.; Medina, v. 60].[3]

The verse is totally misrepresented by both Del Mar and Pound, for it has nothing to do with government or taxes. It is about the People of the Book who are naturally non-Moslems, and it simply states that People of the Book are not all the same. Those People vary in matters of honesty; some are trustworthy, some are not. By implication, the verse calls on Moslems to approach the People of the Book without prejudice, and to accept the individual differences between them. It is a call for tolerance.

Pound's major reference to Islamic history centers on the great Umayyad Caliph Abd-el-Melik, who appears at various points in Cantos 96 and 97. Abd-el-Melik's achievement in monetary system forms the main source of inspiration for Pound's poetic chronicle. This achievement was originally emphasized by Del Mar:

> As usual, the coinage decides the point. The Arabian emirs or caliphs,[4] call them what you will, struck no independent coins before Abd-el-Melik. Their coins bear the stamp of Roman suzerainty; the emblems of the Roman religion; the legends of Roman superstition. These are proofs that until Abd-el-Melik the Arabian caliphs were not independent sovereigns. But the coinage proves more than this: it proves that the temporal sovereignty of the caliphs did not arise from their spiritual authority. This existed from the time of Mohamet, while the temporal sovereignty only began with Abd-el-Melik. Another proof of the correctness of this view is derived from the coinage of gold, which with the Arabs as with the Persians and Romans, was a sacerdotal prerogative. This prerogative belonged to the caliph as the sovereign-pontiff of Islam. The early emirs struck no gold, not even with Roman devices, and when Abd-el-Melik struck gold, the sovereign-pontiff of Rome, who was aware of its significance, immediately declared war upon him. It was the same in Spain. The Spanish caliphs struck no gold before Abd-el-Raman III [pp. 126-127].

It is an oversimplification which Del Mar puts forward here in his history and which Pound incorporates in his poetry. Abd-el-Melik was not a rebel who reformed the monetary system: he merely completed the process of Arabizing the coinage which had been going on for some time. The legends on Arab-Sassanian coins

---
3. Alexander Del Mar, *History of Monetary Systems* (New York, 1903), p. 144. Further references to this source will be made to page number and inserted in the text.
4. Del Mar confuses "emir," who is a local ruler, and "Emir-el-Moumenin," the Caliph, a title given to the Moslem Sovereign.

between A.H. 72-74, for example, were in Arabic script with the exception of the name of the Sassanian ruler, which was written in Pahlavi; and this was just before the dirham was Arabized by Abd-el-Melik.[5] Coins dated by the Hejeerah calendar are known from as early as the reign of Omar Ibn al-Khattab 651 A.D.

It is worth noting that before Abd-el-Melik, Caliphs and other rulers such as Mu'awiyah, Abdullah Ibn Zubir and Hajjaj had minted their own coins, though these were not fully Arabized.[6] These Caliphs and rulers were obviously independent. It is therefore not true "that until Abd-el-Melik the Arabian caliphs were not independent sovereigns."

However, there remains the problem of why the Arab rulers were so slow to Arabize the coinage, despite the fact that they were sovereign powers with independent mints. Two reasons for this have been advanced. One is the suggestion that the Arabs, at the time of the conquest believed that money was especially venerated by the conquered population and that the latter might be incensed by a sudden change in the coinage. Arab rulers appeared to believe that the populace did not associate coinage with sovereignty but cherished it as part of their tradition. It is surprising that Del Mar overlooks this fact when he discusses "Private Coinage" in Chapter XV and claims that Moslem rulers in India violated the coinage prerogative and "deemed themselves at liberty to abuse the coinage, until their issues ceased to command public respect" [p. 387].

The second reason for the delay in Arabizing Moslem money is quite different. It stems from the objections of the *faqihs* (the authorities on religious and theological matters). In the Umayyad period both before and after Abd-el-Melik, these scholars resisted the minting of coins bearing Moslem inscriptions on the basis that a coin bearing the name of God or the Prophet Mohammad might fall into the hands of someone not ritually purified.[7]

Whatever the reasons for the delay, Del Mar fails to realize that the Arabization of the coinage was part of the whole movement of Arabization including that of the *dawawin*, the bureaucracy which was obviously far important.

Del Mar makes, I think, a grave mistake when he states that "the coinage proves more than this (independent sovereignty): it

---

5. Christine Brooke-Rose is wrong in assuming that Abd-el-Melik was the first Umayyad Caliph to have coinage: "Lay me by Aurelie: An Examination of Pound's Use of Historical and Semi-Historical Sources" in *New Approaches to Ezra Pound*, edited by Eva Hesse (London, 1969), p. 245.
6. Mohammad Al-Ush, "Coinage in Islamic Arabic Civilization," *Al-Majallah Al-Arabiyyah Liththa-gafah*, I (September, 1981), p. 184.
7. *Ibid.*, p. 187.

proves that the temporal sovereignty of the Caliphs did not arise from their spiritual authority." In Islam there is no separation between the temporal and the religious authority. The Emir El-Moumenin (the Commander of the Faithful— had full powers in both spheres. Where the responsibility was divided, the temporal ruler was referred to as *'āmil* (laborer). There is no Papacy in Islam.

In fact Abd-el-Melik only moved towards his drastic reforms when he felt his spiritual authority threatened by the rebel Abdullah Ibn Zubir. Interestingly enough, Pound makes a very casual but important remark on the matter in Canto 96 when he says:

> Habdimelich made peace with the 2nd Justinian
> ... contra Zubir and burnt his home and his idols
> with their idolator, sed susciperent, we are getting to
> the crux of one matter [96/657].

This shows that Pound was, at least, aware of the story of Abd-el-Melik and Zubir. However, the brilliant ideogrammatic method, with which Pound feels at home, conceals the fact that he understood the serious implications of this episode. Without knowing the background to this reference, Poundians seem to have dismissed the remark as insignificant and meaningless. Instead, they treat such things as the monetary system and architecture as being complementary aspects in the chronicle of civilization. For example, Bacigalupo turns to the Latin description by Paul the Deacon which Pound includes in Canto 96 and comments:

> ... caliph "Habdimelich," in the course of warring against Justinian II (692), mints his own coin and so attains independence from Byzance, illustrating another authorial aside ..., and indicating that economic autonomy is the necessary premise of art and religion: having coined his money the rebel presently turns to the building of the temple ("et voluit auferre columnas").[8]

I believe that Pound's indication "we are getting to the crux of one matter" can be illuminating despite the ambiguities of the abrupt reference to Zubir and Justinian II. For Abd-el-Melik, and for all the Umayyads, the crux of the matter was always political as well as spiritual. The question of the Caliphate, who should succeed to the leadership of Islam, is at the roots of early Moslem history. The sharp divisions on this matter are too well-known to need any elaboration. What we should note here is that Zubir was a very real threat. He claimed the Caliphate, before and during

---

8. Massimo Bacigalupo, *The Forméd Trace: The Later Poetry of Ezra Pound* (New York, 1980), p. 343.

Abd-el-Melik's time, on the grounds that he was the son of one of those ten who first believed Mohammad's Message and gave Him all support possible. Zubir was a much greater threat to Abd-el-Melik than any foreign power, which explains why the Caliph made peace with Justinian II and even paid him *jizyah*, the poll tax. When Abd-el-Melik felt that the Caliphate was in immediate danger he declared war on Zubir and sent Hajjaj, his most ferocious leader against him. Hajjaj besieged Makkah and bombarded the Ka'abah where Zubir was killed as he was taking refuge in the most holy place of Islam.

With the defeat of Zubir's rebellion, Abd-el-Melik turned to religious and cultural projects. This, I believe, explains the sequence of the reference to Zubir followed by the quotation from Paul the Deacon about "the building of the temple" which refers either to the Ka'abah or to the Sakhrah, or possibly to both. Abd-el-Melik rebuilt the Ka'abah but without following the original design which is associated with the *Kafir* Zubir, who would be called as a result of his claim a *Kharidg* (a deviator from Islam).

Equally important is the building of the Sakhrah, the dome of the holy rock in Jerusalem, built on the spot from which Mohammad ascended to heaven. It is believed by some historians that Abd-el-Melik intended to make the Sakhrah an alternative to Makkah as a place of pilgrimage, *hajj*, if Zubir succeeded in spreading his claim to the Caliphate among Moslems at the *hajj* season. History records that Abd-el-Melik supported his scheme by quoting the Prophet's saying that *hajj* can be made to one of the three most holy Masjids (mosques) one of which is the Masjid of the Holy City near Sakhrah.[9]

---

9. Ya'qubi, an early Arab Historian (A.D. 874) records the following:

> Then "Abd al Malik forbade the people of Syria to make the pilgrimage (to Makkah); and this by reason that 'Abd Allah ibn Zubair was wont to seize on them during the time of the pilgrimage, and force them to pay him allegiance'—which, 'Abd al Malik having knowledge of, forbade the people to journey forth to Makkah.' But the people murmured thereat, saying, 'How dost thou forbid us to make the pilgrimage to Allah's house, seeing that the same is a commandment of Allah upon us?' But the Khalif answered them, 'Hath not Ibn Shihab as Zuhri [a celebrated Traditionist] told you how the Apostle of Allah did say: Men shall journey to but three Masjids, Al Masjid Haram (at Makkah), my Masjid (at Madinah), and the Masjid of the Holy City (which is Jerusalem)? So this last is now appointed for you in lieu of the Masjid al Haram (of Makkah). And this Rock, of which it is reported that upon it the Apostle of Allah set his foot when he ascended into heaven, shall be unto you in the place of Ka'abah.'" Then "Abd al Malik built above the Sakhrah a Dome, and hung it around with curtains of brocade, and he instituted door-keepers for the same, and the people took the custom of circumambulating the Rock, even as they had paced round the Ka'abah, and the usage continued thus all the days of the dynasty of the Omayyads." [Quoted by K. A. C. Creswell, *Early Modern Architecture: Umayyads A.D. 622-750* (Oxford, 1969), I, p. 66.]

Like his predecessors, Abd-el-Melik believed that his family had a right to the Caliphate. He presumably believed that he himself had a special right to it since on a coin of pre-Arabization period he calls himself: "Abd-el-Melik, the Caliph of Allah" whereas all other Caliphs would call themselves the "Caliph of Allah's Prophet Mohammad."

Abd-el-Melik was evidently a most independent Caliph, and his idea of independence went beyond protecting the Caliphate from internal rebels and external enemies (Byzantium). His conviction was that economy formed a strong foundation for the Caliphate whose borders were rapidly expanding with the conquests of new lands in Asia and Africa. Standardization of the monetary system was obviously needed. This naturally brought with it a change in the ratio between silver and gold.

Del Mar's failure to grasp the complex history of the Caliphate makes him puzzled as to "the reasons for establishing this peculiar ratio" between silver and gold [p. 135]. He overlooks the fact that Abd-el-Melik's reform of the monetary system was intended to enforce the integration of the spiritual and temporal spheres in Islam, and he took as the basis for his reform the intricate system of economy which had existed since Mohammad. It is well-known that *Shari'a* in Islam (jurisprudence) has an elaborate system of taxation (to use a tentative modern term). For example, the ratio of one to ten goes back to the time of Mohammad. Neither Del Mar nor Pound is right about Abd-el-Melik going decimal on his own. So Abd-el-Melik's reform was not arbitrary, and it was genuinely aiming at conformity and consistency which the Caliph believed would lead to equality.

Del Mar would have been less puzzled had he been aware of the state of the dirham at the time of the reform. For some time the dirham had been in circulation, "silver being in the hands of people," and with very little control. Unlike the Byzantine, the Sassanian State had ceased to exist at the Moslem conquest, and the Moslems were therefore less worried about the dirham than the dinar. This state of affairs had allowed the dirham to be debased. Abd-el-Melik's leader, Hajjaj, collected all minting experts in Iraq and kept them under close supervision to ensure that they worked with maximum honesty. In these circumstances it was natural to have a new ratio for the new dirham.

However, it is surprising that Del Mar seems to underestimate the economic element as a reason for "the peculiar ratio," and this is apparent in the reduction in the weight of the dinar and the dirham. The Byzantine solido weighed 4.50 gr. and Abd-el-Melik reduced it to 4.25. Similarly the dirham was reduced from 3.98 to

2.98 gr. This obviously meant a loss to the Byzantine State and a gain to Abd-el-Melik's Caliphate, especially since the Moslem treasury had more gold with which to mint dinars than did the Byzantines.[10]

The main reason behind the discrepency in the new weights of the dirham and the dinar is explained by the fact that the Moslem treasury had a surplus of gold which was increasing with the conquest. However, dirhams were in greater demand because commerce was expanding. Something like inflation happened, and the merchants expressed their dissatisfaction by calling Abd-el-Melik's coinage *makrouhah* (loathsome) exploiting the *faqihs'* objection to the new coins which, as already mentioned, was based on the belief coins with the names of Allah and Mohammad should not be handled by people who were not virtually purified.

As for the ratio itself Del Mar creates a confusion [pp. 142-143] which Pound carries into Canto 97. The ratio of six and a half to one is wrong, and positively not the ratio of silver and gold in Abd-el-Melik's currency. The only justification for its presence in Del Mar is a weight ratio with reference to the dang, a persian weight equal to about one sixth of the dirham and one sixth of the dinar.[11] Most probably Del Mar picked up the ratio and lost the reference.

The other ratio mentioned by Del Mar [p. 141] and adopted by Pound is the 12 to 1 of Shafy and Hanbal, the two famous *faqihs*. There is a factual mistake here. Shafy and Hanbal lived in the Abbaside era after Abd-el-Melik's time. The reference is, therefore, superfluous, if not altogether irrelevant. The ratio, as it stands, makes Pound associate it with the similar ratio of the Byzantines, the "Roman Christers," so that he can end up with a witty observation about Abd-el-Melik's "devlish ingenuity" in going decimal. Pound, of course, implies that Abd-el-Melik rejected both the Byzantine ratio and the ratio inherited from the time of Mohammad. While it is true of the former, it cannot possibly be so for the latter.

Another of Del Mar's mistakes, borrowed by Pound, is in taking the sword as a symbol [p. 134]. This, for example, led a Poundian to believe that "Pound's wit, or perhaps Abd-el-Melik's, lies in suggesting that the fine metal content of the coin was at least as serviceable as was the sword in the Mohammadan expansion."[12]

---

10. It may be worth remembering here that Byzantines had to donate a lot of gold to the churches.
11. The *dang* is one *mithqal*. For details, see Walther Hinz, *Islamische Masse und Gewichte* (Leiden, 1970), translated into Arabic by Kimil J. Asali (Amman, 1974).
12. *New Approaches to Pound, op. cit.*, p. 245.

Such a suggestion has no basis in fact. It is a common misconception among Western historians that the sword was a kind of symbol for the war of expansion or part of a coat of arms for Moslems. The sword was never used as a symbol for Moslems, but the closest thing to it is the Prophet's spear, called *harbat rasoul Allah*, the spear of God's messenger (Prophet Mohammad). It was carried by the leader of the army in the front line of the battle. We know that it was lost in the early Umayyad period and recovered in the Abbaside era.

A similar error is Del Mar's quotation, "'I have left to Irak its dinar and to Syria its dirhem,'" on which he comments that this saying "is a boast ascribed to Mohammet, and which, whether true or false, and whether uttered by Mohammet or somebody else of the same era, implies control of the coinage from some centre of administration, either religious or civil" [p. 146]. The main factual mistake here is the placing of the dinar and the dirham in the wrong countries. Iraq always had its dirham in the same way Syria had its dinar. The quotation must have been wrong in the first place. It is presumably taken from a *hadith* (saying) of the Prophet which runs as follows: "One day Irak will have her dirham and *gafeez* abolished, and *al-Sham* (Syria) will have equally her *mudyah* and diner abolished, too."[13]

The saying is a description by the Prophet of the chaos which would one day befall the world. Irak would then have no such regulating aspects of civilization as its dirham and *gafeez* (the measure of weight used in Irak). For the same reason Syria would not have her dinar and her *mudyah* (the measure of weight used in Syria). Had Pound been aware of the original implication, his reference "one fifth to God" which follows the quotation in the text of the canto would have been very witty. In any case it is an undisputed fact that Iraq used the dirham and not the dinar. Pound as well as Del Mar could have avoided this error by making a useful connection between Bassora in Iraq and the dirham which was struck in A.H. 40.

Despite all this misrepresentation by Del Mar, we read Pound's chronicle of Abd-el-Melik with joy in its poetry of wit and rhythm. Fortunately Abd-el-Melik's personality provides a source of attraction and admiration for historians, and Del Mar's history captures the spirit of the Caliph in a way which makes us, as well as Pound, appreciate his efforts in recording the general picture,

---

13. We do not know why Pound quoted only half of the saying. I am grateful to Professor Abdul-Aziz Al-Douri, Professor of Islamic History at the University of Jordan, for enlightening me on this point. His book, *The Economic History of Iraq in the Fourth Century A.H.* (Beirut, 1974) is a valuable reference on the subject.

regardless of the errors of fact. Besides, Pound's ideogrammic method, of which Hugh Kenner frequently reminds us, creates a counter effect making distortions of historical fact acceptable.

BURTON HATLEN

EZRA POUND AND FASCISM

To what extent did Pound commit himself during the 1930s not only to Mussolini as a leader but also to fascism as an ideology? And to what extent do the cantos which he wrote during this period serve as a vehicle for such an ideology? Students of Pound's work have, for the most part, edged nervously around these questions, fearful that the "fascist" label will simply serve to confirm an already widespread prejudice against his poetry, but unable nonetheless to deny his political loyalties. Yet the statement "Ezra Pound was a fascist" seems to me indisputably true, and if I am right then we must begin to confront the meaning of this fact. To do so we must first get straight in our minds the nature of fascism itself, and to this end I want here to advance, first, the proposition that we will seriously misunderstand fascism if we insist on seeing it as simply a "right-wing" political movement. For fascism, I shall here argue, blended an authoritarianism usually associated with the "right" and a "populism" usually characteristic of the "left" into a volatile and ultimately disastrous political mix. In Pound's writings of the 1930s, I shall then proceed to show, we find an analogous interplay of elitist and populist motifs, and to this extent the label "fascist" accurately describes Pound's political position. Yet in the course of the essay my emphasis will gradually shift from political to poetic questions. For while I would be willing to call Pound a fascist, I do not believe that *The Cantos* can accurately be labelled a "fascist poem," simply because Pound's political ideology undergoes a radical decomposition—or, if you like, a deconstruction—as it is transmuted by Pound's ideogrammic method; and to trace this movement from ideology to ideogram will be my ultimate purpose in this essay.

I

All modern political ideologies can best be understood, I believe, as divergent responses to a complex pattern of social and cultural changes that have occurred first in Europe and then gradually throughout the rest of the world during the last three centuries. In these centuries an expanding market economy has transformed a once reasonably homogenous peasantry into an industrial working class. At the same time, economic power has gradually shifted from large landholders to a group of commercial and industrial entrepreneurs to, most recently, a "new class" of professional managers who move freely back and forth among the financial, commercial, industrial, governmental, military, charitable, educational, and media bureaucracies that rule modern societies. These social changes have been accomplished, furthermore, by a decay of traditional religious institutions which have, in all cultures, gradually lost the ability to maintain a general consensus as to the ultimate purpose of human life and the rules that ought to govern human conduct. Faced by this complex pattern of social and cultural changes which I will now, for convenience, label "modernization" we may decide simply to accept all these changes as good, or at least inevitable. I shall call this viewpoint "liberalism." In the 19th century a group of theorists who called themselves "liberals" (Ricardo, the Utilitarians, Spencer) argued that any attempt to restrict the operation of the "free" market or to meliorate the radical transformations which the operation of this market were then (and are now) bringing about in human social life would be as foolish (and as wicked) as trying to repeal the laws of gravity. In our own century this same position has been ably defended by, for example, Milton Friedman—who also, accurately, calls himself a liberal.[1] Alongside such economic liberals, we also find in the last one hundred years a group which we can call the "cultural liberals": theorists who have vigorously argued for the principle of personal self-gratification as the only legitimate rule of human conduct. And this type of liberalism too has been, I would argue (although neither the "right" nor the "left" currently wants to admit the connection), spawned by the expansion of a market economy which offers us an apparently infinite supply of commodities with which to gratify our seemingly insatiable appetites.

Yet the "modernization" celebrated in different ways both by the economic and by the cultural liberals has deeply disrupted

---
1. Milton Friedman, *Capitalism and Freedom* (Chicago, 1962), p. 5.

traditional social bonds, and because of these disruptions the liberal position has been, in the political discourse of the last one hundred years, challenged both from the "left" and from the "right." Indeed it is here, at the point where people recoil from the "modern" with the conviction that "something has gone wrong," that almost all political ideologies of our time—the major exception is, of course, liberalism itself—have been born. In particular, the two most intellectually compelling (in Europe and America at least) of these political ideologies, a principled conservatism that descends from Burke and a revolutionary socialism that derives largely from Marx, originate in a sense that unrestrained modernization threatens to destroy certain bonds of community which alone give meaning to human life. My suggestion that conservatism and socialism emerge from a common matrix would (does) scandalize many adherents of these two movements. Yet conservatives like Burke and Henry Adams and socialists like Robert Owen, Marx, and R. H. Tawney share a common revulsion against the "liberal" vision of a world in which all sense of obligation to others has been replaced by a solitary ethical principle: the duty to—as the title of a book recently very popular in the United States phrases it—"look out for number one." Conversely, both Burkean conservatism and Marxian socialiam give voice to a hunger for the "beloved community," a community founded on mutual trust rather than mutual exploitation, the kind of community which the liberal celebration of the autonomous individual has eroded.

But if conservatism and revolutionary socialism are born out of a common matrix, the two movements have differed with respect to the *kind* of community they have aspired to create (or re-create). Conservatives since Burke have contended that the "beloved community" can be founded only upon legitimate *authority*, while revolutionaries since Godwin and Paine—and certainly since Marx—have instead aspired to create a community of *equals*. Thus despite their roots in a common rejection of liberalism, conservatism and socialism have in our time seen themselves as bitter enemies, and the political discourse of the last one hundred years has been largely dominated by the debate—sometimes a bitter quarrel—between conservatives appalled at the iniquity of anyone rash enough to question the intrinsic authority of kings, bishops, graduates of Oxford, and members of the Adams family, and a "left" which has as often as not reciprocated in kind, by identifying as the enemy such relatively incidental symbols of authority as the policeman on the corner or the teacher who claims to know something that his/her students don't know.

Despite the common origin of conservatism and socialism in a revulsion against the brave new world of liberalism, this quarrel between the two movements over the relative importance of authority and equality has impelled them in divergent directions. By the beginning of World War I, and to a large extent ever since, great conservative and socialist political parties, inspired respectively by a craving for legitimate authority and by a vision of the co-operative commonwealth, confronted each other in most European countries. Yet beneath the apparent conflicts between these parties moved a common revulsion at the social and cultural consequences of the free market, and a common rejection of the philosophic principles of liberalism; and in the political chaos of the post-war years a new political plant would sprout from the anti-liberalism shared by conservatives and socialists, a movement which would claim to be at once "conservative" and "socialist," a movement called fascism.

World War I abruptly and permanently changed the rules of the political game throughout Europe, for the war undermined both the conservative regimes that had led the nations of Europe into the war and the socialist parties which had, for the most part, acquiesced in the bloodbath. The discrediting both of the traditional right and the traditional left created an opening for a nascent fascism which claimed to fulfill both the aspiration of the "left" for an egalitarian community and the demand of the "right" for order and authority. In the trenches a new community at once egalitarian (insofar as all men became brothers in the face of death) and hierarchial (insofar as military discipline demanded absolute submission of each soldier to the will of his commanding officer) came into being, as again and again men proved themselves willing to sacrifice life itself for a "higher" cause. Was this new community of the trenches deeply atavistic, or genuinely revolutionary? Or was it perhaps—as some theorists, including a young former socialist named Benito Mussolini, concluded—at once atavistic *and* revolutionary? In any case, as a widely quoted statement by Mussolini attests, fascism sought to preserve some of the qualities of the community of the trenches in a political movement at once "conservative" and "revolutionary":

> We Fascists have had the courage to discard all traditional political theories, and we are aristocrats and democrats, revolutionaries and reactionaries, proletarians and anti-proletarians, pacifists and anti-pacifists. It is sufficient to have a single fixed point: the nation.[2]

---

2. Quoted from Franz Neumann, *Behemoth* (New York, 1942), pp. 462-463.

So too, the very name of Hitler's party (the National Socialist German Worker's Party) suggests a fusion of "right"-wing nationalism with "left"-wing socialism into a new amalgam. The question of whether or not fascism actually was in any true sense a "socialist" movement has, of course, been the subject of much debate, but I shall not here attempt to enter this debate.[3] Rather I shall simply note that fascism, whatever it did or did not do in practice, sought to—and in considerable measure *did*—satisfy for many Italians and Germans the "socialist" need for a sense of solidarity with loyal comrades.[4] Yet at the same time fascism also tried to satisfy the "conservative" demand for "order"—which meant, in practice, the preservation of existing social inequalities. In this way fascism attempted to tap a revulsion against the liberal state shared by the "left" and by the "right," in order to build a new kind of political movement that would unite the working class and the bourgeoisie in a common task, the creation of a social order neither "capitalist" nor "socialist" but simply "Italian," or "German," or. . . .

Yet if fascism began in a deliberate attempt to blend a "left"-wing egalitarianism with a "right"-wing authoritarianism, this political movement inevitably ended by giving a new meaning to such concepts as "community" and "authority." Fascism sought a principle of community that could serve as an alternative to the international working class community (a community, it should be noted, that defines itself in its struggle *against* the bourgeoisie) envisioned by socialism; and as my quotation from Mussolini suggests, fascism found such an alternative principle in the *nation*, as it defines itself in its struggle against *national* enemies. Yet the "*volk*" like the "proletariat" remains an abstract concept: no one can *see* "Italy" or "Germany." Therefore fascism created a concrete embodiment of the *nation* in the *person* of an all-wise leader ("Mussolini is always right," said a sign on the wall of every Italian classroom) and in the organizational *structure* of an all-powerful party. Fascism, remembering with acute nostalgia the ecstatic self-surrender of life in the trenches, celebrated the power of the leader and the submission of the loyal party member to the leader's will as ends in themselves. Yet while this pronounced authoritarian strain may seem to mark fascism as a "right"-wing

---

3. Neumann and other theorists of the Frankfurt School tend to see fascism as issuing from a confluence of conservative political impulses and the exigencies of a capitalist economy in crisis. On the other hand, George Mosse, in *The Crisis of German Ideology* (New York, 1964), pp. 286 ff., argues that at least in its early stages the Nazi movement included a genuinely socialist thrust, represented in particular by the Strasser brothers.
4. See, for example, Milton Mayer's remarkable *They Thought They Were Free: The Germans, 1933-45* (Chicago, 1955).

political phenomenon, it seems to me important to distinguish between fascist authoritarianism and genuine conservatism. For neither Mussolini nor Hitler claimed power on the strength either of a divine right to rule (as kings have been wont to do) or an an inherent superiority in their "blood" (as hereditary oligarchies generally do). Rather both fascist leaders presented themselves as "men of the people." Thus the *person* of the leader becomes, in fascism, a concrete resolution of the opposing aspirations within the movement: he is at once the "great commoner," the "divine average" *and* the "man apart"; a lonely, heroic incarnation of pure will. In this respect Mussolini's description of fascism as "democratic authoritarianism" seems, if apparently paradoxical, nevertheless accurate. For in blending a "socialist" egalitarianism with a "conservative" authoritarianism, fascism became a new kind of political movement that was neither truly "socialist" nor truly "conservative," neither a "left"- nor a "right"-wing movement, but rather something unique, dazzling—and (in the end) frantically self-destructive.

Fascism's attempt to reunite the socialist and the conservative strains in Western political thought may seem, on the face of it, a laudable enterprise. Yet fascism, born in such promise, ended by declaring universal war on everything that was not itself: first bolshevism, then socialism, then the Jews, then the "decadent" liberal democracies. And as fascism gradually united all the world against itself, it ensured its own destruction. A celebration of the nation as a transcendental principle of unity, a mythology and a political structure that claims to reconcile a quasi-conservative cult of authority with a quasi-socialist cult of "the people"—is there something inherently self-destructive in this mix of political ideas? Not, I think, until we add another crucial ingredient in the fascist brew: a demonized ENEMY. Yet we should make no mistake on this point: without an enemy to whom it could ascribe both superhuman powers and a mindless determination to destroy everything good and beautiful, fascism itself would have dissolved back into its constituent elements. For fascism could not do what it promised to do: above all, it could not resolve the struggle between capital and labor, managerial elites and wage-slaves. Instead it frosted over this conflict with a thick coat of rhetoric, thus introducing into fascism a split between political symbol and social reality that poisoned intellectual life in Italy and Germany throughout the fascist epoch. Refusing to recognize the inevitability of internal struggles within the nation, fascism sought to redirect the energy that might otherwise have gone into the capital/labor struggle toward real or imagined enemies of the nation. For if there are no fundamental conflicts within the nation, how was fascism to explain such undeniable social ills of the epoch as mass unemployment, bankruptcies of small businesses, inflation, etc.? Having ruled out the possibility that these economic ills might result from the structure of the national economy, fascism had no alternative but to blame these problems on something *outside* the nation—other nations which have denied "us" our rightful *lebensraum*—or on enemies who have infiltrated the body politic, to destroy its purity.

Thus fascism finds its logical fulfillment in a militarism directed against the enemy without and an anti-semitism which seeks to destroy the enemy within. As fascism summoned Italians and Germans to arm themselves in order to seize or to defend what was "rightfully" theirs, militarism and a cult of violence became not an accidental but an essential component of this movement. In Mussolini's words:

> Fascism . . . believes neither in the possibility nor the utility of perpetual peace. It thus repudiates the doctrine of Pacifism—born of a renunciation of the struggle and an act of cowardice in the face of sacrifice. War alone brings up to its highest tension all human energy and puts the stamp of nobility upon the peoples who have the courage to meet it.[5]

Once in power, both Mussolini and Hitler immediately began a rapid expansion of their nations' military forces, and both rulers demanded the "right" to use these forces to conquer colonial empires—Mussolini in Africa and Hitler in the Slavic regions east of Germany. And just as fascism sought every possible opening that might serve as a pretext for an attack on the "enemy without," it also sought throughout its history to mobilize "our" forces against the "enemy within" which Fascism everywhere identified as "the Jew." If the "nation"—a community, depending on circumstances, of culture, race, and/or religion—is the supreme reality, then the Jew is almost always sooner or later defined as the alien presence within the nation, the "race" without a homeland in a world where, fascism assumes, only rootedness in a homeland can give substance to our lives.[6] Thus if aggressive war became the logical external culmination of fascism, Auschwitz became the logical internal culmination of this movement: a systematic use of the organized state apparatus to "purge" the nation—and eventually the world—of Jews, to render the body

---

5. Benito Mussolini, "The Political and Social Doctrine of Fascism," in *Fascism: An Anthology*, ed. Nathaniel Greene (New York, 1968), p. 41.
6. For a full discussion of fascism's search for "roots" and its attendant hostility to Jews, see especially Mosse, *op. cit.*, pp. 13-145.

politic "pure" once again. It was the discovery of a common *enemy* that, ultimately, drew the German *volk* together in that experience of brotherhood which they craved; it was the common determination to eradicate "Jewishness," rather than the irresistible will of the Führer, that impelled Germany forward toward the conquest of Europe; it was the trench heaped with naked corpses, the polished boots and the clean gloves of the SS officer staring down with cool contempt at the dead, that became for almost all of us the ultimate symbols of fascism. (And as for Mussolini, his version of fascism has become in the public mind only a more feeble—therefore a less demonic, but therefore also in the end a merely grotesque—imitation of Hitler's.) From an attempt to recover authentic community and legitimate authority to the cooly mechanized mass murder of Auschwitz and Babi Yar: so moves, in brief, the inexorable, terrible dialectic of fascism.[7]

II

Pound received much of his political education—perhaps the most useful part of it—in the editorial offices of the *New Age*. Only one common commitment seems to have united the *New Age* group: all its members detested what they liked to call the "bourgeoisie," and what I have earlier described as the "liberal" view of society. Some of the contributors to the *New Age* criticized modern society from the "right": Belloc and Chesterton, for example. Other *New Age* contributors, including G. D. H. Cole and E. Belfort Bax, are important figures in the history of British socialism. The editor of the journal, A. R. Orage, combined—until he abandoned politics and philosophy for Ouspensky—a devotion to socialism with an admiration for Nietzsche, a writer whose concept of the heroic individual seems wholly antithetical to socialism. The tension between his socialism and his Nietzschianism impelled Orage away from the central tradition of socialism first toward syndicalism and then onward to a distinctive (and, to some post-Gulag socialists, very attractive) political movement that called itself Guild Socialism, which sought to adapt the medieval concept of the craft guild to modern conditions of production. In effect, Guild Socialiam sought to go *forward* beyond capitalism by going *back* to a form of ownership that antedates modern

---
7. My discussion of fascism draws throughout on three classic studies: Mosse, as cited above; Ernst Nolte, *Three Faces of Fascism*, trans. Leila Vennewitz (New York, 1966); and Eugen Weber, *Varieties of Fascism* (Princeton, N.J., 1964). Weber in particular develops an interpretation of fascism that is quite similar to mine.

capitalism. To Guild Socialism, only a collective ownership of the means of production could end both the tyranny of capital over workers and the war of each against all which liberalism sees as the "normal" condition of social life; in these respects even Marx would have been willing to grant the title "socialist" to this movement. Yet at the same time Guild Socialism attempted to avoid those new forms of slavery against which Belloc had warned in *The Servile State* by refusing (against the Fabians) to admit the need for centralized controls over the means of production: instead each "guild" would direct its own affairs. In this respect, Guild Socialism anticipated certain contemporary theories of "worker's control" as well as that emphasis on decentralization which we see, for example, in E. F. Schumacher's "small is beautiful" movement. Thus the Guild Socialist movement refuses to allow itself to be categorized as "conservative" or "radical," "left"- or "right"-wing; and it seems to me significant that some members of the Guild Socialist movement (Cole, Hobson, Tawney) eventually gravitated toward the socialism of the British Labor Party, while others (Penty, the founder and the principal theorist of the movement, de Maeztu, Pound's friend Odon Por) ended as apologists for fascism. Furthermore, to know that during Pound's London years—the years of his youth, the years to which he looks back with such poignancy in the *Pisan Cantos*—the ideals of Guild Socialism dominated political discussion in many of the cafés, drawing rooms, and editorial offices through which he moved can tell us, I believe, something important about the meaning of the commitment to fascism which he would make fifteen years later, after Guild Socialism, like so much else, died in the aftermath of the war.[8]

Pound always insisted that he had never been a Guild Socialist. Nevertheless, when he announced his conversion to fascism in *Jefferson and/or Mussolini*, the political stance which he then adopted claims to reconcile the "left" and the "right" in a manner reminiscent of Guild Socialism.[9] In *Jefferson and/or Mussolini*, Pound consistently sees Mussolini as a man of the "left." Pound quotes with apparent approval a cabinet minister who, alluding

---

[8]. For a succinct history of the role which Orage and the *New Age* played in the development of Guild Socialism, see John Finlay, *Social Credit: The English Origins* (Montreal, 1972), especially pp. 61-84. S. T. Glass, *The Responsible Society: The Ideas of Guild Socialism* (London, 1966) offers a brief account of the Guild Socialist movement.
[9]. In his obituary for Orage, reprinted in *Selected Prose, 1909-1965*, ed. William Cookson (New York, 1973), p. 437, Pound says that "the earlier Guild Socialism . . . had lain outside my view." I am not therefore here implying that at any time Pound "was" a Guild Socialist. But I am arguing that the environment in which he first became interested in economic and political issues was permeated by Guild Socialist ideas. For *Jefferson and/or Mussolini*, I have used the original Stanley Nott edition of 1935. References to this book will be incorporated into my text.

to Mussolini's socialist youth, said of Il Duce, "Once of the left, always left" [p. 28]. And throughout the book Pound describes Mussolini as a "revolutionary"—as, in fact, the prophet of the "continuing revolution." Repeatedly Pound links Mussolini and Lenin as the *two* great modern revolutionaries; and if he prefers the Italian revolution to the Russian, it is less for ideological reasons than because the Italian revolution is more "interesting" [p. 22], and because Pound prefers Italy itself to Russia. Furthermore, Mussolini's economic policies, as described by Pound, seem at least quasi-socialist. These policies rest, says Pound, on three basic principles, the first and the third of which any socialist might assent to:

> I. When enough exists, means should be found to distribute it to the people who need it.
> II. It is the business of the nation to see that its own citizens get their share before worrying about the rest of the world.
> III. When *potential* production (possible production) of anything is sufficient to meet everyone's needs it is the business of the government to see that *both* production *and* distribution are achieved [p. 69].

Here, if you wish, are the fundamental principles of a true "national socialism."

In *Jefferson and/or Mussolini*, however, Pound's "socialist" demand for economic justice is coupled with a distinctly non-socialist call for the preservation of the cultural heritage:

> The fascist revolution was *FOR* the preservation of certain liberties and FOR the maintenance of a certain level of culture, certain standards of living, it was NOT a refusal to come down to a level of riches or poverty, but a refusal to surrender a great slice of the cultural heritage [p. 127].

Here Pound implies a rejection of socialist egalitarianism, in favor of a hierarchical model of society. For to Pound, there is no conflict between a "socialist" demand for an economy directed toward the satisfaction of human needs rather than the accumulation of profits and a "conservative" desire to preserve the "cultural heritage" (which means, among other things, the preservation of existing social inequalities) because *both* these potentially divergent aspirations incarnate themselves in the person of Il Duce himself. Mussolini can play this role, Pound implies, because he is, not an effete aristocrat or a money-loving bourgeois, but a robust, earthy *man of the people*, the

> ... son of a blacksmith, a chap who had edited a terrible left-wing paper, a fellow who had worked eleven hours a day in Lausanne for thirty-two centesimi the hour (pre-War, when 32 centesimi were worth six and a fraction cents) [p. 56].

Yet Mussolini is also for Pound a "man apart," a "genius" [p. 92] capable of going "straight to the center" [p. 66], an artist, a man whose heroic *will* gives him both the right and the power to reshape the inchoate mass of Italy into a thing of beauty. This image of Mussolini, uniting populist and elitist ways of thinking in a distinctive (even perverse) mixture, reveals the poet to be moving beyond the mild Ruskinism of the Guild Socialists, into territories that are specifically fascist. Yet I should at once add that the fascism of *Jefferson and/or Mussolini* remains both temperate and good-tempered. There is no hint of anti-semitism in this book, and no celebration of war as the highest fulfillment of human potentiality. Rather we find here what might be called "fascism with a human face." But, alas, Hitler was already waiting in the wings, and soon enough the human face would give way to a demonic leer.

If Pound's politics *circa* 1933 reflect the relatively positive aspirations of "early" fascism, his political development from 1933 to 1940 parallels the inexorable movement of fascism itself toward nihilism. For in Pound's political thought as in the fascist movement as a whole, the search for a society that would respect both the European cultural heritage and the aspirations of workers and peasants for economic justice gradually gave way to an obsession with the ENEMY: a group of "obstructers" who have, Pound persuaded himself, deliberately and persistently thwarted the attempts of decent people to create a just and orderly *polis*. Furthermore, Pound increasingly tended to identify the "obstructers," the "hoggers of the harvest," as Jews, so that by 1940 the terms "usury" and "kikery" had become, for him, synonymous. To some extent Pound's movement toward a doctrinaire anti-semitism may represent a desire to keep up with his beloved *Duce*. During the 1930s Mussolini fell more and more under the sway of Hitler, whom he had once regarded with contempt. As a consequence, official propaganda in Italy as well as in Germany increasingly described the Jews as the power behind both Boshevism and what Hitler called "finanzcapital," and a survey of Pound's political writings in the last half of the 1930s suggests that he dutifully followed this shift in the fascist party line.[10] Consider the following dates:

> 1933-4: Hitler comes to power in Germany. Mussolini is at first deeply suspicious of this new brand of "fascism." In mid-1934

---

10. My principal course of information on Mussolini's shifting political line has been Ivone Kilpatrick, *Mussolini: A Study in Power* (New York, 1964). For a valuable study of Mussolini's policy toward Jews, see Meir Michaelis, *Mussolini and the Jews* (London and Oxford, 1978).

Italy and Germany come to the verge of war over Austria. Pound, writing *Jefferson and/or Mussolini* in 1933, refers contemptuously to Hitler's "hysterical... yawping" [p. 127].

1935-7: Mussolini and Hitler move steadily toward an alliance, culminating in the Anti-Comintern Pact of 1937. Mussolini increasingly discards the "revolutionary" rhetoric which he had employed as late as the early 1930s. Instead he tends to portray himself as the defender of "Catholic Christian culture" against the destructive threat of "atheistic" or "Jewish" (in fascist rhetoric these terms tend to become interchangeable) bolshevism. He sends armies into Spain and Ethiopia, under the banner of "Catholic Christian culture." In 1937 Pound writes the *Guide to Kulchur*.[11] The positive treatment of Lenin in *Jefferson and/or Mussolini* now gives way to denunciations of "Marxism" as false in theory and destructive in practice [p. 277]. The self-proclaimed worshipper of Venus who had once condemned Christianity itself as a hypocritical fraud now extolls the virtues of "Catholic culture" [p. 26]. (Yet neither Pound nor Mussolini have become "believers." Rather they see Catholicism as a picturesque part of the Italian cultural tradition, and as a useful way of training peasants in habits of obedience.) To his praise of Catholicism, Pound subjoins an attack on Protestantism and on "semitic" ways of thinking [p. 185]. If the *Guide to Kulchur* never explicitly praises war as the health of the state, at least the book ostentatiously ignores Mussolini's invasion of Ethiopia and his increasingly aggressive posture toward Italy's European neighbors.

1938: Mussolini's government adopts a comprehensive set of racial laws, modeled on—if in some minor respects weaker than—the Nuremberg laws, and designed to exclude Jews from participation in any area of Italian life. In 1939, according to Noel Stock, Pound's "attitude towards the Jews" suddenly takes "a turn for the worse," as he begins to display "an unhealthy interest in Jewish participation in any activity whatsoever," and as he spends more and more time reading anti-Jewish tracts and articles of a type which previously he "had barely or never opened."[12]

1940: Mussolini somewhat reluctantly joins Germany in declaring war against Great Britain and France, then a little later the Soviet Union, and then a little later still the United States. In 1941 Pound begins a series of broadcasts over Rome radio in which he acclaims Hitler and Mussolini as defenders of "Europe" against a gigantic Jewish conspiracy and vigorously defends the right of Germany and Italy to conquer and rule over the "inferior" peoples of eastern Europe, Asia, and Africa.[13]

---

11. Ezra Pound, *Guide to Kulchur* (New York, 1970). All references to this volume will be incorporated into my text.
12. Noel Stock, *The Life of Ezra Pound* (New York, 1970), pp. 478-479.
13. See *Ezra Pound Speaking*, ed. Leonard Doob (Westport, Conn., 1978).

As we read through Pound's political pronouncements from *Jefferson and/or Mussolini* through the Rome radio broadcasts, we encounter almost all the major themes of fascist ideology: 1) a generalized unhappiness over the destruction of the social bonds that traditionally joined men and women together and joined both to the soil; 2) a vigorous protest against the inability of the Western nations to end unemployment and make full use of their productive capabilities; 3) a rejection of the Marxist theory that economic distress results from the attempt of capital to preserve its control over labor, and of the Marxist belief that only in a classless society will poverty and unemployment disappear; 4) an attempt to find in the nation-state an alternative to the socialist concept of the working class, as a model of an organic community; 5) support for the use of the full power of the state to stimulate economic development, to end unemployment, and to ensure that the basic needs of people for food, shelter, and clothing are satisfied; 6) a cult of the Great Leader who incarnates the nation and whose indomitable will carries the nation forward toward its destiny; 7) an obsession with the external enemy which denies the nation its "rightful" *lebensraum*, and with the internal "enemy" (i.e., the Jew) who "saps" the nation's strength from within; 8) a celebration of violence as the only effective way of defeating the enemy, and an elaborate ritual of "symbolic violence" centered on the army, the police, and paramilitary party organizations.

Not all these themes are equally important in Pound's political thinking. For example, as an *American* pro-fascist living in *Italy*, he inevitably had a somewhat equivocal relationship to Italian nationalism. Furthermore, the concern for community appears in Pound's writing (but this too is characteristic of fascism) less as an overt celebration of positive forms of community than as a pervasive rage (fascism *is* "the politics of *ressentiment*") against the "usurers" and the "hoggers of the harvest" who have, in the mythology of fascism, "destroyed" an organic way of life that "we" once enjoyed. And rather than celebrating the use of force against "alien" elements within the nation or external "enemies" Pound merely refrains from condemning the brutal tactics which the *squadristi* employed during Mussolini's rise to power, or Mussolini's invasion of Ethiopia, or Hitler's attacks on Poland and Norway, etc. Yet with these relatively minor variations, Pound's political thinking falls into a distinctively fascist pattern. More important, his political thinking also traces through to the end the terrible dialectic of fascism, as it moves from an attempt to create/recover an experience of community to an all-consuming, paranoid fascination with the ENEMY. Once born out of the cauldron of the war, *this* narrow, bitter political persona survived to haunt Pound for another twenty years, making occasional cameo appearances in the later cantos (for example, the evocation of Hitler in Canto 90, and the italicized tirade against the "kikery" of Marx and Freud in Canto 91), until in his last years he finally laid this ghost to rest, in his brief, magnificent statement to Allen Ginsberg: "But the worst mistake I made was that stupid, suburban prejudice of anti-Semitism. All along, that spoiled everything."[14]

III

If Pound's political development carried him inexorably toward a position that is both morally repugnant (*nothing* can excuse the abuse of "kikes" in the Rome radio broadcasts) and sadly futile (for with the defeat of Hitler and Mussolini Pound's fascism became nothing more than a politics of nostalgia), there seem to me some good reasons for trying to *reverse* the process that led Pound to this position—i.e., to work back through the evolution of his political ideas, in the attempt to uncover their gristly roots. For Pound's political commitments *per se* have at this point in history only a biographical and historical interest. Our real concern today is Pound's poetry, which remains alive for us even though fascism has ceased to be a live political option. And as we turn from Pound's political ideology to his poetry, it seems to me important to state at once that, however "closed" and regressive the political system to which Pound committed himself, *The Cantos* remains an "open" text. Pound's mind drove constantly toward closure. What Gertrude Stein called the "village explainer" in Pound was (let us admit it!) always an ideologue: he wanted an Answer, and if at all possible a simple one, something that any man could get in "one day's reading."[15] But Pound's poem retains as much of that quality which Keats called "negative capability"—the capacity to "remain in doubt, without any irritable straining after fact or reason"—as any text in our language. (And, yes, I think Keats was wrong in seeing negative capability as a quality of certain poets; rather it is a quality which we find in texts as various as *Paradise Lost* and *The Cantos*,

---
14. Quoted from C. David Heymann, *Ezra Pound: The Last Rower, a Political Profile* (New York, 1976), p. 298.
15. *The Cantos of Ezra Pound* (New York, 1970), p. 427. Hereafter all references to *The Cantos* will be incorporated into my text. All references will be to the 1970 New Directions edition.

both written by fiercely dogmatic men.) In *The Cantos* Pound's "open" poetic method tends to dissolve fascism, itself an amalgam of disparate political tendencies, back into its constituent parts. *The Cantos* may set out to affirm fascism, but in fact the poem "deconstructs" fascist ideology; and this is, I here shall propose, a principal reason why the poem still lives.

To understand how *The Cantos* "deconstructs" fascism, we need to pause for a moment over Pound's ideogrammic method. As everyone knows, early in his poetic career Pound discovered, with some help from Ernest Fenollosa, that the relationship between the general and the particular (or, shall we say, between the idea and the object, or even between what I am here calling "ideology"—i.e., an organized system of assumptions and explanations—and the phenomenal world) is the central problem of modern aesthetics. And in the ideogram (or, in an earlier version, the "luminous detail") Pound thought he had found a new way of bringing these two dimensions of our world together: in the ideogram, concrete particulars could come together to "configure" an idea. In effect, the ideogrammic method rules out any possibility that "meaning" or "truth" might exist *beyond* the particulars, in a Platonic realm of "ideas" toward which the particulars will, analogically, point. Rather the concept can exist only "in" the particulars themselves, and if we remove one particular, the pattern dissolves, and the rest of the particulars become meaningless. In this respect Pound's ideogrammic method flouts the basic principles both of Platonic and of Aristotelian philosophy: no wonder, then, that Santayana could not understand what Pound was talking about, when the poet tried to explain his theories to the philosopher.[16]

Pound himself, I think, was only sporadically aware of the full consequences of his poetic method, for his own comments generally suggest that he saw the ideogram as nothing more than a new way to communicate old ideas. To Pound, the particulars which he had assembled in *The Cantos* fell into clearly visible patterns; these patterns in turn constituted "ideas" about nature, sex, art, the sacred, the *polis*, etc.; and the total design of the poem in turn sought to draw these various ideas together into a unified picture of the world. It should thus follow that the reader who has absorbed the particulars that Pound has assembled in the proper sequence will come to see the world the way Pound sees it. Because Pound thought that something like this should happen to people as they read *The Cantos*, he was wont to display

---

16. Stock, *op. cit.*, pp. 482-483.

a wild rage against the blind fools who could not *see* in the particulars of his poem the patterns that were so obvious to him. For this reason too, when Pound finally realized that reading *The Cantos* did not lead other people to see the world as he saw it, he could only conclude that his life work was a "failure," a mere jumble. *The Cantos* is not, I am convinced, a failure, but I think that it succeeds for reasons suspected neither by Pound himself nor by those among his critics (and in this camp I would include Pearlman on the positive side, and Stock on the negative) who have sought a specious thematic unity in the poem.[17] The poem "succeeds," I would propose, precisely because the gap between Pound's particulars and the general ideas that he intends to communicate to us will *not* close.[18] Pound tries to force his particulars into the service of a set of general ideas, but the particulars refuse to do what he wants them to do; and the miracle of the poem is that Pound's *method* allows each of these particulars to retain its own "luminous" life, even as his *will* is trying to force them into a (specious) pattern. As a consequence *The Cantos* becomes, as Pound himself described it in *Guide to Kulchur*, a "record of struggle": i.e., a record of Pound's ultimately *unsuccessful* struggle to impose a pattern of meaning upon the particulars of his world. Yet the result is not a mere jumble, for the constant struggle between the poet's centripetal will and the centrifugal will of his particulars energizes the poem, giving it the coherence of a sustained *act*, rather than the mechanical unity of more traditional poems that are organized to "communicate" certain "ideas" and "intentions" which exist prior to the text itself.[19]

For a concrete example of the form which this struggle takes, let us consider the relationship among three of the principal protagonists of the poem: Confucius, Jefferson, and Mussolini. For Pound, it is not enough that all three should embody, more or less imperfectly, the Platonic Idea of the Just Ruler. Rather the archetype must be *absolutely* present in each of the three. For Pound, Mussolini is not "like" Jefferson in certain ways (both governed relatively underdeveloped countries which felt themselves to be on the peripheries of power, but which aspired to greatness;

---
17. See Noel Stock, *Reading the Cantos: A Study of Meaning in Ezra Pound* (New York, 1966) and Daniel Pearlman, *The Barb of Time* (New York, 1969).
18. Michael Bernstein, *The Tale of the Tribe: Ezra Pound and the Modern Verse Epic* (Princeton, N.J., 1980), especially pp. 127-161.
19. My discussion of Pound's poetic method is especially indebted to Hugh Kenner, *The Poetry of Ezra Pound* (Milwood, N.J., 1974, a reprint of the original New Directions edition), especially pp. 25-104; to Eva Hesse, "Introduction" to *New Approaches to Ezra Pound* (Berkeley, Calif., 1969), pp. 13-53; and to Christine Brooke-Rose, *A ZBC of Ezra Pound* (Berkeley, Calif., 1971), especially pp. 93-118.

both sought to expand the territorial boundaries of their countries and encourage economic development, especially in agriculture; both wrote voluminously; etc.) and different in certain other ways (Jefferson was more than any other individual responsible for the development of a two-party system in the United States, while Mussolini suppressed all opposition political parties; Jefferson worked for the establishment of constitutional guarantees for civil liberties, while Mussolini suppressed such liberties; Jefferson tried to keep the United States out of war, while Mussolini eagerly sought to involve Italy in war); such "metaphoric" modes of thinking are, as Herbert Schneidau has brilliantly argued, foreign to Pound.[20] Instead if Pound is to bring Jefferson and Mussolini (and Confucius) into relationship at all, he can do so only by simply conflating them, so that they become, in a way that deliberately subverts conventional "reason," *the same person.* The "and/or" in the title of *Jefferson and/or Mussolini* seems to imply that Pound will here talk about similarities *and differences* between the two men. But actually the slash mark serves to disjoin two ways of thinking. "You, the ignorant, can see only the differences between Jefferson and Mussolini. But we, the members of the 'party of intelligence,' can see the similarities between the two." Such is the implicit message of Pound's tract. And such too is the message of the Jefferson and Mussolini sections of *The Cantos.*

On one level, the conflation of Jefferson and Mussolini (or Adams and Confucius) is ludicrously, dangerously misleading: to the end Pound seemed incapable of imagining that Mussolini's real strength as a leader might be conjoined to some disastrous weaknesses. Yet having rejected those metaphoric patterns of similarity-amid-difference, and difference-amid-similarity, which had been the stock-in-trade of European poetry since the Renaissance, what alternatives did Pound have? He could have left his particulars limply floating in a void, as discrete atoms. In fact, hostile readers are likely to assume that this is exactly what he did do. But I think that instead he attempted, through sheer force of will, to conflate his particulars, to fuse (say) Adams and Confucius in the poem in the same way that he tried to fuse Jefferson and Mussolini in the prose tract. Yet the ideogrammic method of the poem allows us, even *invites* us, to drive apart what Pound has joined together, to seek out the differences which his will has attempted to over-ride. Or to put all this a little differently: the

---

20. See Herbert Schneidau, "Pound, Olson, & Objective Verse," *Paideuma,* 5-1, pp. 15-29.

materials we need to understand the relationship between Adams and Mussolini are all there, *in* the poem; for Pound, this evidence "means" only similarit; both men fully body forth the qualities of the Just Ruler. But if *we*, looking at the same evidence, see differences instead, we have not "misread" Pound's poem. For if *The Cantos* stands as the record of Pound's struggle, at the same time the poem demands that we too "struggle"—and our struggle is in essence the mirror image of his: we must struggle to pull apart what he has joined together, to perceive the "differences" that he has denied, in his quest for identities. Pound, that is, wills his particulars into patterns; our "common sense" resists; and thus the conjunctions within the poem belong to Pound, while the disjunctions belong to us. In this way we become truly Pound's collaborators, for only in the spaces *between* his conjunctions does the poem-as-read, which is the only poem we can know or talk about, come into being.

In the remainder of this essay, I shall attempt to substantiate the generalizations I have made up to this point by examining the ways in which Pound's political ideas interweave in one section of *The Cantos*: the forty cantos that he wrote during the 1930s, a decade during which he was intensely, even obsessively, concerned with political issues. During this decade, as we have already seen, Pound's commitment to a fascist ideology steadily deepened. And in Pound's own mind, I am convinced, the various political ideas that we meet in this group of cantos come together to form a single, vast ideogram, the ideogram *To Kalon*, or Order. And I also have no doubt that in 1940 Pound believed that the ideogram *To Kalon* and the fasces that Mussolini had adopted as the symbol of the Nuovo Ordine were interchangeable. Yet if I am correct in my belief about the way the patterns of similarity and difference work within *The Cantos*, then we not only may but also must, unless we are to shirk our duty as Pound's collaborators, try to pull apart the bundle of sticks that Pound has tied together, "dissociate" (one of Pound's favorite words, borrowed originally from de Gourmont) the patterns of "association" that he has created. In any case, it is precisely such a dissociation of the political ideas in Cantos 31 through 70 that I shall attempt to effect here.

As a first step in this process, I would propose that we can chart as follows the interwoven patterns of political motifs in these cantos:

Demand for a cultural renewal, to "make it new"	Cultural conservatism, desire to "preserve the heritage"

Populism, empathy with masses, especially peasants, desire to be part of "the people"	Celebration of the elite (political and artistic), the "party of intelligence"
Celebration of the impersonal power of love	Celebration of the power of the individual will
Demand for an end to economic exploitation	Belief in private property as essential to preservation of culture
Horror of war	Tolerance of (and sometimes a cult of) violence
Identification with/envy of Jews	Hatred and fear of Jews

To understand the patterns of political ideas and attitudes in Cantos 31 through 70, we obviously must look closely at the tensions that play back and forth between each item in the left column and the corresponding item in the right hand column. Therefore I shall discuss each of these paired sets of motifs. But before doing this it seems to me useful to emphasize for a moment the patterns that emerge if we look up and down these two columns. If we look in sequence at the motifs which I have grouped on the right side of my chart, a frightened authoritarian steps out, terrified at the threat which a rising tide of mass democracy poses to the cultural treasures of humankind, determined to preserve (through violence if necessary, and the unspoken assumption seems to be that it *will* be necessary) the power and the property of a ruling elite, and no less determined to expugn from the nation the alien, subversive influence of Jews. Yet if we read down the left side of my chart, a very different political persona emerges: a "Quaker Pound," committed to the creation of a peaceful and just community, grounded in love and the harmonies of nature. Both these political personae represent, I believe, a response to the steady erosion of the "social affections" caused by the expansion of capitalism. Yet the first persona responds with fear, clinging desperately to institutions and privileges that seem to be dissolving in his hands. The other persona welcomes the new world, confident that history is impelled forward by the eternal generative powers of humankind and of nature. In some of Pound's work, especially the wartime radio broadcasts, we can hear only the first of these two political voices, the voice of the frightened authoritarian. Yet as I am here trying to demonstrate, in *The Cantos* we can hear both the voice of the "Quaker Pound" *and* the voice of the angry reactionary; and it is, I believe, the dialogue between these two voices that makes the poetry which Pound wrote during the 1930s one of the most dynamic—if, also, one of the most problematic—bodies of political poetry in our language.[21]

IV

In this concluding section, I shall try to substantiate the generalizations which I have made above by examining in turn each of the six paired sets of motifs which, I believe, collectively define the "political periplum" of Cantos 31 through 71. Limitations of space means that my attempt to chart the play of these motifs through 268 pages of a richly-textured poetic text will of necessity be somewhat hasty and superficial. Yet I think that I can, at the very least, assemble enough evidence to show that the political stance which Pound assumes in these cantos cannot be summed under a single, simple rubric, whether "conservative" or "radical." Rather, as I shall here try to show, the cantos which Pound wrote during the 1930s are built, thematically, on a series of paradoxes. For example, I think it can be demonstrated that in these cantos Pound presents himself both as a *conservative* and as a *revolutionary*. One of Pound's goals in this group is to recover the roots of the American heritage, in the hope that he will find there a useable political tradition. In this section of the poem, he also seeks to recover a "sane" monetary tradition, represented primarily by the charter of the Siennese Monte di Pasche. And in this portion of *The Cantos* Pound also attempts to penetrate back to the beginnings of the most ancient of all civilizations, China; for in the person of Confucius he has found the incarnation of what he regards as a certain universal principle of justice. In all three of these quests, Pound is clearly seeking *roots*: an "originary moment" in which he can ground his own life, and from which the sane *polis* can also grow. And such a search for roots is profoundly conservative. Yet, paradoxically, the tradition which Pound wants to recover in *The Cantos* is specifically a *revolutionary* tradition, a "tradition" of *breaking* with the past in an endless quest for the *new*. The revolutionary aura surrounding Pound's two principal heroes from the generation of the founding fathers, Jefferson and John Adams, should require no demonstration. Among Pound's

---

21. The usefulness of the principal published discussion of Pound's politics, William M. Chace's *The Political Identities of Ezra Pound and T. S. Eliot* (Stanford, Calif., 1973) is, in my judgment, diminished by Chace's desire to find in Pound a single, consistent political "identity." I would make a similar criticism of John Lauber, "Pound's *Cantos*: A Fascist Epic," *American Studies*, XII, 1, pp. 3-21.

European political heroes, Pietro Leopoldo is offered us as the instigator of radical changes in Italian society. And even the Mussolini of *The Cantos* is an agent of radical change, restructuring Italian society by driving out capitalist profiteers, and even recontouring the Italian earth. This emphasis on revolution even extends into the Chinese cantos and the motto which Tching wrote on his bathtub—"MAKE IT NEW"—echoes not only through Pound's Chinese cantos but through all the cantos that Pound wrote during the 1930s. Furthermore, "making it new"—"it" may be the language, or it may be the *polis*—is clearly the work of a revolutionary. A "revolutionary tradition" then—around this paradoxical, even oxymoronic concept Cantos 31 through 71 largely turn.

A second fundamental polarity within Pound's political thinking is the tension between his "elitist" celebration of the solitary "genius" as the source of artistic and political change, and his "populist" sense of "the masses" as the ultimate agent of history. In the section of *The Cantos* here under discussion, one of Pound's principal examples of the "man of destiny" is Napoleon, whom we see remaking the map of Europe, only to have his work undone by the "league of lice" [50/249]. For Pound, too, the history of China is essentially the history of its rulers and of certain wise counselors, especially Confucius. And to Pound, the history of the United States too is essentially the history of certain powerful personalities (Adams, Jefferson, Van Buren) who decided what needed to be done and *did* it—prototypes, that is, of Mussolini. Yet in Pound's cantos of the 1930s, counterbalancing his celebration of the political "geniuses" who have imposed their will on history, we also find a persistent emphasis on "the people," not only as the raw material upon which the "genius" works, but also in its own right as agent within history:

> The revolution," said Mr Adams,
> "Took place in the minds of the people" [32/157].

These opening lines of Canto 32, repeated in part in Canto 33 and in full in Canto 50, would seem to subordinate the actions of political leaders (including Adams himself) to the movements of some sort of collective consciousness. Furthermore, it is not only in the American history cantos that surges of populism erupt into *The Cantos*. For if the Chinese people sometimes seem little more than clay in the hands of their rulers, nevertheless the ruler who tries to bend that clay into a grotesque, inhuman shape soon warns that the people will rebel against an unjust ruler, thereby taking history back into their own hands. Thus in his treatment of

Chinese as in his treatment of American history, Pound would seem to be an "aristocratic populist," or a "democratic elitist" — committed simultaneously to the ideal of the "great leader" *and* to a firm belief that in the end it is "the people" who make history.

A third polarity within Cantos 31 to 71 is a tension between what I shall call a "cult of the will" and a "cult of love," with the former represented primarily by assertive, active males, and with the later embodied in certain women who are often identified with Nature herself. Confucius, Jefferson, Adams, Mussolini — all are for Pound examples of the *directio voluntatis*, the will directed toward action in the world. But in *The Cantos* Pound also repeatedly invokes certain larger (and always female) erotic powers, which counterbalance male willfulness on a cosmic level, just as on the political level the "will of the people" counterbalances the will of the Great Leader. Pound most openly celebrates these erotic powers in three great cantos: Canto 36, placed at the exact midpoint of *Eleven New Cantos*; Canto 39, placed midway between Canto 36 and the end of the 1934 volume; and Canto 47, placed at the approximate midpoint of *A Fifth Decad of Cantos*. (The careful placement of these cantos suggests their particular importance in Pound's mind.) If we look only at Canto 36, which is largely devoted to a translation of Cavalcanti's "*Donna mi pregha*," it may seem that Pound's primary concern is "intellectual love." But even in Canto 36 Pound moves beyond his Medieval mentors to celebrate a pagan (perhaps Eleusinian, but pagan certainly) mystery: "Sacrum, sacrum, inluminatio coitu" [36/180]. And Canto 39 invites us to enter deeper into this mystery: "With one measure, unceasing:/'Fac deum!' 'Est factus'" [39/195]. Furthermore, the mystery here at issue belongs, Pound insists, to women, or perhaps to Woman. In any event, it is the voices of women that we hear throughout Canto 39, from the girls who "talked there of fucking" in the opening lines, to the final statement of the mystery near the end of the canto:

> His rod hath made god in my belly
> Sic loquitur nupta
> Cantat sic nupta [39/196].

In the last of these three great erotic cantos, Canto 47, Pound enacts for us a grand ritual of death and rebirth, as the male will, personified in Adonis, "dies" into a vast, eternal, erotic, female Nature, to be reborn as the "almond bough puts forth its flame" — reborn, indeed, as Orpheus, "that hath the power over wild beasts" [47/239]. And at this point the power of these "female" natural processes seems at least as strong as the power of those willful men whom Pound celebrates in the more "epic" sections of *The Cantos.*[22]

From the will/love polarity, I move, by a not unnatural transition, to the tension between the sympathy for violence which surfaces sporadically in *The Cantos* and Pound's genuine hatred of war. Pound's ambivalence toward war first became apparent in his response to World War I, and especially to Gaudier's death. The opening sentences of Pound's "Postscript" to his memoir of Gaudier are, in this respect, revealing:

> For eighteen years the death of Henri Gaudier has been un-remedied. The work of two or three years remains, but the uncreated went with him.
> There is no reason to pardon this either to the central powers or to the allies or to ourselves.
> I dare say there was never a man better fitted to serve in trench warfare, and his contempt for war is a message. A contempt for war is by no means a contempt for physical courage.[23]

The sudden leap from bitter sorrow over Gaudier's death to exultation at his skill in trench warfare is startling enough. And when Pound announces, a few sentences later, that "the real trouble with war (modern war) is that it gives no one a chance to kill the right people," we know that this is no pacifist speaking. The sorrow is real enough. So too is the rage, which demands to sate itself in violent action. And a similar ambivalence can be sensed, I would propose, in *The Cantos*. There, Pound's inclination toward violent ways of resolving human conflicts appears primarily in his choice of bellicose individuals as heroes: Malatesta in the opening section of the poem, Napoleon and Mussolini in Cantos 31 through 51, and various soldier/rulers in the Chinese cantos. Yet, strikingly, Pound's American heroes are all distinctly *non*-military types: thus he celebrates Jefferson the farmer-politician, *not* Washington the general, and thus too he focuses on the pacifistic Van Buren rather than on Van Buren's own political mentor, General Andrew Jackson. And even though Pound's treatment of Napoleon is largely positive, he also builds into the poem an "anti-Napoleon" in Pietro Leopoldo, the reformist ruler of Tuscany who devoted himself, not to war, but to husbanding the resources of the nation.

In his cantos of the 1930s, Pound also repeatedly condemns capitalism-as-we-know-it as a cruel and wasteful economic system,

---

22. The classical discussion of the role of these female powers in Pound's work is still Guy Davenport, "Persephone's Ezra," in *New Approaches*, ed. Hesse, pp. 145-173.
23. Ezra Pound, *Gaudier-Brzeska: A Memoir* (New York, 1970), p. 140.

while at the same time he repudiates all collectivist alternatives to capitalism. In Canto 32 we find Jefferson analyzing what Marx would later call "exploitation"—i.e., the extraction of surplus value from workers—and reaching conclusions not very different from Marx's. In Canto 33 Marx himself appears, to offer a page of evidence on the abuse of child workers by 19th century factory owners. Later, Martin Van Buren will excoriate the "landed interests" that would reduce free men to wage slaves. Canto 38 attacks the arms merchants. In Canto 41 we see Mussolini rigorously discipline a gaggle of capitalist profiteers. And Canto 46 sums up "the case for prosecution"—the case, that is, for the prosecution of capitalism-as-we-have-known-it. Despite his hatred of contemporary capitalism, however, Pound continued to believe in the principle of private property. Thus in his list of the achievements of Pietro Leopoldo, Pound tells us that this liberal reformer "split common property among tillers" [44/228]. And Pound admires Van Buren for defending the principle that "land [should go] to [the] actual settler" [37/182]—the basic premise of the Homestead Act. But Pound's rejection of the socialist alternative to capitalism becomes apparent primarily in his insistence that the "enemy" is not capital as such, but rather "finance-capital": that the crisis of the economy is the result, not of a usurpation of control over the means of production by capitalists, but rather of a usurpation of control over the money supply by "usurers": and that what we must seek to extirpate is, not capitalism as such, but "usura." As we follow Pound's progress through the 1930s, we can see "usura" gradually assuming, in his imagination, a truly demonic power, until in Canto 52 he identifies usura with Satan himself. It should be noted that this concept of "usura" does allow Pound to recognize and condemn some of the major abuses of capitalism; thus *The Cantos* is in some serious ways a poem of "social protest." Yet it should also be noted that talking about "usura" rather than "capital" allows Pound to see these social ills as revealing, not that the system of private ownership itself is fundamentally flawed, but rather that certain unscrupulous groups are manipulating this system for their own advantage. Expelling these "obstructors" will require, Pound assumes, a social revolution, but this revolution will restore rather than abolish the private ownership of property. Thus in his economic theory Pound might accurately be called an advocate of a *radical capitalist revolution*.

Pound, I should also here add, makes a serious attempt to resolve this anti-capitalist/pro-private property polarity by invoking what I shall here call the "myth of the peasant free-holder."

At several key points in *The Cantos*, Pound's celebration of eros metamorphoses into a ritual re-enactment of the recurrent rhythms of peasant life, which Pound offers us as a way of "marrying" man and the earth. This theme begins to emerge as early as Canto 44, where Pietro Leopoldo issues decrees to protect the peasantry from usurers. And in the brief, magnificent adaptation from Hesiod which Pound incorporates in Canto 47, the rhythms of peasant life become a "ground base" to all civilization. This theme receives a canto to itself in 49, the "seven lakes" canto, which occupies the same place within *The Fifth Decad of Cantos* that Canto 39 occupies in *Eleven New Cantos*—i.e., midway between the pivotal erotic canto and the end of the volume. And Canto 49 culminates in a ritual enactment of the union of man and nature, which here as in Canto 47 gives man "power over wild beasts." But the theme of peasant life as a ritual marriage between man and nature receives its fullest statement in Canto 52, where after a proud "Know then:" (rhyming with "So that:" at the end of Canto 1?) Pound gives us the Book of Rites—a collection of rules designed, Pound suggests, to regulate the interactions of man and nature, to fit human actions into the total "process" without damaging the harmony of things. And later in the Chinese cantos we learn that wise emperors will also ritually enact the marriage of man and nature, by themselves plowing the earth [61/336]. Implicit in this celebration of peasant life is a "Jeffersonian" political ideal: the image of the independent farmer, holding secure title to his piece of land, and beholden for his livelihood to no one and to nothing except that land. And this myth of the peasant free-holder (anachronistic and sentimental though it may be in an age of massive "public" and "private" organizations) allows Pound to be at once a critic of capitalism *and* a critic of collectivism, both of which threaten the very existence of the independent small farmer.

I come finally, with some trepidation and sorrow, to the last of the six basic polarities which I have isolated in Pound's political thinking, the tension between his fear of, and hatred for, Jews and his (largely unconscious) attraction toward (or even envy of) them. Actually, there are relatively few references to Jews in the cantos which Pound wrote during the 1930s, but these references seem to me very significant. Pound's first extended treatment of this comes in Canto 35, the "*Mitteleuropa*" canto. The tone of this canto suggests a facile, snobbish, but still essentially superficial "social" anti-semitism. Jews here have "funny accents," they have "foreign" names ending in "—ovitch"; and they are more given to family loyalty and to sensual pleasure than are Gentiles. But I do not hear a hatred of Jews in this canto; rather, if anything, I hear a distinct envy of

> ... the warmth of affections,
> the intramural, the almost intravaginal warmth of
> hebrew affections, in the family, and nearly everything else...
> [35/172-173].

On the other hand, Canto 52 opens with a blast of vicious Jew-hatred, worthy of a Hitler. These passages suggest that Daniel Pearlman was quite correct to detect in Pound an impulse to identify with Jews as well as a deep hatred of Jews.[24] Thus the "Jewish theme" in *The Cantos* seems to move, like the other themes I have here discussed, toward paradox.

However, I should here note that anti-semitism plays a unique role within Pound's political system, as it did within fascism as a whole. For to Pound, Jews seem to constitute a kind of parody of *both* of the two political identities which I have sketched above—i.e., the "authoritarian" and the "revolutionary" identities. Indeed, Jews seem to possess *all* of the traits that Pound admired, but always "in excess." Thus he would see Jews as *too* concerned with preserving their "cultural heritage," causing them to neglect the great maxim, "Make It New." At the same time, Pound also seems to see Jews as the agents of a destructive "modernization" of European culture. So too, Pound would see Jews as claiming an elite status, as God's "chosen people"; they "stand apart," but not in the positive creative way of the Great Artist or the Great Leader. At the same time, Pound sees in the loyalty of Jews toward one another an inverted reflection of his own vision of an artistic community. Jews are also, to Pound, *too* concerned with amassing private property, while at the same time they have spawned ideas (socialism, communism) which question the very right of people to own private property. And the allegiance of Jews to a patriarchal God represents for Pound a "cult of the will" gone wrong, while at the same time Jews also, he implies, love in the "wrong" way: perversely, or too intensely. By thus representing in Pound's mind a parody of everything that he himself wanted, Jews came to play a scapegoat function in his thinking, as they did for fascism in general. If we could only purge the world of "Jewishness" Hitler proclaimed, then we would have workers happy in their factories *and* bosses safe in their offices. So

---

24. Daniel Pearlman, "Ezra Pound: America's Wandering Jew," *Paideuma*, 9-3, pp. 461-480. For other useful discussions of Pound's attitude toward Jews, see Charles Berezin, "Poetry and Politics in Ezra Pound," *Partisan Review*, 48, pp. 262-279; and Hyam Maccoby, "The Jew as Anti-Artist: The Anti-Semitism of Ezra Pound," *Midstream*, XXII, 3, pp. 59-71.

too, I think, the idea of a world purged of Jews meant for Pound a world in which true mastery and rightful authority (his own, for example) would be recognized by all men, and in which a loyal band of artist/comrades (Gaudier and Hulme returned from the dead, Eliot escaped from the clutches of the church) would together create that ideal community for which he never stopped longing—a world, in short, wherein authority and community would come together at last, in a joyous marriage.

As the foregoing summary has, I hope, suggested, the political motifs in the cantos which Pound wrote during the 1930s constitute not a single, consistent "system" of ideas but rather an interweaving ("ply over ply") of widely disparate attitudes and ideas, held together less by logic than by certain powerful images— above all, the figure of the just, wise artist/ruler, such as Confucius, John Adams, and Mussolini—and by the force of Pound's own will. Some of the threads that Pound weaves into this fabric, when disentangled, look at least quasi-socialist, as Christine Brooke-Rose has pointed out: "Considering that Pound is generally regarded as (a) a crank and (b) a fascist, it is astonishing . . . how often he seems to echo not only some orthodox socialist thinking but also Marx."[25] And Louis Zukofsky too believed that a doctrinaire prejudice had blinded Pound to the affinities between his own thinking and Marx's analysis of capitalism.[26] At the very least, Pound often speaks as a populist, seeing "the people" (a phrase which is, beyond question, as slippery as any in our language) as an ultimate repository of decency and good sense. Yet at the same time some threads in the fabric that Pound weaves together are profoundly authoritarian, as he seeks a "natural" elite destined by their superior wisdom to rule over others, and as he celebrates the Great Leader who shapes nations as the artist shapes his block of marble. At times, further, Pound speaks as an embattled conservative, determined to defend the cultural heritage of Europe against a new barbarism encroaching from all sides. But at other times he speaks as a cultural revolutionary attempting to transcend the parochial western heritage, in the hope of achieving a new vision that will unite the east and the west, the ancient and the modern. Pound was drawn to fascism, I am convinced, because it seemed (but, alas, *only* seemed) to allow him a way to reconcile all these opposing pulls within him, to be at the same time a populist *and* an authoritarian, to demand both a new and just economic order

---
25. Brooke-Rose, *A ZBC of Ezra Pound*, ed. cit., p. 232.
26. Louis Zukofsky, in a panel discussion on Pound's work, 1975 Ezra Pound Conference, Orono, Maine.

and a preservation of the western cultural heritage—and even to be both a philo-semite *and* an anti-semite. Protean Mussolini, at once (or so he claimed) a reactionary *and* a revolutionary, an aristocrat *and* a democrat, seemed to incarnate, to *enact*, a reconciliation of these opposing political tendencies. In the end, I have here argued, fascism became a destructive political force precisely because it refused to recognize the inevitability of struggle between ways of thought and (yes) between social classes within the nation, thus leaving it no option but to blame all economic distress or internal conflict on "enemies" either without or within the nation. And I would make the same judgment of Pound's politics: ultimately, his refusal to recognize any fundamental conflict between his (idealized) vision of a productive peasantry, their lives rooted in the rhythms of the seasons, and his no less idealized vision of the free, autonomous artistic and political "genius" reshaping the world in accordance with his will, drove him to the conviction that an international conspiracy of "kikes" was preventing him and all humankind from entering the Paradise for which he longed. Yet if the political ideology through which Pound sought to reconcile the quarreling voices within him proved, for him and for the world, disastrous, it does not follow that the aspirations which these voices express (the need for legitimate authority, the longing for the "beloved community," etc.) are unworthy of our sympathy. The problems with which Pound wrestled remain *our* problems, and even if we reject the solution to which he committed himself he still has much to teach us about the angers and the hungers that have shaped the history both of poetry and of the *polis* in our century.

DAVID MURRAY

POUND-SIGNS: MONEY AND REPRESENTATION IN EZRA POUND

"What can drive a man interested almost exclusively in the arts, into social theory or into a study of the 'gross material aspects' videlicet economic aspects of the present?"[1] Pound's own answer to his question helps to explain the nature and limitations of the economic and political views he came to espouse.

> I have blood lust because of what I have seen done to, and attempted against, the arts in my time. . . . The unemployment problem that I have been faced with, for a quarter of a century, is not or has not been the unemployment of nine million or five million, or whatever I might be supposed to contemplate as a problem for those in authority or those responsible, etc., it has been the problem of the unemployment of Gaudier-Brzeska, T. S. Eliot, Wyndham Lewis the painter, E. P. the present writer, and of twenty or thirty musicians. . . [*SP*, p. 23p].

Pound's commitment to cultural morphology, the interrelation of social and cultural forms, leads him to emphasize the importance of the relation of the arts to society: "Artists are the race's antennae. The effects of evil show first in the arts." Clearly, though, artists are more important in Pound's scheme than an advance warning system, a dispensible miner's canary, and in fact Pound's emphasis on individual artists rather than the unemployed millions is an accurate reflection of his elitism. These people *are* more important to society than the masses, and it is important to locate Pound specifically as an artist threatened by a lack of role in a democratic society. Neither traditional patronage nor the market system offered him the upholding of standards necessary for the recognition of creativity, and his attacks on British and American society are in terms not of the social injustice of disparities of wealth as such, but of the *cultural* failure of the rich.

---

1. *Selected Prose*, ed. William Cookson (London, 1973), p. 198. Hereafter cited in the text as *SP*, with page number.

"Those who govern, govern *on condition* of being a *beau-monde* of one sort or another. Their rule cannot indefinitely survive their abrogation of 'culture' in the decent sense of that word" [*SP*, p. 198]. If artists need patronage, the leisure and security to work freely, then that society which best recognizes them and allows them this is to be advocated, not just selfishly but because elites matter to the whole society.

Pound's economic concerns must therefore be placed within a nostalgia for an ordered and hierarchical society, with corresponding concepts of "high" culture, and a rejection of democracy and its apparent threat of "low" culture. This position is not unusual amongst Pound's contemporaries, but Pound's particular combination of general precepts and specific remedies is, and needs clarification. In particular, Pound's longstanding concern with money, which operates almost to the exclusion of other economic issues, needs examination. It has usually been regarded by critics as an eccentric obsession which ruined a lot of his poetry. Some even blame it for his commitment to Fascism.[2] This paper argues, though, that Pound's concern for money relates directly to his major concerns, through money's dual and contradictary role as sign and transforming agent. The particular *terms* in which he chose to express these ideas, though, and his interpretation of historical events to support his theories, are not original to Pound, and are best understood by looking at Pound in an historical context, situated between American Populism and the Depression. The second part of the paper provides this context, with the intention of showing how Pound took over many of the terms and assumptions current among money reformers in America in the late 19th century and applied them to the 20s and 30s, but also how he related these ideas to his most fundamental moral and artistic concerns.

I

For Pound, economics is almost a branch of ethics. His economic thinking tends to presuppose an ordered and largely static society, with a centralized authority which holds a set of ethical assumptions about money, determining the direction of

---

2. See Leon Surette, *A Light from Eleusis* (Oxford, 1979)—who even sees economics as leading Pound into anti-semitism! Surette's study of *The Cantos* is otherwise perceptive about Pound's economics; though from a different standpoint from my own. The only full-length study of Pound's economics is Earle Davis' introductory *Vision Fugitive: Ezra Pound and Economics* (Lawrence, Kan., 1968).

its economic control. For Pound, any economic system or cycle is purely a means to a primarily non-economic end, namely freedom from the physical hardship which would limit the individual's full spiritual and ethical development. A good economic system provides enough for material wants, and leisure (i.e. spare time free from anxiety) for an individual to enrich himself by his own actions as he wishes. This attitude is in direct contrast to the common abstraction of the capitalist tradition of economic thought, that of "economic man." Instead of seeing man as primarily motivated by selfish and *acquisitive* instincts, seen in economic terms as the "profit-motive," Pound goes back to the economic thought of periods prior to the rise of capitalist thought, and especially to the Confucian/Mencian system and the economic doctrine of the medieval Catholic Church. Both of these systems subjugate the economic interests of man to his ultimate spiritual salvation.

The Mencian economic doctrine is an integral part of the whole Confucian conception of man in society and his relation to Process, and is basically concerned with setting up rules for justice in individual commercial dealings, and an equitable tax system designed for an agrarian society. With his stress on an ordered and static society, Mencius sees greed for excessive profit as completely immoral, as Pound points out:

> The profit-motive is specifically denounced. I mean that you will get no more accurate translation of the ideograms in Mencius' talk with King Hwey than "profit-motive." Mercantilism is incompatible with Mencius. Cheap evasion and evasiveness are impossible anywhere near him [*SP*, p. 103].

The reference here is to Mencius Chapter IA where Mencius warns King Hui of Liang against thinking in terms of "profit-and-advantage" (Pound prefers to translate it as "Profit-motive"):

> With this mutual exaction of profit-and-advantage pervading it from top to bottom, your very realm itself is threatened. In a state possessing 10,000 war chariots, the household with 1,000 will become the slayer of its prince. Now possession of ten per cent of power must be considered a large amount, but where propriety is placed second while the considerations of profit-and-advantage are foremost, there will be no satisfaction until one possesses all one hundred per cent. On the other hand, there has never been a case where manhood-at-its-best has neglected its relations. There has never been a case where the follower of propriety considered the interests of his prince secondary. Let your Majesty too use only the terms manhood-at-its-best and propriety! Why must you use that word profit-and-advantage?[3]

---
3. *Sayings of Mencius* (New York, 1960), p. 44.

The same mistrust of personal greed for profit, and belief in a community of interest which should rule such things as the tax-system underlies Chapter 3 of Mencius called "T'ang Wan Kung," where he outlines the ideal policy of a ruler towards maintaining justice in agriculture. The main recommendation is for a flexible tax based on proportion rather than a fixed charge:

> If you would bring order into land-holding nothing is better than the render-help method; nothing is worse than the tribute method.[4]

Both of these passages are brought together by Pound in *The Cantos*:

> "Nowt better than share (Mencius)
>   nor worse than a fixed charge."
> That is the great chapter, Mencius III, I, III, 6
>
> T'ang Wan Kung
>
> pu erh. "Why must say profit
>
>   (the grain cut).
>
>
>   No dichotomy [87/574-575].

For the medieval Canonists, too, economics was a moral issue, taking its place in a much larger context of moral action and organization:

> Man's path in life was a spiritual progress. No one aspect of his existence could properly or safely be separated from the remainder. Economic activity was far from an exception, for if anything a Christian encountered more danger to his soul in buying and selling, in the temptations of avarice, than in most other of life's occupations. To organise life around the quest for unlimited profit was as inconceivable to St. Thomas as the organisation of life around the gratification of sexual passion.[5]

Pound is in agreement with this basic scale of economic values, and, seeing economics in moral terms, he therefore sees the basic issues as unchanging.

He is able, then, to present economic history not as a world of changing and developing resources, and of institutions and practices developing in response to these, but as a series of moral tableaux where one can see acted out repeatedly the struggle between good and evil. *The Cantos* may be an epic, a poem that

---
4. *Ibid.*, p. 44.
5. R. Lekachman, *The Varieties of Economics* (Cleveland, 1962), p. 47.

contains history, as Pound insists, but they "contain" it in several senses. By insisting on an unchanging schema beneath the changing accidentals Pound is denying the importance of historical change and with it the possibility that value-systems might be within history, determined by historical and material changes, contained by it rather than containing it. This is crucial because Pound's insistence on relating the economic to the ethical and religious means that he presents as unchanging ideals, outside history, precepts that are clearly culture-specific. When this is combined with his long-standing concern for rectification of language and clear definition it produces Pound's insistence that clear and simple definitions have been made in the past and need only be rescued. Their relevance has not changed because the basic issues are unchanging. These definitions can be technical and specific, and used by Pound as talismanic reminders (e.g., fragments from Aristotle) or more general, as in the repetition of ideograms for equity, justice, law, etc., from Confucius and Mencius. In both cases, the assumption is that, having been once fixed, these definitions are outside of ideology and change, and can act as bulwarks against slippage of language.

It is this insistence on clear and simple definitions which motivates a great deal of his economic writings, but it is also, when it is combined with Pound's particular style, one of the reasons why these texts are so unsatisfactory. It is worth examining a fairly typical text in some detail to show the characteristic movement of Pound's thought. *ABC of Economics* was published in 1933 but it does not differ substantially in this respect from a later work like *Gold and Work* of 1944. It is a confusing text, partly because of Pound's "ideogrammic" method which he defines here as "first heaping together the necessary components of thought" [*SP*, p. 209]. This relates directly to his concern for precision, and his defense, following Fenollosa, of the ideogram as "scientific" since it works with concrete particulars from which it makes inductions. This method, rigorously used, would of itself, make for discontinuities, and jumps, from one set of data to another, but what really causes the confusion here, and it is an important clue to what happens in Pound's thinking, are the gaps in the assembled data itself. There is a rapid shift from very general moral and political statements to a very limited and specific economic issue, namely distribution. For example, we have on the second page a progression from an assertion of the need for men to have responsibility, "No social order can exist very long unless a few, at least a few, men have such sense" [*SP*, p. 204], to the limitations of democracy, and then, with no preparation; "Probably the only economic problem needing emergency solution in our time is the problem of distribution." A few pages later we have an assertion that

> The science of economics will not get very far until it grants the existence of will as a component; i.e. will toward order, will toward "justice" or fairness, desire for civilization.... [*SP*, p. 210]

followed in the next paragraph by a discussion of money specifically as certificate. This I take to be a very characteristic leap, from ethics to money, involving all sorts of omissions and short circuits, and it is worth examining this leap more closely.

"The question of production is solved" [*SP*, p. 204], Pound asserts. Only distribution needs to be reformed. But reform of distribution does not mean *re*-distribution of wealth (i.e. a political matter and related directly back to production) but to the mechanisms of distribution via *money*. He calls for "ADEQUATE (and more or less just) distribution of credit slips" and adds "I have put 'ADEQUATE' in capitals and 'just' in lower case because that is the order of their importance" [*SP*, p. 220]. This is a particularly explicit example of Pound's curious leap over the political to the limitingly technical, but elsewhere he equates "the orders of an omniscient despot and of an intelligent democracy" in their effect on "the main body of the country's economics" [*SP*, p. 218]. By ignoring production Pound also ignores the larger political issue of who is producing and who is owning. This relates importantly to Pound's tendency to ignore the real changes in the modes of production in different periods of history, itself related to his concern with the recurrent and unchanging.

To insist that Pound's concern is with the *un*changing may seem perverse, given both the mass of historical material from different periods and the theme of metamorphosis in *The Cantos*, but metamorphosis implies both something that changes and something that doesn't, the wave holding its form in the water, the avatar of Aphrodite. As such it posits a world of change, but one informed by unchanging generative sources:

> the deathless,
> Form, forms and renewal, gods held in the air [25/119]

To "make it new" is to change something ("it") that is already there, but this tension between seeing the world as infinitely transformable—a world of energy, and exchange of energy—and only being able to confront this by holding to an unchanging center, an unwobbling pivot, is relevant to Pound's economics as well as his use of literature and mythology. The unchanging center, the key to equity, stability, and justice in economic terms is, for Pound, money and the correct use of it. He even describes it in the same terms as the Confucian ideas which were so important to him: "Money is the pivot. It is the middle term" [*SP*, p. 312], and elsewhere he talks of this pivot wobbling: "A money ticket, under a corrupt system, wobbles" [*SP*, 260]. What he wants money to be in his system of values, is the fixed element in a series of transformations of value. Otherwise the pivot wobbles, the fixed point of certainty disappears. The trouble is, that money has been more usually treated as in itself a repository of value, and an agent of transformation rather than a sign, and Pound's historical materials involve many different types of money.

Money, for Pound, is potentially a threat to values and categories which should *not* be transformable, which should be clearly separated out from each other, and also a potential block, if misused, of the natural exchange of energies. Pound's childhood memories of the Mint at Philadelphia, and the processes of refining and assaying gold and silver have been recognized as influential on his concern for coinage as such ("this spectacle of coin being shovelled around like it was litter—these fellows naked to the waist shovelling it around in the gas flares—things like that strike your imagination"),[6] but I want to stress the image of *transformation* involved in smelting and coining. Values are being transmuted and then fixed before one's eyes—particularly if one believes that either the metals or the coins have an *intrinsic* value—and it is against this idea that Pound endlessly campaigns. He refers in *The Cantos* to the coinage of money as alchemy [18/80], whereby precious metal is created from base metal, in other words, where value is fraudulently created, and sees the creation of money by banks without anything to correspond to it, as being equivalent. Coining as alchemy, though, also relates to the more general transformation involved when gold, silver or paper take on value in *themselves*, that is, when they are substituted for the real sources of value, rather than representing them.

This role of money as *representative* is crucial in Pound. He refers in the Chinese Cantos to Hien Tsong, who dabbled in alchemy, as

    another Lord seeking elixir
    seeking the transmutation of metals
    seeking a word to make change [57/313]

Money can only be a *representation* of value, not valuable in itself, just as any sign is not the thing it signifies. Money actually

---
6. *Paris Review*, 28 (Summer/Fall, 1962), 40.

represents a unit of value, but the source of that value resides elsewhere. Signs cannot have value, words cannot make change. They refer to the real, and should do so clearly. Here, in fact, is the deepest level of connection between Pound's ideas, and it helps also to account for Pound's sweeping generalizations about usury and its effect on the arts, as I show later. Money, then, as the representation of the *relation* between things of value is an abstraction which should remain fixed. As Georg Simmel expressed it,

> As a visible object, money is the substance that embodies abstract economic value, in a similar fashion to the sound of words which is an acoustic-physiological occurrence but has significance for us only through the representation that it bears or symbolises. If the economic value of objects is constituted by their mutual relationship of exchangeability, then money is the autonomous expression of this relationship. . . . Thus it becomes comprehensible that money as abstract value expresses nothing but the relativity of things that constitute value; and at the same time, that money, as the stable pole, contrasts with the eternal movements, fluctuations and equations of the objects.[7]

Only when that pole is stable, or in Pound's terms, the pivot is unwobbling, can the relations of value between things be clarified. If not, the transformations and exchanges of economic life can be deceptive and dangerous, and in Canto 74 he relates this to the transformation of Odysseus' men to swine:

> every bank of discount is downright iniquity
>   robbing the public for private individual's gain
>   nec benecomata Kirkê, mah! κακὰ φάργακ ' ἔδωκεν
> neither with lions nor leopards attended
>   but poison, veleno
> in all the veins of the commonweal [74/437].

This degrading transformation is in contrast to the interrelated images of illumination connected with the recurring and metamorphosing female deities, and the battle between the positive and negative transformations is well illustrated by a passage which combines these mythological materials with Pound's concern for definition—in this case, the single word, taken from Aristotle, *Xpeia*. His primary concern with it is as an example of the obscuring of accurate definition:

> The mistranslation, or rather the insertion of the word "value," where Aristotle said *Xpeia*, demand. Money is not a measure of value. The price is caused by demand.[8]

---

7. Georg Simmel, *The Philosophy of Money* (London, 1978), pp. 120-121.
8. *Guide to Kulchur* (Norfolk, Conn., 1938), p. 357. Hereafter cited in the text as *GK* with page number.

The explanation is necessary to the reader's understanding of the isolated word as it appears in Canto 106, where he uses the word to contrast with the description of the coinage of money in China, but in a context of spiritual illumination:

> coin'd Artemis
> all goods light against coin-skill
> if there be 400 mountains for copper—
> under cinnabar you will find copper—
> river gold is from Ko Lu;
> price from XREIA;
> Yao and Shun ruled by jade
> That the goddess turn crystal within her
> This is grain rite
> Luigi in the hill path
> this is grain rite
> near Enna, at Nyssa:
> Circe, Persephone [106/753].

Pound exploits the connection of Artemis with coinage (as patroness of silversmiths, Diana often figured on coins) to make the connection with the various female deities he uses as images of fertility and natural process, and there is a contrast here between "coin-skill" and images of light and fertility. The basic inorganic commodities, extracted from rivers or out of the ground take on, by being coined, and being treated as having inherent value, the organic qualities of grain, and this contrast between inorganic money and the organic self-reproducing world controls the opposition throughout *The Cantos* and much of Pound's prose, between Usury and Eleusis. Eleusis I am using as an image of energies which are sexual and reproductive, and the seminal energies of artists come into this category. Energy exchanges in this area are productive and life-enhancing, and related to Mencian/Confucian "process" by the images linking the metamorphosing Aphrodite to both fertility and light. Usury is linked to gold, money and to hoarding, described in terms reminiscent of Freud's connection between money and faeces. "Filthy lucre," N. O. Brown calls it, and Pound's scatological language firmly associates money that is hoarded or artificially abstracted from the natural exchanges of energy, with excrement. The "usurer's dunghill," the "putrid gold standard" are standard terms in Pound, and his well-known association of usury with sodomy, as being equally unnatural, "contra naturam," in Canon law corresponds to this division of anal and genital. Usury, then, blocks and corrupts natural energies, substituting for clarity and distinction (visual imagery) the soft and the slimy (tactile imagery), and the passage on "neschek," written about 1941 but not published until *Drafts and Fragments* exemplifies these themes. Having described it as "Syphilis of the State" he continues

> *neschek*, the crawling evil,
> > slime, the corrupter of all things,
> Poisoner of the fount,
> > of all fountains, *neschek*,
> The serpent, evil against Nature's increase [Fragments/798].

The fountain as image of clarity and purity, but also a perpetual and unchanging source of change is related to Nature's increase, poisoned by syphilis, sodomy, excrement.

This broad opposition between natural energies and the stopping of them by the hoarding of purchasing-power has often been recognized in Pound, but the role of labor in this scheme has not been so fully discussed. Grain, which Pound opposes to gold, is not simply "natural," in that it is the product of human labor as well as "nature's increase," and while Pound acknowledges this ("All value comes from labour and nature. Wheat from ploughing, chestnuts from being picked up") [*SP*, p. 264] he is at pains finally to subsume labor under nature: "Work does not create wealth, it *contributes to the formation of* it. Nature's productivity is the root" [*GK*, p. 357]. This appears in *The Cantos* as

> ... the true base of credit, that is
> > the abundance of nature
> with the whole folk behind it [52/257].

The logical landscape which follows this is the "naturalizing" of workers in the fields, the harmony of peasants with nature presented in the Chinese landscapes in *The Cantos*, and the only legitimate source of increase on which money can be advanced is natural increase, like the sheep on which the bank of Monte dei Paschi is founded [43/217-218].

Some distinctions have to be made here, the first being between wealth and value. While it may be true that the wealth (i.e., total goods and services available) is created by nature and labor in interaction (the role of technology will be dealt with later), the determination of *value* is quite different, and it is useful here to return to Pound's use of Aristotle's *Xpeia*. Pound is at pains to point out that Aristotle meant "demand" and not value by it, but he does not pursue Aristotle's thinking any further. Marx did, though, and his remarks are very relevant to Pound's subsuming of labor under nature. Aristotle, Marx tells us, recognizes that exchange cannot take place without some grounds of equality and commensurability, i.e., a standard of value, but is at a loss to locate "that equal something, that common substance"

David Murray 183

which gives one object a value relative to another object. For Marx the missing element is human labor, and he explains why Aristotle could not see this:

> There was, however, an important fact which prevented Aristotle from seeing that, to attribute value to commodities, is merely a mode of expressing all labour as equal human labour, and consequently as labour of equal quality. Greek society was founded upon slavery, and had, therefore, for its natural basis, the inequality of men and of their labour-powers. The secret of the expression of value, namely, that all kinds of labour are equal and equivalent, because, and so far as they are human labour in general, cannot be deciphered, until the notion of human equality has already acquired the fixity in a society in which the great mass of the produce of labour takes the form of commodities, in which consequently, the dominant relation between man and man, is that of owners of commodities.[9]

Pound's strategy in *The Cantos* of ignoring the changes in social organization and in the ways of thinking generated by these changes indicates partly that his ideal society may not be unlike Aristotle's, but also that labor is a term not fully examined by him, and it is worth defining more clearly the differences between the role of labor in different economic views.

Marx's stress on labor and production reflects in a very distinctive form a more widespread conception of value and money which develops with capitalism. Previously wealth had been regarded as a fixed entity which was accurately represented by (because embodied in) coin. Money, then, was a commodity, and the main economic issues were seen as distribution and the just price. Later developments in industry and commerce, though, entailed an emphasis on wealth-creating capabilities, which meant that value was created by labor and technology. As Michel Foucault sees it:

> Value can no longer [after Smith and Ricardo] be defined, as in the Classical age, on the basis of a total system of equivalences, and of the capacity that commodities have of representing one another. Value has ceased to be a sign, it has become a product.[10]

Foucault locates the shift with Ricardo:

> Ricardo, by dissociating the creation of value from its representativity, made possible the articulation of economics upon history. "Wealth," instead of being distributed over a table and thereby constituting a system of equivalences, is organised and accumulated in a temporal sequence: all value is determined, not

---
9. Karl Marx, *Capital* (London, 1970), pp. 59-60.
10. Michel Foucault, *The Order of Things* (London, 1970), p. 254.

according to the instruments that permit its analysis, but according to the conditions of production that have brought it into being.[11]

This has effects directly relevant to Pound's monetarism:

after Ricardo, the possibility of exchange is based upon labour: and henceforth the theory of production must always precede that of circulation.[12]

Pound's attitude to these crucial changes is complicated and ultimately contradictory. On the one hand the changes allow the shift away from a view of wealth reliant on commodity money, the fetishization of metals, and therefore allow a consequent realization of the real meaning of money, as sign. Money then, as Foucault describes it "receives its value from its pure function as sign."[13] Pound should clearly approve of this, but he is appalled by the accompanying shift in attitudes to credit. The very change and expansion which made possible the realization that money was a sign also allowed, in Pound's view, an erosion or obliteration of the real relationship between money and things. Money created "ex nihilo," as in the founding of the Bank of England, took on value *in itself*, rather than being a sign representing something actually extant (goods, labor). As a result Pound dismisses developments since the 15th Century in Europe and since Hamilton in the U.S., as the victory of usury, and praises societies and periods of history which were free of this, but inevitably these are mostly societies based on money as commodity. Pound needs, then, somehow, in combatting the slippage involved in capitalism, to fix sign back on to thing, but not, as in his examples from earlier societies, by means of "hard" money, based on metals. As a result he talks of money as certificate of work done, or certificate of goods available, but the real problem—and it is at the heart of Pound's ambivalence about money—is that money as he wants it to operate is an abstraction, a sign referring to a *relation* between things of value, not to something concrete. By dismissing the importance of production in the creation of value, and the role of credit within it, and returning to the concerns of pre-capitalist economists Pound chooses to ignore crucial historical changes. In particular, his subsuming of labor under nature, as producer of wealth needs to be examined further. For Pound, labor is part of a harmony *with* nature, rather than being for most men the means of their alienation from their full humanity. Although he does

---
11. *Ibid.*, pp. 255-256.
12. *Ibid.*, p. 254.
13. *Ibid.*, p. 176.

acknowledge the role of culture in its fullest terms as opposed to nature, i.e., the co-operation of men in groups, the "increment of association" and the role of transmitted knowledge and skills, "the increment of tradition," his absolute lack of interest in technology means that these ideas and their relation to labor are never really developed. The fact that labor in an unequal society is an alienation of men's energies rather than a free exchange of them, and that money as wealth is an embodiment of that alienation in *itself*, rather than just when accumulated by usurers, is where Pound fails to follow or understand Marx, and he therefore attacks Marx on false grounds:

> Fascinated by the lustre of a metal, man made it into chains. Then he invented something against nature, a false representation in the mineral world of laws which apply only to animals and vegetables. The nineteenth century, the infamous century of usury, went even further, creating a species of monetary Black Mass. Marx and Mill, in spite of their superficial differences, agreed in endowing money with properties of a quasi-religious nature. There was even the concept of energy being "concentrated in money," as if one were speaking of the divine quality of consecrated bread [*SP*, pp. 316-317].

In fact, far from holding these views, Marx makes the same basic criticism of capitalism as Pound. In "The Power of Money in Bourgeois Society," Marx refers to the presentation of money in *Timon of Athens* as "the visible divinity—the transformation of all human and natural properties into their contraries, the universal confounding and overturning of things; it makes brothers of impossibilities." The reason for money's ability to do this, though, is clearly defined by Marx, and his definition surely demystifies the magical element. Its power "lies in its *character* as man's estranged alienating and self-disposing *species-nature*. Money is the alienated *ability of mankind.*"[14]

While both Marx and Pound are opposed to this domination of money-values, Marx differs from Pound in his refusal to idealize what preceded it. He did not look back to an ideal agrarian medieval society as an alternative to capitalism because although he admitted in feudal landed property "the semblance of a more intimate connection between the proprietor and the land than of mere material wealth,"[15] he saw in feudalism the whole basis of the capitalist alienation of man from his labor. Refusing to romanticize the fall of the feudal estates, he sees feudal landed property as:

---
14. Karl Marx, *Economic and Philosophical Manuscripts of 1844* (New York, 1964), p. 152.
15. *Ibid.*, p. 101.

> ... already by its very nature huckstered land—the earth which is estranged from man and hence confronts him in the shape of a few great lords. The domination of the land as an alien power over men is already inherent in feudal landed property. Indeed, the dominion of private property begins with property in land—that is its basis.[16]

Pound, with his respect for the feudal system based on landed property, wrongly interprets Marx's attacks on property as really only attacks on Capital: "Marx attacked 'Capital,' the Russian movement has been perverted into an attack on Property."[17] Pound tries to make a clear distinction between capital and property. Property should be concrete. Anything else is capital:

> The nature of property is radically (at the root, in the root) different from the nature of capital. . . . All such phrases as "capital in the form of" are misleading. Properly understood capital is liquid. The great division is between whatever is a lien on the other men's services, and what is either completely neutral and passive, or constitutes a potential responsibility, whereof the weight leans on the owner. . . . Property does not imply the enslavement of others.[18]

Pound approved of those conservative elements in the U.S. Constitution which guaranteed the rights of property, and several times in *The Cantos* he quotes or refers to Mussolini's "Programme di Verona," a manifesto of the Fascist party, where a right *to* property is guaranteed, but not the rights *of* property: "'Alla non della,' in the Verona statement" [86/564]. In other words, he approves of the possession of private property as long as it is used for the pleasure or convenience of the individual owner, but not when it is used to confer on him power over others. The contradiction here is that the possession of *land* is one of the most obvious forms of power over others, and yet Pound approves of landed estates. He eases his anxiety over the permanence of these estates by an appeal to a key phrase in *The Cantos* taken from Jefferson, "the earth belongs to the living." Pound follows Jefferson in deciding that no debts should continue beyond a generation, but he says nothing of the continuation of land ownership as such, transmitted on hereditary principles.

Pound's misunderstanding of Marx is significant, not only for the differences between them, but for the similarities, and the way that Pound's misreading of Marx relates directly to his support of Fascism. At one level both Pound and Marx respond to the same shortcomings, both in capitalism and in the study of

---
16. *Ibid.*, p. 100.
17. *Impact* (Chicago, 1960), p. 263.
18. *Ibid.*, p. 153.

economics itself. Pound has to go back to the Classical and Canonist writers to find ethical ideas fully applied to economics, and Marx too notes the same shortcomings in modern "political economy":

> If I ask the political economist: Do I obey economic laws if I extract money by offering my body for sale. . . . Or am I not acting in keeping with political economy if I sell my friend to the Moroccans. . . . then the political economist replies to me: You do not transgress my laws, but see what Cousin Ethics and Cousin Religion have to say about it. . . . But whom am I now to believe, political economy or ethics? . . . It stems from the very nature of estrangement that each sphere applies to me a different and opposite yardstick—ethics one and political economy another.[19]

This is exactly the dissociation of different areas of life which Pound is trying to reconcile by means of his "totalitarian" paideuma, but the differences between the two men are instructive. Pound, relying very heavily on organicism, saw any counterforce in the body politic as unhealthy and cancerous, and therefore entertained no idea of class struggle as instrument of necessary change. Indeed, he regarded radical inequalities with equanimity, while reserving for himself, as artist, the right to be outside any particular class.

An examination of the difference between Pound's overall view of history and Marx's shows how he side-stepped the idea of the need for, and historical inevitability of, real structural changes in societies. Calling the present system "usury" or "usurocracy" rather than "capitalism," he personalizes the issues and sees history in conspiratorial, rather than economic determinist, terms. Here we see the crucial importance of Pound's anti-semitism, which, as W. M. Chace argues, was no mere personal quirk:

> It was . . . a way to pin down world troubles on one small fraction of that world's population. It might have had as one source a kind of perverted American Populism. . . . but it was nourished and made even more perverse by his hostility to seeing life in terms of class-structure.[20]

The need then (and in this respect Pound's anti-semitism is classic) is to find an identifiable and personalized scapegoat for the breakdown of society, other than the structure of the society itself, which is felt to preserve necessary order and hierarchy which would be lost in fundamental change.

---

19. *Economic and Philosophical Manuscripts of 1844*, ed. cit., p. 152.
20. W. M. Chace, "Ezra Pound and the Marxist Temptation," *American Quarterly*, XX (1970), p. 724.

In addition, anti-Semitism has the advantage for Pound of relating very directly to his tendency to polarize actions and events in terms of good and evil. Whereas for Marx the selfish actions of a number of individuals make up a larger picture of a system which is beyond their individual control and under which they suffer almost the same alienation as those they exploit, Pound sees the usurers as far too evil and calculating to be suffering from any psychological malaise as a result of their own actions and their own system. He sees usurocracy as an almost irresistible international force which has corrupted all of European life and culture:

> There has been some vague talk in recent months [1944] about an international power, described as financial, but it would be better to call it "usurocracy," or the rule of the big usurers combined in conspiracy. Not the gun merchants, but the traffickers in money itself have made this war; they have made wars in succession, for centuries, at their own pleasure, to create debts so that they can enjoy the interest on them [*SP*, p. 313].

The effect of usury, though, is not just financial exploitation. The corollary of Pound's belief that artists are the antennae of the race is that art should show the sickness in a society. In particular, clarity and definition are at risk:

> Discrimination by the senses is dangerous to avarice. It is dangerous because any perception or any high development of the perceptive faculties may lead to knowledge. The money-changer only thrives on ignorance. . . . An instant sense of proportion imperils financiers [*GK*, p. 281].

Pound's reasons for believing there has been a deterioration since the fourteenth century are nowhere fully given, and in particular there is nowhere a clear model of *how* usury affects the lines an artist draws or the words he uses. In the following passage, where he goes back well beyond medieval society to find the high point of civilization, there is the usual *juxtaposition* of economic malpractice and artistic degeneration, but no more:

> And against usury
> > and the degradation of sacraments,
> For 40 years I have seen this,
> > now flood as the Yangtse
> also desensitization
> > 25 hundred years desensitization
> > 2 thousand years, desensitization
> After Apollonius, desensitization
> > & a little light from the borders:
> > Erigena,
> > Avicenna, Richardus.

> Hilary looked at an oak leaf
> or holly, or rowan
> as against the brown oil and corpse sweat
> & then cannon to take the chinks opium
> & the Portagoose uprooting spice-trees "a common"
> sez Ari "custom in trade" [92/621-622].

The common custom referred to by Aristotle is monopoly, [*Politics*, I 4/5] and the references to the Portuguese and British actions in China to corner the market in spice and opium are examples of this. The "brown oil and corpse sweat" is a reference to the lack of clarity and light in art represented for Pound by painters like Rubens,

> the metamorphosis into carnal tissue becomes frequent and general about 1527. The people are corpus, corpuscular, but not in the strict sense "animate," it is no longer the body of air clothed in the body of fire; it no longer radiates, light no longer moves from the eye, there is a great deal of meat....[21]

These two thousand years of usury are referred to in *Guide to Kulchur* as being a record, set out for those who want to know, of the constant effects of usury to destroy true civilization; but again we are given nothing specific:

> You have 2 millennia of history wherein we see usury opposed to the arts, usury at the antipodes of melody, of melodic invention, of design. Usury always trying to supplant the arts and set up the luxury trades, to beat down design which costs nothing materially and which can come only from intelligence, and to set up richness as a criterion. Short curves etc. "opulence" without hierarchy [*GK*, p. 282].

In general, though, Pound dates the decline of art and thought from the downfall of the authority of the Catholic Church, and he is in agreement with Eliot and Hulme in regarding the Reformation as a disaster in its effects on both art and economic thought:

> The Church slumped into a toleration of Usury. Protestantism as factive and organised, may have sprung from nothing but pro-usury politics.... The "Church" declined and fell on this issue. Historians have left the politics of Luther and of Calvin in the blur of great ignorance.[22]

(Luther was in fact firmly in the Canon Law tradition in his opinion on Usury, and his essay "On Trading and Usury" is hardly distinguishable in attitude from Catholic economic writings, whereas Calvin agreed that certain types of Usury in certain situations were not necessarily sinful. Pound makes no distinction.) He

---

21. *Literary Essays*, ed. T. S. Eliot (Norfolk, Conn., 1968), p. 153.
22. *Impact, ed. cit.*, p. 241.

is aware of the new commercial and industrial developments in the economy at this time but refuses to accept the necessity for new ways of expanding and developing credit facilities. Any divergence from the static controlled medieval system must mean a decline, not only in standards of honesty in economic matters, but in the artistic and intellectual health of the community: "As long as the Mother Church concerned herself with this matter [usury] one continued to build cathedrals. Religious art flourished" [*SP*, p. 293]. The great achievement of the Catholic Church for Pound was the development of gradations of thought and fine discrimination: "things neither perfectly nor utterly wrong, but arranged in a cosmos, an order, stratified, having relations with one another" [*SP*, p. 120], whereas the effect of Protestantism "has been semiticly to obliterate values, to efface grades and graduations" [*GK*, p. 185]. The use of the word "semiticly" here pin-points what so often goes wrong in Pound's analysis of history. He uses the word, in general, not necessarily just to mean Jewish but to stand for an approach to life which is at best unduly individualistic, and at worst murderous in its willingness to create wars and misery for private financial gain—in other words, as here, the opposite of his ideal ordered society with its fine discriminations and gradations, both in art and society. The origins of this use of the idea for Pound may well have been Gaudier-Brzeska's discussion of the characteristic vortices of the past, which Pound summarizes:

> The Paleolithic vortex, man intent upon animals. The Hamite vortex, Egypt, man in fear of the gods. The derivative Greek. The Semitic Vortex, lust of war. Roman and later decadence, Western sculpture, each impulse with corresponding effects on form.[23]

Whereas Gaudier-Brzeska is linking the styles specifically with race here, Pound broadens the definition of the word—but at the same time maintaining his racial hostility for Jews—to include manifestations like Protestantism and earlier individualistic excesses.

It's important, given the generalized schema I used earlier, where Usura was opposed to Eleusis, to insist, with Chace, that Pound's use of usury, and his development of an historical scenario like this is *not* metaphorical. To treat the Usura Canto in isolation as a metaphorical account of corruption is to ignore all the detail in the prose writings and *The Cantos* which insists on the *real* conspiracies, the *actual* changes in the value of gold, etc., in order to make Pound's views more acceptable because more generalized and "poetic." What makes it difficult to take seriously *other* than

---

23. *Gaudier-Brzeska: A Memoir* (Hessle, Yorks., 1960), p. 106.

as metaphor, though, is the absence in Pound of any method of relating artistic standards to social systems, but it is here that the role of money as *representation* may be relevant. In a way that is never fully articulated by Pound himself, it is representation which is the connecting link between economic malpractice and artistic decline. Lack of clarity and definition (of money, of words, of signs) leads to a distortion of the correct proportions between elements of different value and therefore a confusion about what constitutes value, either in economic or in aesthetic terms.

II

So far I have tried to show the particular relation between Pound's social and cultural views, his particular paideuma, and his view of money as sign, and agent of transformation, but the particular *form* his economic ideas take, and the terms in which he expresses them, are also closely related to his own historical position, and the ideas he inherits from his background. Pound's treatment of the monetary controversies in U.S. history stops curiously short at the late 19th Century, and yet this, the period of Pound's own childhood, was the period of the most intense and explicit monetary debate. The terms of this debate account for a great deal of Pound's terminology and for his attitudes towards economic issues in the 20th Century, but their role has been neglected by Pound scholars. As a result I intend to concentrate on this 19th Century legacy rather than Pound's encounter with 20th Century economists, a detailed examination of which is beyond the scope of this paper. It could, in any case, be argued, that it is from the late 19th Century that most of the direction and impetus of his economic thinking comes.

The consistent thread of opposition to industrial capitalism, as it developed after the Civil War, and the analysis of its defects, became focused by the 1890s in the growth of Populism, and in the final defeat of silver interests in the election of 1896. Much of the strength and flexibility of the critique of capitalism was lost by the progressive concentration on the issue of silver, and Pound explicitly dismisses this as a red herring, another fetishization of metal. If we go back behind the concentration on this single issue, though, it is clear that the basic analysis, and many of the remedies, of groups described under the term Populist are very close to Pound's own. Presumably the stress on the common man, combined with the eventual obsession with silver, account for Pound's neglect of the movement, but it is worth pin-pointing his considerable debt to it.

At the heart of many Populist arguments is a basic opposition between producers and financiers. As the former became poorer the latter tightened their grip, so that the two groups became also describable as debtors and creditors. As the U.S. economy expanded, and the demand for money grew, the effect of holding down the money supply, by linking it firmly to gold, which was fairly inelastic in supply, was to increase the value of money in relation to goods, thereby benefitting the creditors, and those controlling and manipulating the supply of gold. Hence the call for inconvertible paper money, the continuation of the greenback, not redeemable in gold, and the unlimited coinage of silver, which had earlier been legal tender in fixed relation to gold. Because of its increasing quantity, and the hope it offered of an increased currency, silver became regarded as "soft" or inflationary money, and the call for it was seen as positively immoral by orthodox business-men and economists, since this new money would have no fixed relation to a real source of value (i.e. gold). For the Populists, though, it had relation to the only real source of wealth and value:

> Labor in its various forms produces the nation's wealth. This is the ultimate truth. The exchange of this wealth constitutes all of the diversified business of the country. The vast throng of busy thousands who produce this wealth also in large measure consume it. If they are now in possession of an ample supply of sound money, they must exchange it for this wealth.
>
> How is it, then, that all men of all classes complain of hard times, and chiefly of the difficulty of obtaining money with which to gratify their wants or carry on business? Why is it that so much of this wealth cannot be exchanged at all? . . . Is it not that money is enormously valuable as compared with property and commodities? And, as money has value in proportion to the quantity of it out, do not such conditions show beyond question that the monetary circulation is insufficient. . . .[24]

Behind this specific monetary proposal, though, which is so similar to Pound's in the 1930s, is a suspicion and fear of the manipulation of the economy which comes close to belief in a large-scale conspiracy. Bankers and usurers use the gold standard to control the finances of America:

> . . . a band of men, with murderous purposes, went—not into the battlefield—but into the very sanctuary of our country, the holy place of government, and there, under the guide of patriot and benefactor . . . plotted the most diabolical scheme of robbery that ever blackened a historic page.[25]

---

24. Norman Pollack, *The Populist Mind* (Indianapolis and New York, 1967), p. 323.
25. *A Populist Reader*, ed. G. B. Tindall (New York, 1966), pp. 57-58.

And elsewhere:

> Monopoly is eating out the very vitals of our existence. Usury and extortion have fastened their iron jaws upon every industry of the land. . . . We are travelling the same road to death that nations gone before have travelled.[26]

The practice of monopoly is particularly concentrated on gold as a commodity because of its other use as a medium, and the ability of the monopolists to increase the value of any commodity relative to others means that they can control the currency by creating scarcity, and then a relative glut, of gold. Pound takes over this idea in toto, as in the following:

> "All metal as barter"
>   Destutt or whomso,
> "Pity to stamp save by weight."
> Always the undertow,
>   gold-bugs against ANY order,
> Seeking the common (as Ari says) [87/572].

The reference to "common practice" is to monopoly and the creation of artificial scarcity. It is significant that the word "gold-bug" used here is standard Populist usage, not only to describe monometallists but to imply, as Pound does here, a whole conspiracy manipulating the economy through gaining a monopoly in gold, as in "the Wall Street, English, Rothschilds gold bug money syndicate," a phrase that could have come from one of Pound's war-time speeches, but is in fact from an 1896 newspaper.[27] Pound's belief that by this century gold has been taken over by the usurocracy who monopolize it, is his main reason for advocating the formation of a new system based purely on the authority of the State rather than precious metals, and it is in this context that he condemns Churchill's return to the gold standard in 1925. He gives as an example the effect it had on Italian farmers who had to pay debts which were suddenly doubled in value:

> "And with the return of the gold standard" wrote Sir Montagu
> "every peasant had to pay twice as much grain
>   to cover his taxes and interest" [77/474].

A way of developing these ideas into a whole interpretation of history was available to Pound in Brooks Adams' *The Law of Civilization and Decay*, which he uses in *The Cantos* and elsewhere. Written at the height of the money controversy in the 1890s, Adams' book offers a wide-ranging account of the movements of

---

26. *Ibid.*, p. 25.
27. Quoted in Norman Pollack, "The Myth of Populist Anti-Semitism," *American Historical Review*, 68 (1962), p. 80.

money and the effects of concentration of capital, which manages to account for the fall of Rome as well as the decline of modern civilization. Its view of history as large-scale transformations of energy, constantly centralizing and then being dissipated was attractive to Pound, and although he criticizes Adams for treating money as *literal* concentration of energy [*SP*, p. 277], he responds positively to the way Adams charts changes in societies in terms of the movement of money. Adams provides the apparent evidence for a conspiracy of bankers working to control the supply of gold:

> These bankers conceived a policy unrivalled in brilliancy, which made them masters of all commerce, industry, and trade. They engrossed the gold of the world, and then, by legislation, made it the sole measure of values.[28]

Although Brooks Adams does not discuss America in the book, his brother Henry was in no doubt about its political relevance or effect, warning him that "The gold-bugs will never forgive you."[29] Certainly the book was used by Populists, just as Pound used it, as evidence for the longstanding manipulation of debtors by creditors, and Adams expresses the issue succinctly in discussing the English Bullion Committee of 1810, in which, he says

> ... the struggle for supremacy between the lender and the borrower is brought out in full relief. To the producer, the commodity was the measure of value; to the banker, coin. The producer sought a currency which should retain a certain ratio to all commodities, of which gold was but one. The banker insisted on making a fixed weight of the metal he controlled, the standard from which there was no appeal.[30]

As the 1890s progressed, the broader arguments about the control of the economy and the power of what was becoming recognizable as monopoly capitalism became subsumed under a more specific argument about the shortage of money, and the need to coin silver. This was a denial of the truth of the orthodox view of the time formulated in Say's law, that it was *impossible* for there to be a shortage of purchasing-power in the economy. The rapid increase in production in nineteenth-century America, or the calling-in of loans, and holding-on to excess reserves by banks (as in the Depression of this century) clearly offered instances which invalidated this supposed law. At times there *is* a need to produce more money—though in itself this hardly constitutes a full response to economic imbalances. In a way very

---
28. *The Law of Civilization and Decay* (New York, 1959), p. 282.
29. *Ibid.*, p. xi.
30. *Ibid.*, p. 267.

similar to the Populists, Pound lets the issue of distribution take over from a larger critique of capitalism, and he quotes with approval a variety of examples of the supply of purchasing-power by unorthodox means. His grandfather, for instance, issued money to his workers:

> No-one, perhaps, has ever built a larger tract of railway, with nothing but his own credit and 5,000 dollars cash, than that laid down by my grandfather. The credit came from the lumbermen (and in face of opposition from the big U.S. and foreign steel monopolists) by printing with his brother the paper money of the Union Lumbering Co. of Chippewa Falls, bearing the promise to "pay the bearer on demand . . . in merchandise or lumber" [*SP*, p. 295].

Similarly the small Swiss town of Wörgl issued its own Stamp Scrip money, and even though the big banks suppressed it, it was really completely valid, since it related to goods in existence and was accepted by its users. The issued money gave the people the ability to buy available goods, and at the same time the issuing bank, in this case presumably the Town Council, claimed tax on the money at 12% which increased the town's revenues and therefore its potential public spending:

> Each month every note of this money had to have a revenue stamp affixed to it of a value equal to one per cent of the face-value of the note. Thus the municipality derived an income of 12% per annum on the new money put into circulation. The town had been bankrupt, the municipality had not been able to pay the school teachers, etc., but in less than two years everything had been put right and the townspeople had built a new stone bridge for themselves [*SP*, p. 284].

The important thing in this context is not Stamp Scrip as such but the issuing of money for the good of the community, corresponding to goods and labor available. Similarly, Pennsylvania, when still a colony issued paper money to the settlers:

> The settlers or colonizers in Pennsylvania and in other colonies irritated by the disappearance of metal money, understood that any other document could be used for book-keeping and as a certificate of what the bearer was entitled to receive in the market. . . . So the governments of several colonies began to lend paper-money for these purposes [*SP*, p. 138].

On the whole, though, in spite of these examples of good private money the best guarantee members of a society can have is that the money is backed by the State itself. Sovereignty in the issue of money is the key to all state power. Once it loses this it has lost all effective power, and this is why Pound sees the U.S. Bank War as so crucial to the rest of American history. Instances of shortage of purchasing-power are seen by Pound simultaneously as instances of a conspiracy *and* evidence of an inevitable *structural* imbalance in capitalism, and he uses 20th Century economists to support this view. Major Douglas' A & B theory, for example, appeared to him an ideal model to explain the breakdown of the system. Douglas argued that the cost of producing something consists of wages and dividends paid out, *and* the cost of reinvestment and overheads. This means that the money paid out to the actual producers of goods is always less than the total cost of the goods to produce, reflected in the price, leading to a permanent disparity between the cost of goods and the purchasing-power of the producers of those goods. The debt to Marx's theory of surplus-value is clear, but the crucial element which needs to be added, to give this simplified theory any sort of sophistication or relation to economic reality is the *rate* of distribution, and this is why Pound becomes interested in Gesell's Stamp Scrip ideas, since increased *flow* of purchasing-power has the same effect in this area as increasing the amount. Keynes' analysis of the situation was similar in many respects, and Pound's hostility to Keynes and to the New Deal seems to be based partly on a premature judgment of Roosevelt's policies, as well as Pound's increasing inability to revise his views as the 30s progressed. Roosevelt's Federally-funded works programs and deficit financing at least should have appealed to Pound, given the similarity to some of Mussolini's programs.

In general it is clear, though, that *monetary* policy appealed to Pound more than any more substantial social changes, since it allowed him to ignore the real nature of modern societies, and allowed him to equate widely disparate social systems. By emphasizing distribution rather than production he is able to bypass larger political issues, and in this respect Pound fits Galbraith's description of

> . . . a long line of monetary reformers extending to Professor Milton Friedman in our own day who have hoped that their changes would make other and more comprehensive government action unnecessary. They are monetary radicals because they are political conservatives.[31]

In this respect, too, aspects of Populism are relevant to Pound. Populism, as Lawrence Goodwyn has argued,[32] ultimately became deflected by emphasis on the one issue of money from its broad and longer-standing critique of capitalism, and its ultimate defeat

---

31. John K. Galbraith, *Money: Whence it Came, Where it Went* (London, 1975), pp. 210-211.
32. Lawrence Goodwyn, *Democratic Promise: The Populist Movement in America*, (New York, 1976), pp. 516-517 and *passim*.

involved a consequent narrowing of the concerns of American politics. I have tried to demonstrate that something similar happens to Pound. His concern for economics, his criticisms of his society and its manipulation of wealth were not in themselves freakish or peripheral, or unworthy subjects for a poet, but his failure to follow through his arguments at crucial points meant that they became increasingly separated both from his other major concerns and from political reality.

INDEX OF PERSONS, PLACES AND THINGS

ABC of Economics (Pound), 30, 177
Abd-el-Melik, 135-143
Adams, Brooks, 193, 194
Adams, Charles Francis, 109
Adams, Henry, 147, 194
Adams, John, 75, 79, 80, 113, 161, 162, 164, 165, 166, 171
Agassiz, Louis, 54
Analects, The (Confucius), 103, 104, 105, 106
Analysis of Sensations, The (Mach), 46, 49
Annunzio, Gabriele d', 58
Aristotle, 182, 183, 189
"As for Imagisme" (Pound), 42, 49
Asquith, Margot, 121, 122, 123

Bachelard, Gaston, 45
Barry, Iris, 95
Barthes, 62
Bax, E. Belfort, 152
Beardsley, Aubrey, 131
Beckett, Samuel, 17
Bell, Ian F. A., 38, 39, 46
Belloc, Hilaire, 152, 153
Bernstein, Michael André, 63
Binyon, Laurence, 99, 101
Blackmur, R. P., 87
Blake, William, 60
"Blandula, tenulla, vagula," 86, 87
BLAST, 27, 100
Booker, Peter, 38
Born, Bertrans de, 41
Bornstein, Daniel, 54
Bouvard et Pécuchet (Flaubert), 16, 17, 18, 19
Bracciolini, Poggio, 58
Broglio, 55

Brooke-Rose, Christine, 38, 42, 43, 171
Browning, Robert, 58, 131
Buchan, John, 53
Bunting, Basil, 51
Burckhardt, Jacob, 57
"Burgos, a Dream City of Old Castile," 9
Burke, Edmund, 147

Calvin, John, 189
Cantos, The, 9, 10, 11, 12, 15, 17, 18, 19, 20, 21, 22, 23, 24, 26, 27, 28, 30, 32, 33, 39, 51, 53, 54, 55, 56, 60, 61, 62, 63, 67, 70, 71, 72, 73, 74, 82, 103, 104, 105, 111, 116, 119, 121, 122, 123, 132, 133, 145, 158, 159, 160, 161, 162, 163, 164, 165, 166, 167, 168, 169, 170, 176, 178, 179, 181, 182, 183, 186, 190, 193
Canto 1, 32, 61, 107, 169
Canto 2, 41, 50, 61
Canto 3, 21, 50, 58
Canto 5, 58
Canto 7, 28, 66, 67, 68, 69
Canto 8, 11, 55, 63, 67, 70
Canto 10, 71
Canto 12, 58
Canto 13, 100, 104, 107
Canto 17, 31
Canto 18, 179
Canto 25, 178
Canto 31, 11, 75, 76, 77, 78, 79, 80, 81, 109
Canto 32, 109, 165, 168
Canto 33, 165, 168
Canto 35, 169, 170

Canto 36, 123, 124, 166
Canto 37, 168
Canto 38, 123, 168
Canto 39, 166, 169
Canto 40, 28
Canto 41, 168
Canto 43, 182
Canto 44, 168, 169
Canto 45, 129, 130
Canto 46, 107, 168
Canto 47, 31, 130, 169
Canto 49, 105, 130, 169
Canto 50, 165
Canto 51, 130
Canto 52, 33, 112, 168, 169, 170, 182
Canto 53, 112, 114
Canto 54, 112, 114
Canto 55, 112, 113, 114, 115
Canto 56, 112, 113, 114, 115, 116
Canto 57, 112, 117, 179
Canto 58, 112
Canto 59, 112
Canto 60, 112
Canto 61, 112, 116, 117, 169
Canto 74, 49, 180
Canto 76, 133
Canto 77, 33, 193
Canto 80, 119, 120, 121, 123, 124, 125, 126, 127, 128, 129, 130, 131, 132
Canto 81, 119, 120, 125, 127, 128, 129, 132
Canto 84, 125
Canto 85, 19
Canto 86, 186
Canto 87, 99, 176, 193
Canto 90, 42, 158
Canto 91, 158
Canto 92, 189
Canto 93, 133
Canto 96, 12, 135, 136, 138
Canto 97, 12, 135, 136, 141
Canto 98, 22, 30, 71, 133
Canto 99, 133
Canto 102, 133
Canto 106, 181
Canto 116, 22, 32, 33, 42
Canto 117, 10, 25
Cardinal, Peire, 60
Castro, Ignez da, 58
Cathay (Pound), 101, 102, 103

Catullus, 58, 86, 87, 88, 95, 98
"Cavalcanti" (Pound), 39
Cavalcanti, Guido, 124, 166
Chace, W. M., 187
Chavannes, 109
Chesterton, G. K., 152
Child, John Steven, 38
Chine, ou description historique..., (Pauthier), 104, 108, 111
Chinese Written Character as a Medium for Poetry, The (Fenollosa), 42, 49, 102, 103
Chu Hsi, 104, 105, 109, 110, 113, 116, 117
Cid, El, 55, 58, 60
Civilization of the Renaissance in Italy, The (Burckhardt), 57
"Classic Drama of Japan" (Pound), 101
Cocteau, Jean, 131
Cole, G. D. H., 152, 153
Confucii: Chi-King (Lacharme), 108
Confucius, 12, 35, 55, 60, 100, 104, 108, 110, 115, 116, 117, 160, 161, 164, 165, 166, 171, 175, 177, 179, 181
Confucius et Mencius: Les Quatre Livres de Philosophie Morale et Politique de la Chine (Pauthier), 100, 104, 105
Cory, Daniel, 135
Couvreur, F. S., 109
Cranmer-Byng, L., 99, 100
Creekmore, Hubert, 33
Cromwell (Buchan), 53
Cronaca Universale (Broglio di Tangelia), 54
Cunard, Nancy, 121
Curie, Marie & Pierre, 40

Dante, 55, 58, 60, 111
"Date Line" (Pound), 24, 72, 87
Davie, Donald, 39, 40, 42, 43, 94
de Gourmont (see Gourmont, Remy de)
Dekker, George, 65
Del Mar, Alexander, 12, 135-143
de Maeztu, Ramiro, 153
de Mailla (see Mailla, J-A-M Moyriac de)
de Rachewiltz (see Rachewiltz, Mary de)

Index

Derrida, 62
Dionysus, 55
Divine Comedy, The (Dante), 111
Doctrine of the Mean (Confucius), 105
Dolmetsch, Arnold, 41, 49, 131
Donne, John, 84
Douglas, Major C. H., 60, 114, 196
Draft of XVI Cantos, 104
Draft of XXX Cantos, 105, 121
Drafts and Fragments (Pound), 11, 33, 181, 182
Dulac, Edmund, 131
Duncan, Robert, 17, 18
Durant, Alan, 39, 77

economics, 24, 28, 29, 57, 106, 114, 146, 150, 151, 154, 157, 167, 168, 169, 171, 173-197
Einstein, Albert, 40
Eleven New Cantos XXX-XLI, 105, 166, 169
Eliot, T. S., 24, 53, 65, 66, 67, 101, 105, 122, 124, 133, 171, 173, 189
Emerson, Ralph Waldo, 42
Empirio-criticism, 46, 47, 48, 49, 50, 51
Epochs of Chinese and Japanese Art (Fenollosa), 101
Erigena, Scotus, 60
Este, Isabella di, 58
"Ezra Pound: America's Wandering Jew" (Pearlman), 170

Fascism, 12, 23, 28, 145-172, 174, 186
Fenollosa, Ernest, 12, 28, 29, 31, 60, 100, 101, 102, 103, 105, 108, 109, 130, 159, 177
Fenollosa, Mary, 100, 101
Fifth Decad of Cantos XLII-LI, 105, 107, 166, 169
Flaubert, Gustave, 10, 15, 16, 17, 20, 22
Flight of the Dragon, The (Binyon), 99
Ford, Ford Madox, 30, 48, 104, 131
Foucault, Michel, 18, 62, 183, 184
Four Books, 103, 105, 106
Frazer, Sir James, 60

Freret, Nicholas, 110
Freud, Sigmund, 37, 38, 51, 158, 181
Friedman, Milton, 146
Frobenius, Leo, 60
Fu I, 100

Gaudier-Brzeska, Henri, 131, 167, 171, 173, 190
Gaudier-Brzeska: A Memoir, 48, 190
Gesell, Silvio, 196
Giles, Herbert, 12, 100, 106, 107, 108, 111
Ginsberg, Allen, 158
Godwin, William, 147
Goethe, 19, 42
Gold & Work (Pound), 177
Gourmont, Remy de, 49, 60, 162
Great Learning, The (Confucius), 104, 105
Grosier, M. l'Abbe, 110
Guide to Kulchur (Pound), 39, 63, 106, 120, 124, 125, 126, 156, 160, 188, 189, 190
Guild Socialism, 152, 153, 155

Hadrian, 87
Hardy, Thomas, 94, 131
Harper, Michael, 68
Hart, Bernard, 49
Hell Cantos, 60
Hertz, Heinrich, 45
Hesiod, 130
Heydon, John, 41
Histoire Générale de la Chine (de Mailla), 109, 111, 116, 117
"History and Ignorance" (Pound), 24
History of Chinese Literature (Giles), 100, 108, 111
History of Monetary Systems (Del Mar), 12, 135-143
Hitler, Adolf, 149, 150, 151, 152, 155, 156, 157, 158, 170
Hobson, S. G., 153
Homage to Sextus Propertius (Pound), 11, 26, 59, 83, 84, 85, 86, 88, 91, 95, 96, 97, 98
"Home Thoughts from Abroad" (Browning), 131
Homer, 55, 60, 91
Horace, 84, 85, 88, 95

How to Read (Pound), 70
Hugh Selwyn Mauberley (Pound), 15, 24, 26, 132
Hulme, T. E., 60, 171, 189

Ideogram(-mic), 12, 25, 30, 33, 40, 56, 57, 58, 59, 62, 70, 76, 102, 138, 143, 145, 159, 160, 161, 162, 177
"Imaginary Letters" (Pound), 103
Imagism, 25
Imitations of Horace (Pope), 83
"Immediate Need of Confucius" (Pound), 106
inductive method, 70, 71, 72, 73, 159
Instigations (Pound), 103
"An Introduction to the Economic Nature of the United States" (Pound), 25

Jakobson, Roman, 38
James, Henry, 66, 69
James, William, 49
Jameson, Frederic, 77, 78
Jefferson and/or Mussolini (Pound), 12, 153, 154, 155, 156, 157, 161
Jefferson, Thomas, 72, 75, 78, 79, 80, 81, 160, 161, 164, 165, 166, 167, 168, 186
Johnson, Samuel, 84
Jonson, Ben, 84
Joyce, James, 24

K'ang-hsi, 110
Keats, John, 158
Kenner, Hugh, 40, 42, 43, 101, 103, 105, 143
Keynes, John Maynard, 196
Korg, Jacob, 38
Korn, Marianne, 61
Kublai Khan, 113, 115

Lacan, Jacques, 51
LaCharme, A., 108
Law of Civilization and Decay, The (Brooks Adams), 193
Lawes, Henry, 131
Leavis, F. R., 24, 37
Legge, James, 12, 106, 107, 108, 109

Leibnitz, G. W., 102
Lenin, Vladimir, 50, 51, 154, 156
Leopoldo, Pietro, 168, 169
Letters of Ezra Pound, 1907-1941, 32, 33
Lewis, Wyndham, 16, 77, 78, 122, 131, 133, 173
"The Liberal: Request for an Effective Burial of Him" (Pound), 29
Li Po, 100, 101, 116
Literary Essays (Pound), 41
Lodge, Oliver, 45
Logopoeia, 11, 90, 91, 97, 98
Lorenzaccio, 67
Lukács, 68, 69
Lun Yu (Analects), 103
Lustra (Pound), 86
Luther, Martin, 189

Mach, Ernst, 46, 47, 48, 49
Maeztu, Ramiro de (see de Maeztu, Ramiro)
Mailla, J-A-M de Moyriac de, 12, 109, 110, 111, 112, 113, 116, 117
Malatesta Cantos, 10, 11, 63, 70, 73, 167
Malatesta, Sigismundo, 35, 54, 55, 56, 60, 67, 71, 72, 73, 167
Mallarmé, Stéphane, 19
Manet, Edouard, 128
"Mang Tsze (Ethics of Mencius)," 106
Marconi, Guglielmo, 40, 45
Martial, M. V. M., 86
Marx, Karl, 37, 38, 51, 147, 158, 168, 182, 183, 185, 186, 187, 188, 196
Materialism and Empirio-Criticism (Lenin), 50
Maxim, Hudson, 49
Maxwell, Clark, 45
Medici, Allessandro de, 67
Mencius, 100, 106, 108, 175, 176, 177, 181
Mencius, The Book of, 105, 107
Mendel, Gregor J., 40
Merleau-Ponty, 51
metaphor(s), 25, 28, 30, 32, 33, 41, 42, 45, 50
metonymy, 76, 77, 80, 81, 82
Milton, John, 61
Modernism, 20, 23, 25, 37

Index

money, 12, 136, 137, 138, 140, 141, 142, 174, 178, 179, 180, 181, 182, 183, 184, 185, 190, 191, 192, 193, 194, 195, 196
Monroe, Harriet, 99, 102
Morrison, Robert, 12, 106, 107
Mottram, Eric, 43, 44
Mu Ch'i, 105
Murray, David, 39
Mussolini, Benito, 35, 72, 106, 145, 148, 149, 150, 151, 152, 153, 154, 155, 156, 157, 158, 160, 161, 162, 165, 166, 167, 168, 171, 172, 186, 196

Naidu, Sarojini, 101
Nänny, Max, 76
Napoleon, 165
"Near Perigord" (Pound), 10, 41, 54
New Age, 12, 152, 153
Nietzsche, Friedrich, 19, 152

Odysseus, 55, 107
Orage, A. R., 131, 152, 153
Orwell, George, 19, 73
Ossian, 102
Ovid, 55, 95
Owen, Robert, 147

"*paideuma*," 38, 112
Paine, Thomas, 147
Paradise Lost (Milton), 158
Paterson (Williams), 18
Pauthier, M. G., 12, 100, 103, 104, 105, 108, 111
Pearlman, Daniel, 42, 67, 107, 160, 170
Pearson, Karl, 46
Penty, A. J., 153
persona, 9, 26, 84, 85, 96
Phenomenology, 43, 44, 45, 46, 50, 51
Pindar, 95
Pisan Cantos, 119, 125, 126, 129, 132, 133, 153
Pius II (*Commentaries*), 68
Poema de Mio Cid, 54, 56
Poetry, 99, 101
Poggio, 55
Poincaré, Henri, 46, 49
Polite Essays (Pound), 27
Polo, Marco, 118

Pope, Alexander, 83, 84, 85
Populism, 12, 191, 192, 193, 194, 195, 197
Por, Odon, 153
Propertius, Sextus, 83, 85, 86, 88, 89, 90. 91, 92, 93, 94, 95, 96, 98
Prufrock and Other Observations (Eliot), 124

Quinn, John, 55, 58

Rabaté, Jean-Michel, 38
Rachewiltz, Mary de, 132
realism, 16, 30, 68, 69, 70
referentiality, 17, 18, 19, 20, 21, 27, 28, 29, 30, 31, 40, 41, 42, 54, 55, 71, 72, 73, 76, 79, 80, 81
Ricardo, David, 183, 184
Richards, I. A., 24
Riddel, Joseph, 80
Ring and the Book, The (Browning), 58
Rock-Drill, 121, 132, 133
Roosevelt, F. D., 106, 196
Rouse, W. H. D., 32
Rummel, Walter, 121

St. Victor, Richard, 41
Sargent, John, 127, 128, 131
Sartre, Jean Paul, 51
Sayings of Kung the Master, The (Cranmer-Bing), 99
"Scented Leaves from a Chinese Jar" (Upward), 99
Schneidau, Herbert, 38, 76, 77, 161
Seafarer, The (Pound), 56, 59
"The Serious Artist" (Pound), 27, 41, 49
"Sestina: Altaforte" (Pound), 9
"Seven Lakes Canto," 105, 106
Shih Chi, 109
Shih Ching (The Book of Odes), 108
Smith, Colin, 56
Smith, Paul, 77
Smuts, Jan, 42
Sordello, 41, 60
Sordello (Browning), 58
Spirit of Romance, The (Pound), 11, 41, 86

Ssu-Ma Ch'ien, 109, 116
Ssu-Ma Kuang, 109, 115, 117
Stein, Gertrude, 158
Stendhal, 70
Stock, Noel, 160
Sullivan, J. P., 83
Sung Lao, 109
Surette, Leon, 119

Ta Hio (see Ta Hsueh)
Ta Hsueh (The Great Learning), 104, 105, 106
Tawney, R. H., 147, 153
Terrell, Carroll F., 65
Textes Historiques (Weiger), 109
textuality, 16, 17, 20, 21, 22, 25, 26, 54-62
Thrones, 121, 132, 133
"Through Alien Eyes, I" (Pound), 39
Tibullus, 98
"To a City Sending Him Advertisements" (Pound), 95
tradition, 24, 31, 32, 37, 38, 40, 41, 53, 65, 84, 107, 131
translation, 26, 32, 40, 54, 55, 56, 58, 60, 61, 62, 79, 80, 81, 83, 84, 86, 87, 88
T'ung-Chien Kang-Mu, 109, 110, 111, 113, 116, 117
Tzu-Chih T'ung Chien, 109

Upward, Allen, 39, 40, 50, 60, 99, 100
Ur-Cantos, 58, 70

Value of Science, The (Poincaré), 46
Van Buren, Martin, 165, 167, 168
Varchi, 55, 59
Velásquez, 124, 125, 126, 127, 128, 129, 130
Virgil, 88, 95
"A Visiting Card" (Pound), 32
voice (poetic), 20, 21, 25, 26, 27, 33, 35, 54, 55, 56, 60, 61, 62, 82, 97, 98, 121, 122, 123, 124, 125, 126, 127, 131, 132, 133, 163, 164, 169, 172
Voltaire, 102
vortex, 27, 39, 40
"Vorticism" (Pound), 48, 49

Wang An-shih, 114, 115, 117
Wang Mang, 116
Waste Land, The (Eliot), 25, 65
Weiger, L., 109
Whistler, James, 131
White, Hayden, 73
Williams, W. C., 18
Wilson, Stephen, 39
Winters, Yvor, 39, 46
"The Wisdom of Poetry" (Pound), 48, 49
Works of John Adams, The, 109
Writings of Thomas Jefferson, The, 109

Yeats, W. B., 122, 131, 133
Yriarte, Charles, 54

Zukofsky, Louis, 171